Enriching Hymn and Song Stories
of the Twentieth Century

AMBASSADOR

BELFAST, NORTHERN IRELAND
GREENVILLE, USA

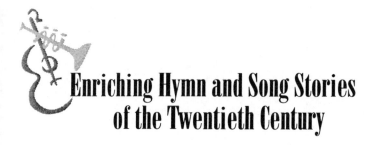

Enriching Hymn and Song Stories of the Twentieth Century

by
PAUL DAVIS

Introductions by Dave Bilbrough (UK) & Linda Hargrove (USA)
Foreword by Andrew Selous (UK Member of Parliament)

AMBASSADOR

BELFAST, NORTHERN IRELAND
GREENVILLE, USA

ISBN 1   84030 126 0

Ambassador Publications
a division of
Ambassador Productions Ltd.
Providence House
Ardenlee Street,
Belfast,
BT6 8QJ
Northern Ireland
www.ambassador-productions.com

Emerald House
427 Wade Hampton Blvd.
Greenville
SC 29609, USA
www.emeraldhouse.com

This keepsake book is ideal for the pastor, preacher, teacher, student, layperson, music fan, the Christian reader and the casual reader.

From worldwide sources, these songs were heavily recorded and published throughout the last Century.

Each inspirational song-story is preceded by an appropriate Bible text and songs, scriptures and song-writers are listed alphabetically.

List Of Contents

Foreword *by Andrew Selous MP* 11
Introduction *by Dave Bilbrough* 13
Introduction *by Linda Hargrove* 15
Alphabetical Hymn and Song Index 17

ARE YOU WASHED IN THE BLOOD? (Have You Been To Jesus?) 21
BEYOND THE SUNSET 27
FATHER GOD 33
GOD IS GOOD ALL THE TIME 39
GOD OF GLORY, WE EXALT YOUR NAME 45
HALLELUJAH, FOR THE LORD OUR GOD THE ALMIGHTY REIGNS 50
HAVE THINE OWN WAY 56
HE LIVES! (I Serve A Risen Saviour) 62
HE TOUCHED ME 67
HERE I AM WHOLLY AVAILABLE 73
HOW DEEP THE FATHER'S LOVE 79
I AM A NEW CREATION 85
I HAVE RETURNED 91
I WISH WE'D ALL BEEN READY 97
I'LL FLY AWAY 102
IN HEAVENLY ARMOUR (The Battle Belongs To The Lord) 107
IN TIMES LIKE THESE 113
IT TOOK A MIRACLE 118

JESUS IS LORD OF ALL 123

JESUS STAND AMONG US 128

KING OF KINGS (HE CAME TO EARTH) 136

LIVING HE LOVED ME (One Day When Heaven Was Filled With His Praises) 142

O HAPPY DAY 147

O LORD YOU'RE BEAUTIFUL 152

ROOM AT THE CROSS 157

SEARCH ME O GOD 162

SHOUT TO THE LORD 166

STANDING ON THE PROMISES 172

TAKE MY HAND PRECIOUS LORD 177

TAKE THIS BREAD I GIVE TO THEE (Communion Song) 182

THE GLORY SONG (When All My Labours And Trials Are O'er) 188

THE HEART OF WORSHIP 193

THE LORD IS GOOD 198

THEN JESUS CAME 203

THERE IS POWER IN THE NAME OF JESUS 209

THIEF IN THE NIGHT 215

THOU DIDST LEAVE THY THRONE 220

THROUGH IT ALL 225

TILL THE STORM PASSES BY 230

TO GOD BE THE GLORY 236

TODAY I FOLLOWED JESUS 241

UNTIL THEN 246

WE'LL UNDERSTAND IT BETTER BY AND BY (Trials Dark On Every Hand) 250

WE'VE COME TO WORSHIP YOU, LORD 255

WE SHALL BEHOLD HIM 260

WE WILL GLORIFY THE KING OF KINGS 266

WHEN THE ROLL IS CALLED UP YONDER (When The Trumpet Of The Lord) 271

WITHOUT HIM 277

Alphabetical Songwriter Index 283

Scripture Index 285

 # Dedicated to

My Dear Wife -
Hazel

Our Wonderful Children & Grandchildren -
Anita & Ed McGirr
(& Nathanael and Rachel)
Laura & Paul Ewers
Wes & Sue Davis

Our Faithful Parents -
Helen & Tom Davis
Rose & Walter Scott

Our Loving Church -
Leighton Christian Fellowship, England
and Worldwide

All Our Friends -
In The World Of Music

# Acknowledgments

Pat & Dave Bilbrough/Jim & Judy Leigh/Debbie & Harley Rollins/David Moody/Erv Lewis/Jerry Arhelger/Anne & Cliff Barrows/Miriam & James Blackwood/Francine & Cecil Blackwood/Sir Cliff Richard, OBE/ Bill Gaither/Sue & Wes Davis/Karlene & George Beverly Shea/Adelaide & George Hamilton IV/Joy & Samuel Purdy/Jessy Dixon/Marijohn Wilkin/John Pantry/Chris Bowater/Robert Lamont/John Nice/Roger Hill/Paul & Susan Hansen/Linda Hargrove/Jo and Jimmy Payne/Harvey Thomas, CBE/Andrew Selous, MP/Matt Redman/Laura & Paul Ewers/Hazel Davis

# **F**oreword *by Andrew Selous MP*

In answer to the question "What is the chief end of man?", the Westminster Confession says "Man's chief end is to glorify God and to enjoy Him for ever." We glorify God through lives of love and service but also in our worship.

I believe that the sort of worship represented in these hymns and songs is playing and will continue to play a big part in the future growth of churches. Many of these hymns and worship songs enable us to gain a greater intimacy with Jesus and indeed to "enjoy Him for ever". So from Westminster, I commend Paul's book to the widest possible readership.

Andrew Selous MP

Introduction *by Dave Bilbrough*

As I sat, guitar-in-hand meditating on my desire to know the Father's love in a deeper way, I allowed the chords to flow in the direction of the melody going around my head. Little did I know that the song that was being brought to birth on the scrap of paper in front of me, 'Abba Father', was to be the beginning of a personal quest to learn the craft of songwriting. Years on and countless scraps of paper later, the aspiration-to-learn and create is still just as strong as ever.

A good song can be so powerful and can capture so much. To the uninitiated, it can seem so simple, and yet as any songwriter worth his salt would say *'songwriting is a lifelong apprenticeship'*. Saint Augustine once said, *'he who sings, prays twice, first with the words then with the melody'*. Good songs are a unique form of expression and can be the key to unlocking emotions that at times are hard to articulate. They enable us to capture a glimpse of the majesty of Christ in the midst of our own frailty and humanity, and are capable of evoking feelings that range from 'unconfined joy' to 'heartfelt lament'. Really great songs like many of these in this collection have and will stand the test of time.

Under the guidance of the Holy Spirit, songs have the power to move, change and shape the thinking of the listener or participant, often becoming a reference point for many defining moments of one's life. Paul Davis has helpfully chronicled the stories behind many of the contemporary songs-of-praise that we love to sing. Packed with interest and surprises this contemporary musicologist provides us with some fascinating insights proving that the process of songwriting is often as important as the song itself.

I have known Paul and his family for many years. Diligently and sometimes at great personal cost, Paul has sought to make known the work of writers and performers who hold out the light of Christ to this hurting world, in a manner that manages to skillfully avoid fuss or pretension. Christian music and *'the proclamation of Christ'* genuinely excites him. I cannot think of a better man than Paul Davis to compile these pages.

Dave Bilbrough (Singer/Songwriter/Worship Teacher)
London, England

Introduction *by Linda Hargrove*

I am honoured and pleased to write a few words of introduction for my long time friend and Christian brother, Paul Davis about this newest book *'Enriching Song-Stories Of The Twentieth Century'*.

I met Paul on my very first visit to Great Britain in the spring of 1981. He was, in fact, quite instrumental in that first visit and subsequent evangelistic trips that my husband, Charlie Bartholomew and I made to England.

Having spent the 1970's in Nashville pursuing and building a 'secular' songwriting and recording career, my records and songs had obtained some notoriety in Great Britain. But in 1979, I had an encounter with Jesus Christ that forever changed the focus and direction of my life. In 1981, I traveled to Great Britain with a group of other well-known country artists *not* to promote the music I had created to serve my career and myself, but to proclaim the Good News of Jesus Christ and to play gospel music for the first time at the famous Wembley Country Music Festival. Paul was the facilitator of that undertaking. Later that year in October, Charlie and I returned to England for our first solo international evangelistic ministry trip and became even closer to Paul and Hazel and their lovely family, as they helped us greatly in our efforts to proclaim the gospel of Jesus Christ.

The stories of how these great inspirational songs of the twentieth century were conceived and brought forth in their time is testimony to the creative power of God's-Word-in-man. Here you will read how a simple phrase from another's lips caught the ear and the heart of a consecrated writer and inspired him to compose a song and psalm that has blessed us in our Christian heritage. Here you will also learn of the phrases, rhymes and melodies from which we have received such solace and comfort in Christ that were forged in the crucible of human experience. The stories that Paul has researched, compiled, and written about these great Christian songs that have had such an impact on us and our faith in God will simply bless you and inspire you.

In the secular world (if such a division of secular and spiritual exists) these songs are accounted for as 'hits' — attributed to by not only their great popularity, but by the income their sales have accumulated over time. We, in this time and space of eternity, acknowledge their greatness by our acceptance of their messages and themes. Those writers that are still living with us receive our praise of God for their good works. So likewise, I praise God for the good work that my friend and brother, Paul Davis has done in setting forth these stories to teach us, inform us, comfort us, and bless us.

Well done, my friend!

Linda Hargrove (Singer/Songwriter/Record Producer)
Florida, USA

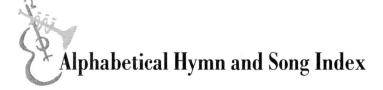

Alphabetical Hymn and Song Index

1	ARE YOU WASHED IN THE BLOOD? (Have You Been To Jesus?) 1 John 1:4-7 / Revelation 1:5	ELISHA ALBRIGHT HOFFMAN
2	BEYOND THE SUNSET 1 Corinthians 15:54-58	BLANCHE & VIRGIL BROCK
3	FATHER GOD Romans 8:14-17 / II Thessalonians 2:16	JACK HAYFORD
4	GOD IS GOOD ALL THE TIME Psalm 34:1-8	DON MOEN & PAUL OVERSTREET
5	GOD OF GLORY, WE EXALT YOUR NAME Philippians 2:5-11	DAVE FELLINGHAM
6	HALLELUJAH, FOR THE LORD OUR GOD THE ALMIGHTY REIGNS Revelation 19:5-8	DAVID & DALE GARRETT
7	HAVE THINE OWN WAY Jeremiah 18:1-6	ADELAIDE ADDISON POLLARD &GEORGE STEBBINS
8	HE LIVES! (I Serve A Risen Saviour) Revelation 1:18	ALFRED HENRY ACKLEY

9   HE TOUCHED ME   BILL GAITHER
     Matthew 8:1-2

10   HERE I AM WHOLLY AVAILABLE   CHRIS BOWATER
     Isaiah 6:1-8

11   HOW DEEP THE FATHER'S LOVE   STUART TOWNEND
     Luke 15:11-24

12   I AM A NEW CREATION   DAVE BILBROUGH
     2 Corinthians 5:16-17

13   I HAVE RETURNED   MARIJOHN WILKIN
     Isaiah 55:7

14   I WISH WE'D ALL BEEN READY   LARRY NORMAN
     Matthew 24:38-44 / I John 2:28

15   I'LL FLY AWAY   ALBERT BRUMLEY
     I Thessalonians 4:16-18 / I Corinthians 15:52-55

16   IN HEAVENLY ARMOUR   JAMIE OWENS COLLINS
     (The Battle Belongs To The Lord)
     Ephesians 6:10-17

17   IN TIMES LIKE THESE   RUTH CAYE JONES
     II Timothy 3:1-13 / Hebrews 1:1-2

18   IT TOOK A MIRACLE   JOHN PETERSON
     Genesis 1:1-5, 14-19

19   JESUS IS LORD OF ALL   MARILYN BAKER
     Acts 10:34-36

20   JESUS STAND AMONG US   GRAHAM KENDRICK
     John 20:19-23

21   KING OF KINGS (HE CAME TO EARTH)   JOHN PANTRY
     Revelation 19:11-16

22   LIVING HE LOVED ME (One Day When   J. WILBUR CHAPMAN
     Heaven Was Filled With His Praises)   & CHARLES H. MARSH
     I Timothy 1 :14-17

23   O HAPPY DAY   EDWIN HAWKINS
     Psalm 146:5-8

24   O LORD YOU'RE BEAUTIFUL   KEITH GREEN
      Psalm 27:4-6

25   ROOM AT THE CROSS   IRA STANPHILL
      Ephesians 2:13-18 / John 19:25-26

26   SEARCH ME O GOD   JAMES EDWIN ORR
      Psalm 139:23-24

27   SHOUT TO THE LORD   DARLENE ZSCHECH
      (My Jesus, My Saviour)
      Psalm 96 : 1-13

28   STANDING ON THE PROMISES RUSSELL   KELSO CARTER
      2 Peter 1: 2-4

29   TAKE MY HAND PRECIOUS LORD   THOMAS DORSEY
      Psalm 139:7-10 / Mark 9:27

30   TAKE THIS BREAD I GIVE TO THEE   BARRY McGUIRE
      (Communion Song)
      1 Corinthians 11:23-26

31   THE GLORY SONG (When All My Labours   CHARLES HUTCHINSON
      And Trials Are O'er)   GABRIEL
      Colossians 3: 1-4

32   THE HEART OF WORSHIP   MATT REDMAN
      1 Samuel 16:7 / Psalm 9:1-2

33   THE LORD IS GOOD   PAUL & SUSAN HANSEN
      Ephesians 5:19-20 / Psalms 106:1

34   THEN JESUS CAME   OSWALD JEFFRAY SMITH
      Mark 10:46-52   & HOMER RODEHEAVER

35   THERE IS POWER IN THE NAME OF JESUS NOEL RICHARDS
      Romans 13:1 / Daniel 4:34-35

36   THIEF IN THE NIGHT   PAUL FIELD
      II Peter 3:8-14

37   THOU DIDST LEAVE THY THRONE   EMILY ELIZABETH
      Philippians 2:5-8   STEELE ELLIOTT & IRA
                                               SANKEY

38   THROUGH IT ALL   ANDRAE CROUCH
      Acts 14:22-23

39   TILL THE STORM PASSES BY   MOSIE LISTER
      Luke 8:22-25

40   TO GOD BE THE GLORY   FANNY CROSBY &
      Jude 24-25   WILLIAM H. DOANE

41   TODAY I FOLLOWED JESUS   ERV LEWIS
      Romans 7:18-20

42   UNTIL THEN   STUART HAMBLEN
      Revelation 21:1-3 / Hebrews 12:22-23

43   WE'LL UNDERSTAND IT BETTER BY   CHARLES A. TINDLEY
      AND BY (Trials Dark On Every Hand)
      II Corinthians 1: 3-7 / II Corinthians 13:9-13

44   WE'VE COME TO WORSHIP YOU, LORD   DAVID MOODY
      1 Chronicles 16:8-9

45   WE SHALL BEHOLD HIM   DOTTIE RAMBO
      Zechariah 12:9-10 /Revelation 1 :7-8 / Matthew 24:29-30

46   WE WILL GLORIFY THE KING OF KINGS   TWILA PARIS
      Psalm 50:23

47   WHEN THE ROLL IS CALLED UP YONDER   JAMES MILTON BLACK
      (When The Trumpet Of The Lord)
      Revelation 3:5 / Revelation 20:12-15 /Revelation 21:23-27 /Revelation 22:19-21

48   WITHOUT HIM   MYLON LEFEVRE
      John 15:4-5 / Philippians 4:13

Are You Washed In The Blood?

(Have You Been To Jesus?)

Elisha Albright Hoffman

"And these things write we unto you, that your joy may be full.
This then is the message which we have heard of Him, and declare unto you,
that God is light, and in Him is no darkness at all.
If we say that we have fellowship with Him,
and walk in darkness, we lie, and do not the truth:
But if we walk in the light, as He is in the light,
we have fellowship one with another,
and the blood of Jesus Christ His Son cleanseth us from all sin." 1 John 1:4-7
Grace be unto you, and peace, from Him which is, and which was, and which is to come;
and from the seven Spirits which are before his throne;
And from Jesus Christ, who is the Faithful Witness,
and the first begotten of the dead, and the prince of the kings of the earth.
Unto Him that loved us, and washed us from our sins in His own blood,
And hath made us kings and priests unto God and his Father;
to Him be glory and dominion for ever and ever. Amen.
Revelation 1:5

Hymnwriter, Elisha Albright Hoffman was born in a small town with the strange name of Orwgsburg, Pennsylvania on May 7th 1839. On that day, his pious parents decided to give their new baby the unfashionable name of Elisha because they were impressed by the exploits of Elisha, the Old Testament prophet.

The baby grew and became musically inclined. Elisha was educated in the public school system of Philadelphia and later studied in the 'Union Seminary of the Evangelical Association'. Then for eleven years he was associated with the 'Evangelical Association' publishing house of Cleveland, Ohio. Highly motivated by Christ's Great Commission to tell the 'good news' at every opportunity, he was ordained as an evangelical pastor. Accordingly, he served many churches as a 'Minister of the Gospel' including the First Presbyterian Church of Benton Harbor, Michigan.

In spare times, Elisha concentrated on the ministry of sacred song, editing numerous song collections and authoring some enduring songs such as 'Are You Washed In The Blood?', 'Down At The Cross Where My Saviour Died' and 'Leaning On The Everlasting Arms'. The latter song starts with the words *"What a fellowship, what a joy divine leaning on the Everlasting Arms"*. These lyrics were conceived when Elisha Hoffman was conversing with his acquaintance, Anthony Johnson Showalter. Sadly, Anthony told Elisha that he had just received letters from two heartbroken dear friends. Both of them were recently widowed. In a great show of sympathy, Anthony and Elisha shared their deep concern for their widowed friends. Wise Elisha thoughtfully said, *"Never forget brother Anthony, the promise of Deuteronomy 33:27 is that the eternal God is thy refuge, and underneath are the everlasting arms! He upholds us all through every trial!"*

"What a wonderful theme for a hymn, Elisha," said Anthony. Soon the inspired duo were conspiring to create a new hymn-of-comfort.

In contrast, Elisha's hymn 'Are You Washed In The Blood?' (inspired by the First Epistle of John) was not meant to comfort but rather to stir and challenge. Elisha knew that the Apostle John set-out two purposes for writing his three epistles. Elisha declared *"My hymn confirms that a believer's fellowship with God and with his fellowman essentially hinges on being first cleansed by the Blood of Christ. The Apostle John's first purpose in writing his epistle was that Christian readers may always enjoy fellowship with other believers. The second purpose was that individual Christian readers would have joy that was full and complete!"*

Each purpose that the Apostle John set-out rested on the necessity of the application of the Blood of Christ, the Lamb of God who takes away the sin of the world. Indeed, both of the Apostle John's two purposes centred on the necessity to answer - in the affirmative - Elisha's opening questions of his hymn: *"Have you been to Jesus for the cleansing power? Are you washed in the blood of the Lamb?"*

Right at the start of His earthly ministry, Jesus was called the Lamb of God by John the Baptist, emphasizing the redemptive character of the work of Christ. More than a score of times in the Book of Revelation the Lamb is used as a symbol of Christ. The Passover Lamb in the book of Exodus became in time a picture of redemption from sin. The substitutionary use of the unblemished Lamb in sacrifice led to the idea of the Suffering Servant, who as a Lamb died in the place of sinners

Elisha clearly understood that the Apostle John's use of the pronoun 'we' in 1 John 1:4-7 assured the readers in the generation of believers that followed Christ chronologically. The message of the Epistle was being proclaimed by someone who had personally heard the Gospel with his own ears. He had even touched Christ with his own hands, a reference to His Resurrection appearances. In Verse 3 of 1 John 1, John introduced the purposes of the Apostle's letter: *"that you also may have fellowship with us. And our fellowship is with the Father and with His Son, Jesus Christ."* Like the Apostle John, hymn-writer Elisha was convinced that true fellowship was only possible via the application of Christ's blood by faith. ∖

Experts tell us that the Greek word rendered 'fellowship' (*koinonia*) is not easy to translate into English. Its meaning embraces, in addition to 'fellowship', 'communion' and 'joining-in'. Indeed, it is nothing less than the sharing of a 'common-life' and 'partnership'. The Greeks used this word group (*koinonia*) to describe 'partners-in-business', 'joint-owners-of-a-piece-of-property', or 'shareholders-in-a-common-enterprise'. Like the Apostle, hymnwriter Elisha wanted *koinonia* to be the abundantly fulfilling, supernatural life that all Christians could share. *"Our abundant eternal life"*, he said, *"comes from our Father and matures into the life shared individually and corporately by the company of believers. Oneness with God is what causes the oneness of faith."*

Elisha Albright Hoffman's great hymn, 'Are You Washed In The Blood?' clearly shows that a believer's fellowship-joy is inseparable from his salvation in Christ. Often Elisha would preach on the subject. *"Joy, my friends, is a gift of the Father, even as the Son is a gift of the Father. Joy is attendant wherever the fellowship truly becomes visible. If we as believers are to have fellowship with the Father and with the Son, we must grasp what makes this possible. We must know who God is in Himself and, consequently, who we are as children of God."*

The preacher went on to explain how the Apostle John loved to describe the moral constitution of God in terms of light. *"The genuine proof for 'fellowship with God' or 'walking in the light' is threefold. Firstly, we believers have fellowship with one another. Secondly, we are cleansed in the blood of Christ (upon confession of sin), granting pardon and purification. Thirdly, we believers have assurance that if we do sin then we have Jesus Christ as our attorney and offering for our sins. Brothers, the Apostle John stressed that God's light was pure and holy in a Christian. It demands that our character should conform accordingly...If people turn from the light or love darkness rather than light, it is because their deeds are evil!"*

'Are You Washed In The Blood?' is a great favourite of Pastor Rex Landon who is based in Bedfordshire, England. Much of his time is spent visiting the elderly and the sick in hospitals and nursing homes in the rural villages and country towns. Rex says that *'it is important that our forgiveness is always up-to-date and the hymn helps keep the matter high on the agenda'*.

The same Apostle John who wrote the three epistles, years later in Revelation 1:5 again stressed the necessity of the Blood. Upon his consideration of the person and offices of the Risen Christ, he burst into sweet praise to His Saviour. *"Unto Him that loved us, and washed us from our sins in His own blood, and hath made us kings and priests unto God and hath made us kings and priests unto God and His Father; to Him be glory and dominion for ever and ever. Amen!"*

Elisha Albright Hoffman wrote both the words and music to his hymn, *'Have you been to Jesus for the cleansing power? Are you washed in the blood of the Lamb?'* It was first published in 1878 in Cleveland, Ohio by Elisha and J. H. Tenney in the book entitled 'Spiritual Songs For Gospel Meetings And The Sunday School'. The British publication of Ira Sankey's 'Sacred Songs And Solos' in 1881 further popularised the hand-clapping song. As the years past, Elisha became increasingly convinced like the Apostle John that Christ's love was unmistakably made public in His atoning death. He preached that Christ purchased release from the penalty and servitude of sin to all who come to Him in repentance and faith. Indeed even today, Christ's kingly strength is still chiefly revealed in His ability to transform individual lives through His cleansing blood. Through His death on the cross, He defeated the devil and those who follow Christ in the battle against the devil share His victory.

Elisha Albright Hoffman lived a full life, dying at ninety years of age in the year of the 'Wall Street Crash' of 1929 that ushered in the Great Depression that clouded the world in economic gloom for almost a decade .

Have you been to Jesus for the cleansing power? Are you washed in the Blood of the Lamb?
Are you fully trusting in His grace this hour? Are you washed in the Blood of the Lamb?

Are you washed in the Blood, in the soul-cleansing Blood of the Lamb?
Are your garments spotless? Are they white as snow?
Are you washed in the Blood of the Lamb?

Are you walking daily by the Saviour's side? Are you washed in the Blood of the Lamb?
Do you rest each moment in the Crucified? Are you washed in the Blood of the Lamb?

When the Bridegroom cometh will your robes be white?
Pure and white in the Blood of the Lamb?
Will you soul be ready for the mansions bright, and be washed in the blood of the Lamb?

Lay aside the garments that are stained by sin, and be washed in the Blood of the Lamb;
There's a fountain flowing for the soul unclean, oh be washed in the Blood of the Lamb.

Elisha Albright Hoffman

Beyond The Sunset
Blanche & Virgil Brock

'So when this corruptible shall have put on incorruption,
and this mortal shall have put on immortality,
 then shall be brought to pass the saying that is written,
Death is swallowed up in victory. O death, where is thy
sting? O grave, where is thy victory?
The sting of death is sin; and the strength of sin is the law.
But thanks be to God, which giveth us the victory through
our Lord Jesus Christ.
Therefore, my beloved brethren, be ye steadfast,
unmoveable,
always abounding in the work of the Lord,
forasmuch as ye know that your labour is not in vain in the
Lord.'
(1 Corinthians 15:54-58)

Husband and wife, Virgil (1887-1978) and Blanche Kerr Brock (1888-1958) were an enterprising songwriting duo. They passionately believed that in 1 Corinthians 15, the Apostle Paul pronounced his deep faith that 'beyond the sunset' of life, there is 'the sunrise-promise of resurrection' for every believing Christian.

The Brocks' beautiful sacred song, 'Beyond The Sunset' became one of the most popular gospel songs of the 20th century recorded hundreds of times by artistes including Pat Boone, Elton Britt, George Beverly Shea, Burl Ives, Jo Stafford & Gordon MacRae, Red Foley,

Roy Rogers & Dale Evans and even comedian Jimmy Durante. Indeed, the evergreen 'Beyond The Sunset', when already an immortal hymn, was further popularised by the 'Hillbilly Shakespeare', the late Hank Williams, singing and narrating as 'Luke The Drifter' in the late 1940s.

'Beyond The Sunset' is by far the Brocks most well known and recorded composition although they wrote many other beautiful inspirational songs such as 'Today Is Mine - Tomorrow May Not Come' (recorded successfully by Slim Whitman and others).

Clearly the Brocks understood that God's people must have more than their physical bodies of flesh-and-blood to receive their inheritance in the eternal heavenly kingdom of God. Virgil Brock stated that like his present humanity, his mortal body was perishable and could not inherit that which was imperishable. Thus he said, *"The saved must have their bodies changed beyond the sunset before they can enter heaven. Unsaved unbelievers cannot be in heaven at all,"*. He added, *"The scriptures assert that all believers will receive newly changed-bodies (when Christ comes back to Earth on that great Resurrection Day) and summons His family at the stirring sound of the last trumpet."*

Theologians call this crescendo of an event 'the rapture'. It will be a dramatic change that will transpire instantaneously and thoroughly for all Christians, whether living or dead. The change will take place from one kind of body to another. The old perishable body will become an imperishable one. The Brocks loved to read together 1 Corinthians 15:54-58 with its strong emphasis on the words 'victory' and 'sting'. In it the Apostle Paul explodes into an ecstatic song of triumph: *"Death is swallowed up in victory. O death, where is thy sting? O grave, where is thy victory?"*

"For Christians, death certainly does not have the final mastery", said Virgil, *"as the Apostle Paul's glorious closing exclamation proclaims. 'But thanks be to God, which giveth us the victory through our Lord Jesus Christ!'"*

Virgil said that beyond the sunset only Heaven itself gives the believer final comfort and final victory through his Lord Jesus Christ's provision. *"Indeed, the Church of God can state here and now that there is 'good news'. 'Beyond the sunset', there is victory even over death and the grave. It was won at Calvary through our Lord Jesus Christ. He died and rose and is coming again!"*

Virgil and Blanche Brock blessed millions with their singing and hymn-writing even before 'Beyond The Sunset' was composed by them. The duo often featured as special guest duetists at the inspiring evangelistic crusades of the 1920's and 1930's held throughout the USA and Canada by the outspoken preacher, Billy Sunday and singer, Homer Rodeheaver.

Evidently, as well as being beautiful singers, Virgil and Blanche were also very gifted in the area of composition. They become prolific creators of spiritual songs. They said that they drew their inspiration from all kinds of situations and experiences …a-scripture-verse, a-personal-occurrence, a-family-tragedy, God's-wonderful-creation and such. When duly inspired, they would interrupt whatever they were involved-in to document the inspired words and music, even getting up during the wee small hours of the morning to put pen to paper. Usually, Virgil wrote the lyrics whilst Blanche composed the tunes.

'Beyond The Sunset' was written in 1936. The couple at the time were guests at the home of world famous evangelistic song leader and composer, Homer Rodeheaver. Homer's home, Rainbow Point, overlooked the beautiful Winona Lake. Situated on the eastern side of the lake, it afforded the opportunity to observe beautiful sunsets as the glorious sun set in the western sky.

On this particular visit, one of the other house guests, Horace Burr (who was blind) made a remark that surprised them all in the house. He said, *"Wow, my friends, I have never seen a more beautiful sunset!"*

As the golden sun dipped, there was a sudden hush among the sun-flushed guests aghast at the observation. All eyes were on the blind man. Staggered and somewhat taken aback by the remark, after a few seconds, Virgil asked in a kindly but inquisitive voice, *"How can you say that, Horace, when you cannot see, my brother?"*

The sightless man answered confidently with a broad smile, *"Oh, I've seen the sunset, Virgil, through the eyes of others!…I even see beyond the sunset by God's grace!"*

Fellow guests looked at each other in amazement as they watched the blind man view the sunset through sightless eyes. As Virgil and Blanche too continued to observe that particularly beautiful sunset, they were both inspired by what they saw and heard, and the artistic juices started to flow.

So the combination of the awe-inspiring sunset across the lake and blind Mr. Burr's remarks triggered thought-processes in the Brock duo's minds. *"Beyond the sunset....,"* he repeated, *"Beyond the sunset..."*

Quietly, the drama then began to unfold as Virgil began humming a new tune. Improvising, new words, the basis of a new sacred poem flowed from his lips as he did. Listening quietly to the process was his wife Blanche. Inspired, she rose from her garden chair quietly and left the other guests. She walked into the nearby house. Sitting down at the piano, she picked out the immortal melody and lyrics and began to sing.... *"Beyond the Sunset, O blissful Morning! When with our Saviour heaven is begun!"*

Later Virgil wrote, *"That evening, to us the sunset seemed matchless in its beauty. The rapidly changing shades, deepening hues and blending colours, impoverished our vocabulary in an attempt to describe it. From inadequate words, we spoke of the artist's possibility of catching its beauty in the colours of his palette. We decided to penetrate to the truth behind what our eyes saw. There we stood entranced, enjoying the hospitality of the householder at Rainbow Point, and watched the Householder of Heaven draw down the multi-coloured curtains over His latticed windows. Our rapture moved to the inescapable questions, 'What lies beyond the wondrous sunset? What will it be like when our work is done and the experience of heaven is begun?'...So amid the afterglow of the sunset, and still in the wonderland of its beauty, the poem took form and was set to music. To us it seemed as if a light of truth streamed through that open western window into our hearts and became a song to answer our question."*

Years later after the song was well known nationwide, the Brocks remembered their minister preaching at Easter-time on 1 Corinthians 15 in their local church. He posed a challenging question to his congregation. *"What difference should Christ's victory over death and the grave make to us as believers today?"*

The excited preacher continued. *"Brothers and sisters! In 1 Corinthians 15, speaking of the resurrection beyond the sunset, the Apostle Paul not only gives out a glorious outburst of eloquent praise! He concludes with a practical, down-to-earth exhortation for us all....It's almost as if Saint Paul was speaking personally to all the Christians of the city of Corinth to whom his epistle was written. Indeed, his practical advice rings true even for believers today... Brother Paul said, 'Come on now, my brothers and sisters! In the light of these inspiring truths, be unwavering in accomplishing the Lord's work. We know that He will recompense us fully at His coming - beyond the sunset!'"*

Of course, for Virgil it was a very sad day when he said his earthly goodbye to his dear wife as she passed beyond the sunset ahead of him. Indeed, he wept when Mrs. Blanche Kerr Brock died in 1958 and was buried in Warsaw, Indiana. But there in the cemetery, he arranged on her tombstone an inspiring inscription of their hymn's comforting words-and-music of promise. There, for all the world to see, were engraved the lyrics of one of the world's all-time favourite gospel songs, 'Beyond The Sunset'. On the day of the funeral, Virgil said that the precious sentiments expressed in the fourth stanza of the song became even dearer to him that day than when he wrote them in 1936. Standing at the graveside, he contemplated a reunion with his blessed Saviour and wife in Glory... *'Beyond the sunset, o glad reunion with our dear loved ones who've gone before!'*

Slowly during the subsequent twenty years, Virgil Brock came to terms with his loss. He continued to be actively involved as an evangelistic singer and songleader long after his wife's death. He in due time passed 'Beyond The Sunset' too when he died in 1978.

Beyond the sunset, O blissful morning, when with our Saviour, heaven is begun;
Earth's toiling ended, O glorious dawning, beyond the sunset, when day is done.

Beyond the sunset no clouds will gather, no storms will threaten, no fears annoy;
Oh, day of gladness, O day unending, beyond the sunset, eternal joy!

Beyond the sunset, a hand will guide me to God the Father, whom I adore;
His glorious Presence, His words of welcome, will be my portion on that fair shore.

Beyond the sunset, O glad reunion, with our dear loved ones who've gone before;
In that fair homeland we'll know no parting, beyond the sunset, forever more!

Father God
Jack Hayford

> *"For as many as are led by the Spirit of God, they are the sons of God.*
> *For ye have not received the spirit of bondage again to fear; but ye have received the Spirit of adoption, whereby we cry, 'Abba, Father'.*
> *The Spirit itself beareth witness with our spirit, that we are the children of God:*
> *And if children, then heirs; heirs of God, and joint-heirs with Christ;*
> *if so be that we suffer with Him, that we may be also glorified together."*
> *(Romans 8:14-17)*

Yielding to scriptural revelation, one understands that God is 'Father' in more modes than one! Firstly and obviously, in a specific and unique recognition, He is the *Father of Jesus Christ*. Secondly, generally he is known as the *Father-Creator* of the cosmos and of the human race. Thirdly, the New Testament also declares that He is the *Father of His spiritually-born children*. He is the Father who begets and takes care of His 'born-again believers' making them His spiritually-born children. It is that special family tie of father and son that Jack Hayford's beautiful chorus addresses.

Located in Van Nuys, Los Angeles, California, the *Church on the Way* is pastored by radio and television preacher, author and songwriter - Jack Hayford. Tall, soft-spoken and intellectually strong with penetrating brown eyes, originally his church numbered merely a dozen-or-so persons when he took-over! It grew eventually to more than a thousand members under his outstanding leadership, Bible teaching and preaching ministries!

International speaker, Jean Darnell remembered well the first time that she attended the *Church on the Way.* When she arrived in the neighbourhood at eight o'clock on a Palm Sunday morning there was a Sunday morning 'sleeping-in-late' hush. The wide city boulevards were almost devoid of traffic. To her amazement as she turned into the street that housed the *Church on the Way,* she encountered a vast but disciplined crowd on the church steps over-spilling onto the pavement. She recalled how a few days earlier, Jack Hayford had wisely warned her to get there as early as 8:00 a.m. if possible. *"Would that be the Sunday School time?"* she asked quizzically.

"Why no!" The pastor-friend retorted with a smile, *"That's the service time, Jean. You see, we have multiple crowds that demand multiple services if they are going to be accommodated!"*

Eventually, Jean parked the car and joined the throng entering the chapel. Predictably, the sanctuary filled quickly. Taking her seat, she noted that Pastor Jack was already at the front ready to lead the worship. Years before, Jack had been an associate of hers at the Angelus Temple. She smiled to herself as she remembered him as a *"strong, confident and active extrovert brim-full of optimism and drive"*. She said, *"Jack was always able to inspire people, stimulating everyone to be as enthusiastic as himself."*

Born in 1934, Jack Williams Hayford's immediate family members were already earnest in their Christian convictions. However, as Jack declared, *"Although I came from a Christian home, I discovered that God has no grandchildren, just children. I had to have a personal one-on-one relationship with Christ Jesus to qualify for sonship with God. I for my part had to respond to God positively through Jesus!"*

Amidst a very busy life-long ministry, Jack found time to compose hymnal choruses such as 'Father God' and 'Majesty'. The seeds of his songs were divinely sown in lives during the so called 'Jesus

People' movement of the 1970s. As he explained, *"The songs were inspired by my 'walk with God'. I saw them as psalms to the majestic Lord, the Great Father King! The songs exalt Him for His mighty acts and benevolent virtues, the glory of His kingly rule. It's apt that all believers praise God's mighty acts, which display His greatness and His goodness in creation, providence and redemption. Praise of God's benevolent virtues, should move all creatures to celebrate the glory of His kingdom!"*

Jack's touching chorus 'Father God' was lovingly written after he prepared and preached a sermon on the subject of the Fatherhood-of-God. In his sermon study and preparation, he noted that scripturally, 'Abba' was an endearing Aramaic word from Bible days meaning 'Father'. As he studied, he discovered that in Jewish tradition it had three uses. Firstly, it was always a conventional title used of God in prayer. Secondly, 'Abba' was also found in the Babylonian Talmud where it was the address applied by a child to his father. Lastly, it was also used as a type of entreaty to rabbis. In essence, it was commensurate to using the endearing term of 'Daddy' or 'Papa' in modern culture.

Fascinated, as Jack researched the subject further, he did some deeper and deeper examination of the engaging subject. His study unearthed that down the centuries, the Jews found it too audacious and nearly blasphemous to use the word 'Abba' when speaking to God in prayer. They would therefore never address God in that fashion! But in the New Testament, Christ Jesus boldly called God 'Abba Father' and gave that same right to us, His discipled born-again children. Later, the learned Apostle Paul saw 'Abba" as symbolic of the believers' Christian adoption as children of God and of their possession by the Holy Spirit!

In the last quarter of the 20th Century, the name Jack Hayford and his 'Church On The Way' became increasingly known for preaching and teaching ministries. The Church was a trail-blazing pioneer in the blossoming contemporary worship movement of the USA. Initially, aid came to him from some of his church members. These included the hit-making crooner of the 1950s and 1960s, Pat Boone plus the husband-and-wife songwriting duo, Jimmy and Carol Owens.

With their skills and Jack's innovative hymns and choruses, they helped rejuvenate the jaded, banal church music scene of the day. The Christian public warmed to Jack's theologically-challenging lyrics and uncomplicated melodies. The worship songs spoke in dignified yet unpretentious language. Consequently, Jack and his 'Church On The Way' members blazed the trail of the contemporary worship movement on both sides of the Atlantic. In 1972 'Come Together', a musical written by Jimmy and Carol Owens was a special innovation in gospel music led by Pat Boone. It notably altered the traditional image of church use of contemporary Christian music-in-worship. Some of Jack Hayford's songs absorbed into the mainstream of hymnody.

An experienced choir conductor and music arranger (for movies, TV and audio recording) at the time, Mississippi-born Jimmy and his wife, Carol with their two teenage children, daughter Jamie and son Buddy attended Jack's church. While the Owens were eating together at Jack's house after Sunday night church, Jack dropped a casual suggestion into the chat. In his sonorous tone he asked, *"Why don't you write a musical about our church?"*

Jimmy remembered that initially, neither he nor Carol took the suggestion very seriously, but by the next morning, he said, they knew it was their next 'assignment from the Lord'. It was to be a musical not 'about' the church, but setting forth the principles of 'Church On The Way' ministry to be shared with other churches.

Jimmy and Pat Boone worked together on the exciting project, Jimmy conducting the singers and Pat leading the worship. The presentations spread widely. In local churches, each provided local musicians and local worship leaders. Soon the impact of this innovative presentation made itself known in other parts of the world.

In the in the summer of 1973 the Owens were invited to England by Jean and Elmer Darnell to promote 'Come Together' in some 400 presentations. Jimmy remembered, *"It was at the height of severely damaging exposes of sex scandals involving some United Kingdom government ministers. At the time, the condition of the United Kingdom was spiritually and socially in crisis. British churches were often small and their relationships contentious. Socially, inflation, unemployment, and crippling strikes and riots were rampant."*

'Come Together' brought many diverse denominations together for worship and ultimately gave new unity and strength to the nation. Pat Boone remembers, *"On the River Thames, opposite the Houses of Parliament, London's Westminster Central Hall, was packed to capacity the first night with over a thousand people unable to get in! Undaunted, the crowd outside nevertheless joined in with the spirit of 'Come Together' and held their own worship celebration, singing and praying in the falling rain!"*

Bringing the flavour of Jack Hayford's church, the Christian musical went ahead in the largest halls and cathedrals of the land. Local mass choirs, totaling thousands, sprang-up. It was a pivotal time in the church - the early days of the *'Jesus Movement'*, the *'Charismatic Movement'*, the *'House Church Movement"* and the *'Praise and Worship Movement"*. 'Come Together' from Jack's church in California became an effective vehicle to help spread all these new movements.

Thoughtfully, Pat recalls, *"The 'Come Together' presentations included songs and dialogue mainly of scripture. There was an informality, freedom-in-worship without it becoming frivolous or sacrilegious, with a strong emphasis on keeping discipline. I'm told that many attendees found a new liberty in their style of worship that still carries on today!"*

Throughout his many years of ministry, Jack Hayford enjoyed preaching on the Fatherhood of God. The reason was, as he explained, very clearly. *"I sincerely believe that 'Father God' is a term that still can easily communicate to a believer that great sense of warmth, intimacy and respect for his or her Heavenly Father! I'm delighted and amazed when I see how my chorus 'Father God' is sung nowadays by Christians all over the world!"*

Although popularised and promoted by Jack's edifying weekly television and radio shows, the real secret of the chorus' success lies, in its child-like, sing-along simplicity. The sentimental chorus has an honest prayer-like quality and boldness!

Now our Lord Jesus Christ Himself, and God, even our Father, which hath loved us, and hath given us everlasting consolation and good hope through grace,

Comfort your hearts, and establish you in every good word and work.

II Thessalonians 2:16

God Is Good All The Time
Don Moen & Paul Overstreet

"I will bless the LORD at all times: His praise shall continually be in my mouth.
My soul shall make her boast in the LORD:
the humble shall hear thereof, and be glad.
magnify the LORD with me, and let us exalt his name together.
I sought the LORD, and he heard me, and delivered me from all my fears.
They looked unto him, and were lightened: and their faces were not ashamed.
This poor man cried, and the LORD heard him, and saved him out of all his troubles.
The angel of the LORD encampeth round about them that fear Him, and delivereth them.
taste and see that the LORD is good: blessed is the man that trusteth in him.
O fear the LORD, ye his saints: for there is no want to them that fear him.
The young lions do lack, and suffer hunger:
but they that seek the LORD shall not want any good thing.
Psalm 34:1-8

Historically, there has always been a great chorus of God's saints joyfully celebrating God's goodness, what He has done on behalf of

His own. Talented songwriters, Paul Overstreet and Don Moen took note that commonly in the Bible, apart from the general use of the word 'good', the word was used predominantly as a description of the Triune-God Himself. Indeed, the scriptures declared that the Father, the Son (Christ Jesus), and the Holy Spirit alone are truly good all the time.

Ace country singer-songwriter, Paul Overstreet as he looked upon nature, observed an entire universe displaying the 'good' work of God's creative power. As he declared, *"All God made was good!"*

Worship leader, Don Moen also perceived that God's self-revelation of His perfect character and divine will, His word, and His law are good too. Thus together, the songwriting duo declared the Gospel as good tidings and good news! Furthermore, both could witness that, as well as the gifts, the way God establishes and maintains relationships with people is always good. Truly, as their song declared, He was good to all people all the time. The Overstreet-Moen duo's composition expressed increasing amazement at how God gives to all out of the providential care that He exercises over them.

The ancient psalmist of Psalm 34 (David – the shepherd-boy who became king) preludes his words with personal praise in the form of a hymn. Seemingly, like God's goodness, a believer's 'praise- of-God' should be around-the-clock. Such worship should be God-centered, the output of an obligated heart. Such a praise-offering the Lord would not decline. The psalmist's individual response to hardship and rescue in Psalm 34 was to advocate that the afflicted people of God seek Him diligently. Wise and mature, the psalmist testified well from experience. He had known alarm but also attested to how God's saints diffused great assurance and delight in Him. Anticipating the light of His smiling face, they are blessed with the plenteousness of His unfailing goodness.

An inventive force in Christian music, and a gold-disc award artist with a worshiper's heart, Don Moen was brought-up in Minnesota. He left for Tulsa, Oklahoma to attend college at the Oral Roberts University. It was during his studies at ORU that his musical abilities caught the eye of Terry Law Ministries. Don was mustered as a musician for the evangelistic ministry, to play guitar, trombone and on occasion, violin. During ten years with the ministry, he became responsible for many of the group's arrangements and music productions.

Don met, fell in love, and finally married a pretty girl called Laura. Together, Don and his wife, located their family home in Mobile, Alabama and raised five children. In the latter part of the 20th century, he became very well-known in two arenas of activity. Firstly, as a musician, songwriter, singer and worship-leader. In the 1980s-1990s, he earned discriminating acclaim and many citations for his musical efforts. Secondly, he served as an executive Vice President of 'artistic creativity' at the successful 'Integrity' record and music publishing company. Indeed, he had a hand in producing or exercising authority over numerous projects that helped make the company a leader in the Christian-music-industry. Don stated, *"In both my roles, I am realising a dream of reaching thousands worldwide with music tools to bring them into the manifest presence of God."*

In 1984, Michael Coleman the enterprising president of 'Integrity Incorporated' approached Don about aiding his new recording company as the worship leader on the seventh 'Hosanna! Music' live praise and worship recording. The sequential project, 'Give Thanks', became one of 'Integrity''s most popular recordings and was said by many to be a benchmark for the 'praise and worship' genre, selling more than 850,000 copies.

In his developing role at 'Integrity', Don's spiritual impact was felt greatly not only in the company, but also among hundreds of thousands of believers worldwide. They were beneficially influenced by the progressive sounds of 'Integrity Music'. They in turn influenced the on-going hymnology of local churches.

As the 'Creative Director', Don Moen planned the strategy of the music direction of numerous high-profile Christian artists and their projects. In this role, he worked closely with the A & R (Artist & Repertoire) department and music publishing department in the development of Integrity Music's worship, choral and children's products. Don also served as the executive producer for many 'Integrity' CD releases, working with fellow songwriters and worship leaders and focusing on the research and development of new products.

Even though he was, as he stated, *"...elbow deep in product development"* at 'Integrity', Don still took quality time for his own creative pursuits. In the 1990s, he received several 'Gospel Music Association' Dove Award nominations for his songs including 'God Will Make A Way' and for the album, 'Worship with Don Moen'. In 1994, he won a Dove Award for the musical 'God With Us'. Later popular releases included 'God For Us' and 'God Is Good' that he penned with Paul Overstreet. Don declared, *"Being a creator, I want to pour my life into giving birth to new things. I want to find new artists and new niches for the future of Integrity. I contend that a heart of worship can be found in many styles of music. My vision is that, within a broad-based media of creative products that reach an expansive audience, my songs and musicals offer believers live praise and worship combined with powerful testimonies of God's goodness."*

Multi-cultural, the musical, 'God Is Good' was jointly recorded by Don Moen and Paul Overstreet 'live' at the well-known conservative Liberty University in Lynchburg, Virginia. It featured a praise team and mass choir, along with a full orchestra and ace guest musicians Justo Almario and Abraham Laboriel. Don himself played piano and even picked up a fiddle for the song 'God is Good' with Paul Overstreet. The musical featured other classic songs such as 'Praise Looks Good On You', 'God Will Make A Way', 'We've Come To Bless Your Name'. It also featured 'Our Heart', a duet by Don with fellow worship-leader, the infectious Ron Kenoly.

Country-to-the-core, Paul Overstreet was born on March 17th 1955 in Newton, Mississippi. From an early age Paul was surrounded by music. It was gospel music mostly which he heard in church. Also at his local church, he was taught how in the Old Testament, the Lord God unveiled His goodness in His relationship to, and treatment of His People, Israel. His preacher often declared that the scripture announced that *'wise folks taste God's goodness for themselves'* by taking refuge in Him and by submitting their way-of-life to His plans and purposes. The congregation was encouraged to follow the psalmist's example and confess that *'blessed are those who find refuge in the Lord because they taste and see that the Lord is good'!*

Living in the rural Deep South, the early secular entertainment influence was raw country or hillbilly music as some would call it, making great use of guitar, mandolin, fiddle and banjo. Paul's stepfather played mandolin but his main instrument was the guitar. Paul taught himself to play by watching him. Thus Paul soon began to compose songs too. In 1981, Paul's big break came when country star, George Jones recorded one of his compositions that soon hit the charts. Other hits followed by the Forrester Sisters, Randy Travis and others in the same decade.

Sadly, alcohol was having a profound detrimental effect on Paul Overstreet's personal life. But in 1985 the years of heavy drinking suddenly came-to-a-head after a dreadful night at a New Year's Eve party. Sick-sober-and-sorry, Paul awoke the next day with what he described as a terrible head-banging hang-over. Coming at last to his senses, at that point, Paul decided by God's grace that it was time to quit his drinking before it destroyed him. He said that it was a decision owed to the fact that he wanted to became a born again Christian.

Slowly but surely, his prayers were answered and Paul's life was miraculously changed for the better as his aspirations became centred and built around his new-found faith in God. Paul came to understand that on account of sin, human beings have no goodness that is admissible in God's sight. They can, however, take possession-of and become channels-of the wonderful goodness of God. From then on, Paul would now insist on always praying to God first about any new venture and then acting on it. Clearly, the blessing of a strong loving-marriage strengthened his faith with a spouse and children whom he deeply loved and adored. This family bond was often reflected in many of his positive country hit-songs. By the turn of the new Millennium, Paul was a big star in country music. However, better still by far in his eyes, he pursued a spiritually profitable career in the Christian sphere where he gained great respect working with evangelists such as Franklin Graham.

God is good, all the time, He put a song of praise in this heart of mine.
God is good, all the time through the darkest night,
His light will shine, God is good, God is good all the time.

If you're walking through the shadows and there are shadows all around
Do not fear, He will guide you He will keep you safe and sound
He has promised to never leave you nor forsake you and His Word is true.

We were sinners so unworthy, Still for us He chose to die
Filled us with His Holy Spirit Now we can stand and testify
That His love is everlasting and His mercies, they will never end.

Though I may not understand all the plans You have for me
My life is in Your hands and through the eyes of faith I can clearly see.

God Of Glory, We Exalt Your Name
Dave Fellingham

'Let this mind be in you, which was also in Christ Jesus:
 Who, being in the form of God, thought it not robbery to be
equal with God:
But made Himself of no reputation, and took upon Him the
form of a servant,
and was made in the likeness of men:
 And being found in fashion as a man, He humbled Himself,
and became obedient unto death, even the death of the cross.
Wherefore God also hath highly exalted Him,
 and given Him a Name which is above every name:
 That at the Name of Jesus every knee should bow,
of things in heaven, and things in earth, and things under
the earth;
And that every tongue should confess that Jesus Christ is
Lord, to the glory of God the Father."
Philippians 2:5-11

British-born, Dave Fellingham's worshipful chorus, 'God Of Glory, We Exalt Your Name' was initially inspired by the general expressions of praise in the Old And New Testament. He appreciated especially the picture painted by the Apostle Paul in Philippians 2 of Christ's humiliation and subsequent exaltation. Dave's chorus, like the scripture, was intended to encourage in Christians in every generation into an attitude of Christ-like humility in worship. Dave was aware that the Apostle Paul was declaring that those folks identified as Christ's followers, must make evident His characteristics in addition to exalting Him. Indeed, Paul's entreaty was that Christians should seek to live a life of meekness. Furthermore, it also comprised an important 'word-to-the-wise'. As Christ illustrated, triumph follows abasement. God's glory will at length prevail.

Even in Sunday school, Dave Fellingham was taught that in Bible times, the concept of the word 'name' employed an importance it does not have nowadays. In modern times, a person's name is generally merely a tag without special meaning. Back then in Bible times, a name was given only by a personage in a status-of-authority. The given-name indicated that the person named was appointed to a particular position, function, or relationship. The name given was often determined by some circumstance at the time of birth. Sometimes the name expressed a hope or a prophecy. Clearly, in the Scriptures, there is the closest conceivable association between a person and his name, the two being virtually equivalent. So strong is this association, to remove the name was to extinguish the person.

In the case of God, to forget God's name was seen as a departure from Him, the opposite of 'God Of Glory, We Exalt Your Name'. In Biblical teaching, 'the name', moreover, was 'the person' as he had been revealed. For example, the term, 'name of the LORD' signified the Lord in the attributes that He had manifested. These included His holiness, His power, His love, and such. Additionally, often in the Bible 'the name' signified 'the presence of the person' in the character revealed.

Dave Fellingham's worshipful chorus 'God Of Glory, We Exalt Your Name' addresses Jesus Christ who although He was God took on the nature of a servant. Clearly, His divinity could not be dispensed with, for God could not cease to be God. Rather, He took on the very form of a lowly servant when He entered human life in His incarnation. Plainly too, Christ became part of suffering humanity, being made in human likeness. Externally, He appeared as a mere human being, no different from other people. Committed to the Father's plan, He obeyed God's purposes even as far as death, the disgraceful death by crucifixion. Such a death was not allowed for Roman citizens and to Jews it was indicative of the curse of God.

In resurrection, God elevated Christ to the highest position, granting Him 'The Name Above All Names'! 'God Of Glory, We Exalt Your Name'. Thus exalted to the highest place, Christ is today super-exalted following His humiliating death. This exaltation will finally climax at the end of the Age when His lordship will be acknowledged by every being.

Born in 1945 just after the end of World War II in Europe, Dave grew-up surrounded by the verdant English countryside of Horsham in Sussex. Dressed smartly in their uniforms, his mother and father served faithfully as Salvation Army officers. After sundry postings with the Salvation Army, the Fellingham family at length settled down in the village of Tongham located between Aldershot and Guildford. David's youthful heart warmed early in life to the 'call of the gospel'. In boyish straightforwardness, he recollects that he was 'born again'.

Christianity as an adolescent youth meant becoming actively involved in the musical life of the local Salvation Army corps. Outfitted in the dashing, traditional blue uniform of General Booth's Tongham brigade, the teenager discovered 'music-and-faith'. As he matured, they seemed to mix as comfortably as fish-and-chips or strawberries-and-cream!

David obtained a profitable post-war education at George Abbot School For Boys in Guildford, Surrey. Leaving after his sixth year at the School, he toiled between shelves of books as a librarian for a year. Incapable of settling, he then determined to make ready to be a teacher. After hard study, he was conferred with an honours degree in education by Sussex University in 1968. His musical abilities, however, never lapsed from consciousness.

Becoming an associate of the Royal College of Music, he majored in the trumpet. In July 1968, matrimony bells rang out as David married Rosemary Downer, daughter of Eric Downer. David's new father-in-law was converted under the ministry of the famous pentecostal pioneer, George Jeffreys and served as the secretary of Great Britain's Elim Churches' conference.

David's vocational history proceeded with a condensed interlude of teaching music at Newhaven Tideway followed by his assignment as the Director of Music at Longhill until 1976.

Now spiritually highly motivated, he was instated into the Christian ministry as a lay pastor in an Anglican Church. In early 1979, he became a positive component of the leadership team of what became called the 'Church of Christ the King' on England's south coast. He successfully developed his music skills and by the commencement of the 20th century, David was recognised as an internationally acclaimed songwriter, worship-leader, author and speaker. His ministry at the 'Church of Christ the King' was essentially as an evangelist, heading up the 'Alpha Program For Beginners In The Christian Faith'. He was also charged with organising creative outreach events and exercising authority in worship within the Church.

Most of Dave Fellingham's wonderful worship choruses tend to be inspired by 'exaltation of Christ' but he does not solely write worship music. He is also a writer of contemporary classical music and has many works performed by orchestras, chamber groups and choirs. Zealous to sustain an even keel in life, Dave says that he catches time for other things too! Outdoors and indoors, a serious sports devotee, he takes pleasure from playing squash, soccer and skiing.

When relaxing at home, he says that he takes pleasure in watching western movies on video and perseveres with an enthralling engrossment in history. He also confesses that he derives great joy from cooking-especially fish dishes! He says that garlic, peppers, mushrooms and cream, together with a little *'je ne sais quoi'* are the foundation for any good meal that anyone can cook.

David and Rosemary parented two sons, Luke and Nathan. Both are now married and are part of a full-time Christian music ministry, commonly playing music at major Christian conferences worldwide. Together with his dear wife-Rosie, David says that he gets heavily absorbed in crisis-counseling especially in the area of 'spiritual deliverance'. In David's home Church, he has advanced many connections with other churches that furnishes opportunities for him to minister periodically in North America, Europe and the Far East.

In his 'God Of Glory, We Exalt Your Name' chorus, Dave understood that 'The Name Above All Names' is the equivalent of the Old Testament term, 'Lord'. Nowadays, Dave declares that

Christ's exaltation categorically manifests His Lordship as the word 'exaltation' is a term used exclusively as a reference to God. *"The universal expectation of Christ's exaltation is that all beings might bow in affirmation of The Name confessing Jesus Christ as Lord. Ultimately, this universal admission will include the angels, the saints in heaven, the people on earth, the satanic hosts and even the lost of humanity in hell. Thus compliance will be expressed by verbal confession from even Christ's enemies. His Name with all its nobility and divine prerogatives will eventually be recognized by every creature!"*

God Of Glory, we exalt Your name, You who reign in majesty.
We lift our hearts to You And we will worship, praise and magnify Your holy name.
In power resplendent You reign in glory, Eternal King, You reign forever.
Your word is mighty, Releasing captives,
Your love is gracious, You are my God.

Hallelujah, For The Lord Our God The Almighty Reigns

David & Dale Garrett

"And a voice came out of the throne, saying,
 Praise our God, all ye his servants, and ye that fear him,
both small and great.
And I heard as it were the voice of a great multitude,
and as the voice of many waters, and as the voice of mighty
thunderings, saying,
 Alleluia: for the Lord God omnipotent reigneth.
Let us be glad and rejoice, and give honour to Him:
 for the marriage of the Lamb is come, and His wife hath
made herself ready.
And to her was granted that she should be arrayed in fine
linen, clean and white:
 for the fine linen is the righteousness of saints.
Revelation 19:5-8

Under the inspiration of the Holy Spirit, after much internal and external searching, King Solomon declared three thousand years ago that there was nothing new under the sun! Although by no means new, the fashionableness of the use of the 'Scriptures in Song' genre overflowed into most mainstream churches in the second half of the 20th century. The enthusiastic New Zealander, Dale Garrett is to be credited for doing most of the melody-writing of the new 'Scriptures in Song'.

World-wide from the late 1970s onwards, a very popular worship chorus (with a most lengthy title) was 'Hallelujah For The Lord Our God The Almighty Reigns'. Although penned by the husband-and-wife duo, David and Dale Garrett. it was inspired, of course, by Revelation 19:5-8 and the Book of Psalms.

Dale was born in 1939 in New Zealand. At the time, her nation, along with all the British Empire, was thrust into the hostilities of World War II, following the German attack on Poland. Dale, the new baby's name, was being popularised world-wide by Hollywood's western-movie duo, Roy Rogers and Dale Evans. The fame of the 'Queen of the West' even spread as far as New Zealand. At play at 'cowboys and Indians', it felt good to be named after a silver-screen hero.

As a young girl, she came under considerable Christian teaching that challenged her lifestyle. But like most youngsters when she reached her teenage years experienced some rebellion against the establishment. Eventually, along with her husband David, Dale yielded more and more fully to the claims-of -Christ upon her life.

Growing more mature in her Holy Faith, Dale was challenged in her inner spirit to actively contribute to the worship of her local church. Slowly over several years, she developed in her homeland an evident love of hearing the ancient scriptures sung to the contemporary pop sounds of the 1970s. Enthusiasm grew and in the years that followed Dale and her husband, Dave succeeded in laying the foundation of what became the world-wide 'worship chorus' phenomenon in the latter part of the 20th Century.

From their New Zealand base, song books to accompany the Garretts' 'Scriptures-in-Song' record albums were produced and exported to many parts of the world. Many churches of varied denominations experimented in the use of the Garretts' 'Scriptures-in-Song' as tools in their congregational worship. Indeed, Dale and her husband, Dave matured into outstanding pioneering promoters, songwriters and worship leaders in what became the 'Scriptures-in-Song' genre.

Looking backwards, across the decades and commenting on the results of the 'Scripture-in-Song' concept from New Zealand, Dale took great pleasure in observing that their songs were blessing so many Christians across the world. *"As we continue to listen to what the Holy Spirit is saying, we are able to put tools in the hands of God's people that are life-changing. We disciple people in using music in a prophetic way. Later, they too can train and teach others. Whatever we're doing that is 'of God' will be multiplied!"*

The enterprising Garretts said that they discovered that the old English word 'Hallelujah' transliterated a Greek word, which in turn transliterated the Hebrew expression 'hallelu yah'. This meant in plain terms – 'Praise the LORD!' This transliteration cropped up once in the Revelation book of the New Testament, but it was a very frequent word too in the Old Testament psalms. To the Garretts, this plainly explained by example the correlation of the Early Church's liturgical worship with the synagogue and temple worship of the first century. Clearly, 'praise psalms' ceaselessly forged a significant part of Jewish festival celebrations.

The old Hallel was dubbed 'The Hallel of Egypt'. This was by virtue of the reference in it to the 'Exodus of God's People from Egypt' following the Passover night. Indeed, the Hebrew psalms enjoyed a special role in the Feast of Passover. Most Jewish specialists associate the Hallel with 'the destruction of the wicked', precisely as this scripture excerpt from Revelation does. These Hallel psalms were what Christ Jesus and His disciples sang after their Last Supper (the Passover-Eucharist observance). Then they left for the Mount of Olives on the night before His arrest. This close connection between the Hallel, the Passover Lamb, and the death of Christ no doubt demonstrates why all the Early Church liturgies incorporated the Hallel into the Easter and Easter Week liturgies. They venerate the good news of salvation in the victorious triumph of Christ. In Revelation 19 an ultimate Hallel is pronounced by an angelic voice from the Throne. *"Hallelujah For The Lord Our God The Almighty Reigns...Praise our God, all you His servants. You who fear Him, both small and great!"*

The Garretts clearly felt that this 'call-to-worship' fused together all socio-economic classes in concordant veneration of God by the church. In the Apostle John's vision, ultimately, the cycle-of-praise is achieved with the echoing sounds of great multitudes. John saw that the church's garments were white linen, the expensive cloth used to make the garments worn by priests and royalty illustrating brightness and cleanness. Such radiant qualities at that celebration depicted glorification, purity, loyalty, and faithfulness. In his written account the Apostle John was asserting that the fine linen stands for the righteous acts of the saints. Dave recalled, *"Such scripture prophecies greatly inspired us in New Zealand as a songwriting husband and wife team."*

From a huge family, Dave was born in Wellington, the capital city, the second of eleven children. His hard-working father started out as a carpenter by profession but then managed a firm trading in chemistry appliances. Dave's earliest Christian persuasion came by way of his parents whom he described as *'convinced fundamental evangelicals'*. Looking rearward to his boyhood and adolescence years, he observed how very real was their faith! *"That's something I realised as a boy!"*

Ceasing his school studies, Dave's early professional life was in the tea business on-the-road extensively to the beggared tea-producing countries. These eye-opening excursions, he said, challenged him greatly as he observed just how emaciated was the condition of many human beings in the world. It was an affront to his social conscience but it also made him appreciate deeply the blessings he enjoyed.

At An eventful 'New Zealand Youth For Christ' meeting in the North Island city of Auckland, Dave and Dale originally became romantically mindful of each other. On the platform, Dave was performing while Dale listened attentively in the young audience. Prior to that significant rendezvous, they had worked together beforehand as singers. As he told me, Dave theorized that the timing of their second encounter was crucial in both their lives. *"I am sure it was the timing of God because when we did fall in love, it was right! Prior to that, it could have been a diversion for us!"*

Subsequently as husband and wife, the twosome linked together to scribe many 'Scripture In Song' gospel songs. David credited Dale as doing most of the melody-writing but he said that he sometimes recommended new ideas for themes and scriptures. He also said that there were times when he would burst into a spot of what he described as spontaneous singing!

In 1968 the duo started recording some of their new scripture songs and coined a new term. They called them 'Scriptures in Song'. The simple concept was to use original King James scriptures verbatim to pop melodies. Rather than a new idea it was a re-discovery. The Garretts were aware that many times throughout history, hymn and gospel song-writers used written raw scripture as their bedrock. When asked where the Garretts' rediscovery of this historic practice came from Dale said, "*It was really just something the Lord dropped on us! Several years before we were praying for a musical way to express ourselves and communicate to people things that had more meat than the sort of popular 'Sweet Bye and Bye' type of song. We heard some of the first Scripture Songs and felt we should put them on record. That was the simple beginning!*"

When the unpretentious albums were released, the uncomplicated yet graceful songs were described as 'anointed' by some people. When asked about the rationalization of this insight, Dale replied, "*I guess we tried to respond to what the Holy Spirit said to us! If what one does is motivated by God, one can expect the Lord to bless it! That's the way it was! Neither of us were musicians, we were congregational singers rather than performing artists. At the same time, we become a demonstration to people in the area of praise and worship. We were able to use songs to teach in a prophetic sense and deliver something of God's Word to people! God's Word teaches that His Word will never return unto Him void. That is to say whenever the Word is proclaimed it will accomplish that purpose it was meant to do!*"

Taking their songs abroad, Dave and Dale Garrett became recognised as skilled trailblazers. They pioneered the use of the 'Scripture-in-Song' music style of the last quarter of the 20th century. The Garretts are convinced that the use of Christian songs—especially 'Scripture In Song'— is an effective means of worshipping, communicating and of learning God's Word. They deeply believe that as Christians sing truths via 'Scripture In Song', it imparts spiritual food into individuals who are hungry and thirsty to receive and learn. The twosome enthusiastically asserted that the Word of God is food for all! As a result they tried to always guarantee that the substances of their scripture songs were worthy of both singing and learning. David would often quote the words of Christ, *"Man does not live by bread alone but by every word that proceeds from the mouth of God!"*

Hallelujah, for the Lord our God the Almighty reigns.
Hallelujah, for the Lord our God the Almighty reigns.
Let us rejoice and be glad and give the glory unto Him.
Hallelujah, for the Lord our God the Almighty reigns.

Have Thine Own Way
Adelaide Addison Pollard & George Stebbins

> *"The word which came to Jeremiah from the LORD, saying,*
> *Arise, and go down to the potter's house, and there I will*
> *cause thee to hear my words.*
> *Then I went down to the potter's house, and, behold, he*
> *wrought a work on the wheels.*
> *And the vessel that he made of clay was marred in the*
> *hand of the potter:*
> *so he made it again another vessel, as seemed good to the*
> *potter to make it.*
> *Then the word of the LORD came to me, saying,*
> *'O house of Israel, cannot I do with you as this potter?*
> *saith the LORD.*
> *Behold, as the clay is in the potter's hand, so are ye in*
> *mine hand, O house of Israel.'"*
> *Jeremiah 18:1-6*

The gentle hymnwriter, Adelaide Addison Pollard was born in Bloomfield, Iowa on November 27th 1862, the daughter of James and Rebecca (Smith) Pollard. The bouncy baby-girl was bestowed with the cumbersome name of Sarah Addison Pollard. However, later as a child, she took a dislike to the name Sarah. Determinedly, she adopted the new name Adelaide in lieu and answered to no other. By her teens, all her friends and relatives knew her as Alelaide.

Refined and a high achiever, she was educated at the 'Denmark Academy' located in the region of Denmark, Iowa, and later at a school in Valparaiso in Indiana. To top all that quality education, she opted for a three-year course in elocution and physical culture at the Boston School of Oratory. Now extremely well qualified, she relocated in the 1880s to Chicago where she taught in several schools for girls.

Adelaide's close friend, Miss Lily Waller introduced her to the evangelistic work of John Alexander Dowie. Soon Adelaide was involved in his healing services and indeed she testified that she received divine deliverance from her diabetes. Later Adelaide and Lily moved to New England initially in support of the evangelistic preacher, Pastor Sanford who majored on preaching on the subject of the Second Coming of Christ. Highly motivated in spiritual matters, for a while Adelaide treasured plans to go to Africa to serve as a foreign missionary. Disappointingly, her plans failed and she opted instead to serve her Saviour as a teacher at the Missionary Training School of New York City.

Prior to World War I that broke out in Europe in 1914, Adelaide fulfilled her dream by sailing to Africa to advance the Christian cause. When fierce fighting commenced in earnest in mainland Europe, she sailed north to the United Kingdom's bonnie Scotland where she spent her war years. They were days when 'votes for women' were being earnestly campaigned. When peace came in 1918, she was free to return to her homeland. So she sailed to New York and when she arrived headed for more Christian work in New England.

Mystically-inclined and in frail health, Adelaide's devoutly orthodox Presbyterian family often despaired of Adelaide's seeming fascination with what they saw as extreme theology and unorthodox religious sects. One day, after returning home from a prayer meeting, in great distress of soul because of her failed missionary service dreams, she settled into an armchair to read. While she was reading the 'Parable Of The Potter' in Jeremiah 18:1-6, she was very deeply challenged. As she dug deeper, she learned that 'The 'Potter's House' was the most familiar of the prophet Jeremiah's literary illustrations. But she also found that it was also located elsewhere in Scripture in Job, Psalms, Isaiah and Revelation. In the passage of Jeremiah, she saw a true but mysterious blending of God's divine sovereignty and mankind's human responsibility. She declared aloud, *"The Lord used the potter to illustrate how He deals with humanity!"*

There and then, Adelaide knew that God the Divine Potter was not to be seen as an arbitrary Sovereign. Rather, the deeper level of meaning spoke of His grace that even under-girded the coming disasters to befall the Biblical nation of Judah.

She read how the divine command came to Jeremiah to go down to the pottery, where it was the Lord's intention to give him a message for the people. So he went there from the temple that was in the upper part of the city. The potter's house was probably on the slopes of the Valley of Hinnom (south of Jerusalem), where water and clay were traditionally found. Here the prophet was to be taught the principles of the divine government. At the pottery, Jeremiah saw what was already familiar to him. The potter was fashioning a vessel on the wheels, the upper and lower discs made of stone and wood. The lower one was worked by the foot of the potter and was attached by an axle to the upper one, on which the clay was worked. The discs were in a horizontal position. In Adelaide's mind-eye, the scene was almost alive.

As happened regularly in the daily life of a potter, the clay did not turn out quite right. Often in throwing the clay, some defect would become evident. The potter then rolls the clay into a lump to begin his task again to make a more suitable product. Here the chief elements in the teaching illustration to be noted by Jeremiah were twofold. Firstly, the potter retains power over the clay. Secondly, the potter is patient and persevering. Ultimately, the clay is in his hand and under his control. Jeremiah noted that the defects were in the clay, not the hands of the potter.

Now as Adelaide read on, Jeremiah is taught the meaning of the lesson. The infinite power of the Lord is compared with that of the potter over his clay. Just as the potter remade the clay to conform to his purpose, so the Lord's will and power continue to mould His people until they conform to His plan. *"I understand now!"* Adelaide spoke quietly to herself. *"The Lord will never be defeated even if His people turn from His way for them. There is a conditional element in His dealings with His people. Repentance can always change the Lord's decree of judgment, for His threatenings are never unconditional."*

As she meditated, it seemed the Holy Spirit was cautioning her. The parallel between humanity and the clay must not be carried too far. Human 'clay' is not passive. Upon a person's repentance, God can rework him or her into a vessel of honour. The position is not one of absolute fatalism (blotting out human freedom), nor is it one where God's sovereignty is wholly dependent on a person's choice. Ultimately, no human being is free. God in His mysterious working in human life has ordered it so that humanity may freely choose.

Inspired, Adelaide rose from her comfortable chair by the fireplace and moved to her office-desk. Taking paper and pen she wrote as truth dawned on her soul…. *"Thank God that He does not exercise His omnipotence arbitrarily or capriciously but conditions everything ethically."*

She understood clearly that the parable of the potter was meant principally for the people of Judah. Yet she also understood that God deals similarly with all nations and with all people, corporately and individually… *"All people are given the opportunity to repent and conform to God's purpose. When the Scriptures speak of His 'relenting' or 'repenting', we must understand this in the light of Numbers 23:19. The verse says, 'God is not a man, that He should lie; neither the son of man, that He should repent: hath He said, and shall He not do it? or hath He spoken, and shall He not make it good?'"*

That day, Adelaide realised firstly, the truth that in this parable the prophet was holding out the opportunity for the nation and individuals to repent. Secondly, when the term 'repentance' is used about God, it never means what it does for a human being, for God has never done anything wrong. Looking heavenward her thoughts turned to praise. *"Oh I thank You Lord that You always decide to act differently toward men and women when they turn from disobeying You to obeying You…. Oh thank You, Lord that with You, repentance is not a change-of-mind. I see now that it's Your consistent response in accord with Your changeless nature. Thank You Lord for responding in love to the changes in an individual heart or in a nation's conduct."*

Adelaide penned a prayerful poem entitled 'Have Thine Own Way', continuing to be inspired by her experience,. Later, the poem became a hymn when George Coles Stebbins added a suitable melody. He included it in several publications including two songbooks in 1907: 'Northfield Hymnal with Charles Alexander's Supplement' and Ira Sankey's 'Hallowed Hymns, New And Old'. George Stebbins was born in Orleans County in New York on February 26th 1846 and died in Catskill, New York on October 6th 1945. A prolific songwriter, George studied music in the New York cities of Buffalo and Rochester. As church music directors, he located to Chicago in 1869 and then Boston in 1876. This was followed by twenty-five years of work in evangelistic song.

Adelaide Addison Pollard died in New York City on December 20th 1934, five days before Christmas. The Christmas gift that she left for future generations was her prayerful hymn-poem, 'Have Thine Own Way'. She successfully applied the 'Parable of the Potter' to Christian believers in her song. She was convinced that responsibility for repentance clearly rested on them. When the Righteous Lord declared that He is 'preparing' a calamity of judgement for His People, the Hebrew verb was the same as the word for the work of a potter; so there is a play on words. In Jeremiah's day, the threatened calamity was the nation's exile to Babylon.

What was the nation's reaction? The people claimed that it was hopeless to try to dissuade them from their ways. Sadly, having gone too far in sin to turn back, they condemned themselves. Their intractability showed how deep-seated their love of idolatry was. After all His loving pleading, what a disheartening response it was for Jeremiah to receive!

Have Thine own way, Lord! Have Thine own way!
Thou art the Potter; and I am the clay.
Mould me and make me after Thy will,
While I am waiting yielded and still.

Have Thine own way, Lord! Have Thine own way!
Search me and try me, Master, today!

Whiter than snow, Lord, wash me just now,
As in Thy presence humbly I bow.

Have Thine own way, Lord! Have Thine own way!
Wounded and weary help me, I pray!
Power - all power - Surely is Thine!
Touch me and heal me, Saviour Divine!

Have Thine own way, Lord! Have Thine own way!
Hold o'er my being absolute sway!
Fill with Thy Spirit till all shall see
Christ only, always, living in me!

He Lives! (I Serve A Risen Saviour)
Adelaide Addison Pollard
& George Stebbins

'*I am He that liveth, and was dead;*
and, behold, I am alive for evermore, Amen;
and have the keys of hell and of death.'
(Revelation 1:18)

American-born hymn-writer, Alfred Henry Ackley was greatly encouraged by these powerful words in Revelation 1:18 from the resurrected Christ Jesus, recorded by the Apostle John in exile on the Isle of Patmos. *"I am He that liveth, and was dead; and, behold, I am alive for evermore, Amen; and have the keys of hell and of death!"*

Under the inspiration of the Holy Spirit, these divinely-uttered words inspired Alfred to write one of the most triumphant Easter anthem-choruses of all time. The very-singable ballad-style verses of the hymn aptly document why the Christian should 'rejoice-and-be-glad' in the life-changing truth that 'He Lives!'

John Calvin (1509-1564) was a French-born legendary Reformation preacher and theologian. He settled in Geneva, Switzerland as a political and religious leader. He once spoke powerfully about the Resurrection. *"We have complete salvation through Christ's death because we are reconciled to God by it. But it is by His resurrection, not His death, that we are said to be born again to a living hope."*

As a keen student of scripture and a Christian minister, Alfred Henry Ackley clearly saw this living hope that John Calvin spoke of so eloquently. In unmistakable terms, Alfred understood that the risen Jesus ascertained to the Apostle John that His true identity was that of 'The Christ', the Messiah - the Anointed One. Indeed, His words connected John's vision of the glorified Christ with His past existence as the Lord of All History. Songwriter, Alfred recognised that the awe-inspiring vision of John was seen in the light of the Eternal One. It was God speaking Himself, in the first person. Alfred commented, *"John knew that Christ's title of being 'the First and the Last' was one that pertained solely to God. On the island of Patmos, the resurrected Christ Jesus was declaring to him in vision that He alone was the great Creator God - the absolute Lord-of-History."*

At the fearful sight of this awesome Supernatural Being, the Apostle John— stricken with trembling and fear, as had prophets before him— fell at His feet as though dead! Instantaneously, Christ positioned His hand on the Apostle and vouched that he would not die. Christ's words, *'Do not be afraid!'* comforted and cheered. Christ also declared that He was *'the Living One'*—the One who never changes. Such divine attributes of His Person, He associated with His earthly life-span in first-century Palestine as He declared, *'I was dead, and behold I am alive for ever and ever!'*

Alfred Henry Ackley accepted fully that the Apostle John's written theological panorama of Christ Jesus orbited around His Cross and His Resurrection and needed to be documented in an appropriate hymnal anthem. He said that these significant events won Christ the right to own the 'keys of death and the grave'. Victoriously, he said that this grants Him as the Key-holder access to 'death's inner-parts' and the 'contents of the grave'. Since Christ Jesus alone conquered death and the grave, He alone now determines who will enter death and who will be delivered. Alfred declared, *"He has the keys so for the Christian, death can only be seen now as the servant of Christ Jesus, our Lord! Hallelujah!"*

In his 'Forty Gospel Hymn Stories', George W. Sanville says that Alfred claimed that he wrote both the words and music of 'He Lives' following a chance encounter. Alfred said that the song came after an experience witnessing to a young Jewish man about Jesus of Nazareth, the Messiah of Israel known to his followers as Christ Jesus. Indignantly, the young man cornered Alfred with a startling question. *"Tell me why I should acknowledge and worship Jesus? He's only, after all, a dead Jew?"*

Alfred's answer was immediate, inspired and inspiring. *"The reason is simple but profound, my friend!...Jesus Christ is alive today!...He lives!...The glorified Christ is the Lord of All History!"*

Later at home settled comfortably in his favourite armchair, Alfred pondered over the lively discussion. Seizing his well-thumbed Bible, he returned to the scriptural accounts of the eyewitnesses to the Resurrection including the Apostle John's account. After reading the Bible story again, the lyrics and tune of 'He Lives' were divinely conceived: *"I serve a Risen Saviour who is in the world today!"* It was published in the 'Triumphant Service Songs' collection in 1933.

Alfred Henry Ackley was born in Spring Hill, Bradford County, Pennsylvania on 21st January 1887 while Queen Victoria reigned over the British Empire that boasted that a quarter of the globe was under its sway. Alfred saw many changes in his lifetime of seventy-three years. Under the shadow of nuclear warfare, at the height of America's Cold War with Russia, he died in Whittier, California on July 3rd 1960, the day before the annual Independence Day celebrations in his hometown.

As a very teachable child, Alfred Henry Ackley always enjoyed music and received his first instruction from his dear father, Stanley F. Ackley. Later to add to his domestic teaching, Alfred studied harmony and composition in New York and London. It was little surprise that he became such an expert musician majoring on the cello coached by the accomplished cellist, Hans Kronold. Alfred proudly graduated from the Westminster Theological Seminary in Maryland seeking a vocation in the Christian ministry. By the time of the Great War that broke out in Europe in 1914, Alfred was ordained into the Presbyterian ministry. He served in as pastor in townships from Wilkes-Barre, Pennsylvania to Escondido, California. Later he served in pastoral responsibilities at the Shadyside Presbyterian Church in Pittsburgh, Pennsylvania.

Alfred never strayed far from his love affairs with music and scripture, maintaining a keen interest in the composing of inspirational lyrics and hymn tunes throughout his life. He claimed that during the years he amassed a self-composed collection of no less than fifteen hundred pieces that ranged from hymns, gospel songs, kiddies sing-along pieces, and secular ditties to college glee-club anthems. For many years, Alfred's brother, Benton D. Ackley supported the famous evangelist Billy Sunday as the pianist for the famed soloist, Homer Rodeheaver. This gave Alfred great exposure for his music compositions.

An impactive performer of gospel songs, Homer was born in 1880. He became evangelist Billy Sunday's song leader in 1909. Homer realised early-on the importance of gospel songs as a vital part of revival meetings. He was endeared to songs such as those penned by Alfred Henry Ackley including 'I serve a Risen Saviour He's in the world today!'. This new emphasis on gospel songs was to change the face of evangelistic meetings.

At the age of fourteen in 1923, the veteran soloist, George Beverly Shea recalled the great thrill of hearing Homer for the first time singing on record. The inspiring sound came from a wind-up Victrola phonograph, a mahogany instrument highly prized at the time. It belonged to the Beardsley family who lived opposite the Sheas in Metcalf Street, Ottawa. Years later, Beverly remembered personally meeting with Homer at Winowa Lake. He found Homer to be a short, stocky, smiling individual whose sincerity was infectious.

Homer favoured 'sing-along-songs' such as those often penned by the Ackley brothers. In his many years of service, Homer developed to the full the art of audience-participation in gospel singing. His innovative style and his God-given ability to draw even the most reluctant individuals into taking part in the services was a totally different style to that of other song leaders before his day. He would often prelude the meetings with a musical quiz or parts-singing drawing on the audience to participate. An accomplished trombonist, Homer's trombone with piano accompaniment, provided dramatic background to the gospel singing not heard of before in revival meetings.

Hymn-writers like the Ackley brothers were huge influences on soloist George Beverly Shea especially in the decade before World War II. Predictably, both the Ackley brothers were deeply involved with the Rodeheaver Publishing Company as Homer Rodeheaver popularised so many of their compositions. Under their auspices many collections of gospel song collections were published accordingly. Such songbooks popularised the Ackley brothers' songs internationally.

I serve a risen Saviour, He's in the world today;
I know that He is living, whatever men may say.
I see His hand of mercy, I hear His voice of cheer,
And just the time I need Him, He's always near.

He lives, He lives! Christ Jesus lives today!
He walks with me and talks with me along life's narrow way.
He lives, He lives, salvation to impart!
You ask me how I know He lives?
He lives within my heart!

In all the world around me I see His loving care;
And though' my heart grows weary, I never will despair.
I know that He is leading thro' all the stormy blast;
The day of His appearing will come at last.

Rejoice, rejoice, O Christian, Lift up your heart and sing
Eternal hallelujahs to Jesus Christ, the King!
The Hope of all who seek Him, The Help of all who find,
None other is so loving, so good and kind.

He Touched Me
Bill Gaither

"When He was come down from the mountain, great multi-tudes followed Him.
And, behold, there came a leper and worshipped him,
saying, Lord, if thou wilt, thou canst make me clean.
And Jesus put forth his hand, and touched him,
saying, I will; be thou clean.
And immediately his leprosy was cleansed."
Matthew 8:1-2

'He Touched Me', written by American songwriter, Bill Gaither was a powerful song that received renewed interest in the 21st century via his award-winning male quartet, the Gaither Vocal Band. Yet it was written in the early 1960s, one of the first songs that Bill ever wrote, and it was recorded hundreds of times down the decades since. Probably, however, the first recorded version of the song heard by most people was by the Bill Gaither Trio composed of Bill, Gloria (his wife) and Danny (his brother). The song was sung widely in the 1970s and 1980s at Trio concerts and Billy Graham Crusade meetings.

In the Four Gospels there are many historic incidents when Christ Jesus (who was 'Emmanuel-God with us') physically *touched* people with miraculous results. Indeed in those times past, many of the miracles involved a 'touch from Jesus'. However, the 'touch' in Bill

Gaither song 'He Touched Me' is more up-to-date and personal because it refers to contemporary believers touched in every generation.

Attending church every Sunday in the 1940s and early 1950s, Bill remembered time-and-again hearing his local preacher declaring from the pulpit that the old disease of leprosy in the Bible was usually an illustration of the sinful condition of every human heart. Preaching on the subject was common. He retold the story first recorded by the ex- tax collector, St. Matthew in his Gospel account. Dramatically one day, a poverty-stricken and diseased leper came to Christ requesting healing. The preacher encouraged the congregation to search the scriptures with reference to the subject of leprosy. *"You folks will discover that the condition in Old Testament times was looked on as 'unclean' whether it was in people, houses, or clothing. The old religious law of the day obligated the individual proclaimed leprous by the priest to identify himself in an appointed manner and to disengage himself from society. When any member of the public drew near to a leper, the leper was to cry, 'Unclean, unclean!'"*

Clearly, the preacher said that leprosy was very contagious and therefore, detailed instructions were given for dealing with this disease. *"In the New Testament, the cumbersome procedures of defilement were further developed by the scribes and Pharisees, which Christ condemned.... "Do NOT touch!" was the clear emphasis and instruction of Old and New Testament teachings regarding anything designated as 'unclean'....This great religious obsession boldly emphasised the different attitude and contrast of the loving Christ's gracious standpoint. No wonder the on-looking crowd was utterly amazed at His willingness to touch the untouchable!"*

The congregation was spellbound as the preacher continued. *"In Matthew 8, Matthew recorded that when Christ came down out of the hills (fresh from where the Sermon on the Mount had been delivered), great masses of people still tracked after Him. Then a poor 'unclean' leper knelt before the Great Physician and worshipped Him addressing Him as Lord. Readers of Matthew cannot help but conclude that that this leper spoke and acted better than he perhaps knew. His words, 'If you are willing...', reflected the leper's great faith. It was this that induced Christ's miraculous healing activity."*

Listening attentively, Bill noted that the needy leper did not question Christ Jesus' healing power, fearing only being passed-by. Christ confirmed His willingness to heal, already having the authority and power to act. Lovingly, Jesus stretched to touch the leper, as the individual would not dare venture closer as he was 'unclean'. The preacher continued, *"According to Hebrew law, to touch an unclean leper rendered Jesus ceremonially defiled. But at Christ's touch, nothing remains contaminated, He makes the unclean pure! Praise His glorious name!"*

Both Jesus' words and touch were effective. His authority was vested in His gospel message as well as in His divine person. Then Jesus commanded the cured man to follow the Mosaic formula for lepers claiming healing. This showed that Jesus submitted Himself to God's law. The awesome consequence was that from that time 'the law' achieved a new relevance. It pointed to Christ Jesus. Concurring with the law, the 'touched' cured-leper becomes the opportunity for the law to confirm Christ Jesus' authority! Standing before the Jewish authorities being quizzed on his healing, the cured-leper declared for all to hear, *"He touched me!"*

Back in Gaither's home church, the minister then passionately emphasised more about the divine miracle itself. *"Jesus put forth His hand, and touched him!* The drama of those few words went deep into Bill's psyche. For Bill it was more than an interesting and challenging sermon that Sabbath morning. A new sacred song was conceived. *"The greatest miracle of all"*, Bill thought to himself, *"is not the healing of a dreadful disease, great as that experience may be. The greater miracle is when God touches a life full of sin and performs a life-giving change in a man or a woman."*

Arriving home for Sunday dinner, at the dining table the farming family discussed the powerful sermon. Bill's loving farming parents spoke of the necessity for all to come to the point of personal faith. His mother then declared, *"Every person must come to Christ just like that leper and receive His divine touch."* .....Her comments were measured and calm. In the process it had the affect of starting the creative juices to flow freely in Bill's mind. Retiring to his bedroom after the home-cooked meal, the lyrics and melody started to take shape.

Bill Gaither was born on the 28 March 1936. Meanwhile overseas and half a world distant, on that same day, the German people gave Hitler a 99% approval rating in the plebiscite. Caught midway between the Great Depression and the gathering storm-clouds of World War II, Bill grew up contentedly in the small farming community of Alexandria, Indiana. Derived from such a rural farming background, Bill was a true country boy who delighted himself in the commonplace such as the indispensable farming task of milking the cows. Years later, he said that he thought that this rustic background helped to proverbially *'keep his feet on the ground'*. However, Bill never intended to take up farming as a career because as he jokingly stated, *"I have always had a bad case of hay fever! That's always been a problem to me even as a child working outside!"*

As a maturing youth, in Bill's heart evolved a real love for God. It was manifested more-and-more in his love of Christian music of the Southern gospel genre. Feeling inspired, he tried his hand at writing poetry and making up melodies in his head. However, to be realistic, he did not entertain the idea of making it a serious career after high school. Surprisingly, he says that he never found himself coming top of the class in things like poetry. Looking back, he says that nowadays his school buddies are amazed at the way he developed his talent so successfully. He thought that he was positively not good enough to do it full-time.

The love for Christian music, however, burned brightly. He recalls that when he was a fourteen years old adolescent, he first listened to the Blackwood Brothers' Quartet on record. As he explained to me, he became enraptured! *"As a boy in 1950, I cannot begin to tell you the impression those records made on my young life. I could not wait to get home from school in the evening to play them. I had many dreams to one day be able to sing like that!"*

In his teens, Bill perceived that there was not that many opportunities for a young person attracted to full-time music as a career. He decided the best course was to go to college and major in English to pursue a teaching career. He did so and consequently, he taught English in public high school for seven or eight years, planning to do that for the rest of my life. He did not foresee how meeting a blonde called Gloria would change his future paths.

Gloria Sickal (his wife-to-be) was born in Battle Creek, Michigan on 4th March 1942. Bill laughingly recalls that she was far more academic than him graduating from Anderson College with honours in French, English and Sociology. They met when she was teaching school at the same place as Bill. Cupid's arrow met its mark, they fell-in-love and married. Then they started writing successful original songs together. It was clear when the songs became popular that their teaching career days were numbered. When Bill finally became a successful Christian songwriter, he never once regretted the experiences of teaching school or his old experiences down-on-the-farm. Indeed, he stated that even the experience with the animals helped him enormously. He said that in those years, the experiences helped him acquire *'a sensitivity to new life'* and for the *'caring of the new-born'*. With a broad smile he said, *"When someone speaks about simple, everyday things I know what they are talking-about!"*

In the final quarter of the 20th century, the Gaithers wrote many hundreds of successful gospel songs. They were recorded by almost every conceivable genre of artists from Elvis Presley to George Beverly Shea. Their volume of repertoire-production seemed a large number but it was not a lot when compared to Charles Wesley and Fanny Crosby who wrote thousands! The consequential songwriters of foregoing generations, of course, came to their highest attention after they died. In contrast, today times have changed. With the capacity of today's media available, the Gaithers have become a legend in their lifetimes. Time to write thousands of songs, like Wesley and Crosby, is on the Gaithers' side, grace permitting!

I asked Bill how it makes him feel to be classed among the ranks of history's great hymn writers. *"You know, Paul"*, Bill modestly stated, *"in something as sensitive as Christian ministry I don't think one can even think about that very long because the Lord blesses and the Lord adds to the increase. The only reason we are here in the first place is because God chose to bless the ministry!'*

I then asked whether the pressure of success dulls the edge of their spiritually. Bill spoke positively on this matter. *"There are basic tenets of our faith that are big! They are the theological principles that we believe and hear from the pulpit every Sunday. The basic objective of our ministry is how to put heavy theological ideas that we all believe, into everyday terms that make a difference in people's day to day lives and decisions!"*

To their credit the Gaithers have been uncompromising in their approach to their Christian music ministry down through the years. They have maintained a consistency and an integrity that have helped them to remain spiritually sharp and culturally relevant. Nowadays, people sometimes ask Bill to explain where his poetry comes from in his music. He replies, *"Well, I think it has to be born in you!...I think you can fan the spark, but there must be a natural inclination to understand poetic things, understand the power of poetic suggestion, and to understand signals. I've often said I think everybody has to have a little bit of poetry in him to even make it these days!"*

> *Shackled by a heavy burden, 'neath a load of guilt and shame*
> *Then the hand of Jesus touched me, and now I am no longer the same.*
>
> *He touched me! Oh He touched me, and oh the joy that floods my soul;*
> *Something happened and now I know, He touched me and made me whole.*
>
> *Since I met this blessed Saviour, since He cleansed and made me whole,*
> *I will never cease to praise Him. I'll shout it while eternity rolls.*

Here I Am Wholly Available
Chris Bowater

"In the year that king Uzziah died I saw also the Lord sitting upon a throne,
 high and lifted up, and His train filled the temple.
Above it stood the seraphims: each one had six wings;
 with twain he covered his face, and with twain he covered his feet, and with twain he did fly.
And one cried unto another, and said,
'Holy, holy, holy, is the LORD of hosts: the whole earth is full of his glory'.
And the posts of the door moved at the voice of Him that cried, and the house was filled with smoke. Then said I, 'Woe is me! for I am undone; because I am a man of unclean lips, and I dwell in the midst of a people of unclean lips:
for mine eyes have seen the King, the LORD of hosts.'
Then flew one of the seraphims unto me, having a live coal in his hand,
which he had taken with the tongs from off the altar:
 And he laid it upon my mouth, and said,
'Lo, this hath touched thy lips; and thine iniquity is taken away, and thy sin purged.'
 Also I heard the voice of the Lord, saying, 'Whom shall I send, and who will go for us?'
  Then said I, 'Here am I; send me!'
Isaiah 6:1-8

Cheery and stocky, the talented Englishman, Chris Bowater wrote this challenging song. He says that it is a *'call-to-discipleship'* or a *'call-to-service'*. The song is a reminder that all Christian believers should know that each has a personal vision and calling from the Holy One Himself. Inspired by the prophet Isaiah's vision found in the sixth chapter of his book, Chris' powerful song, 'Here I Am Wholly Available' is about service in the Kingdom of God.

The date of the event of Isaiah's vision was the time of good King Uzziah's death. For Isaiah, the experience was nothing less than a vision of God the Almighty King at a time when an earthly king's reign of over fifty years had come to its end. Possibly, the prophet was present at an act-of-worship in the temple. Certainly, the Apostle Paul evidently believed that angels are present at Christian worship. His references to angels likewise deal with 'veiling and unveiling' in the presence of God.

Interestingly, this is the only biblical passage where heavenly beings are called 'seraphs'. In the biblical account, there is no indication of the number of seraphs seen by Isaiah. Part of the great variety of heavenly beings created by God (along with others such as angels, archangels, principalities, powers, and cherubim), the seraphs are called 'bright creatures'. The Hebrew translation means 'burning ones'; yet in Isaiah's vision, they hide their faces from the greater brightness displayed in the glory of the Lord. The prophet watched as the heavenly beings covered their feet suggesting humility before God. On that subject, the great American preacher of Victorian times, Dwight L. Moody (1837-1899) stated, *"We may easily be too big for God to use, but never too small!"*

In the holy presence of God the heavenly creatures cried unto another, *"Holy, holy, holy, is the Lord of hosts!"* This worshipful threefold ascription of 'holiness to God' was interpreted by the Early Church Fathers in the 'fuller light of the New Testament' as a reference to the Trinity. Clearly, divine holiness greatly impressed Isaiah in his vision. When called to prophetic service, the man-of-God never forgot that sense of awesome purity.

Isaiah then declared that *'the whole earth is full of His glory'* as God manifested Himself to His creatures. Although the full essence of God's deity is unfathomable, Isaiah saw something of His glory that day as it pleased God to disclose it . Amazingly, in John 12:41, after quoting Isaiah 6:10, the Apostle John said that Isaiah *"saw (Jesus) glory and spoke about Him"*. This startling statement is in fact altogether consistent with the teaching of the other New Testament writers, for Christ Jesus was God incarnate. He is the same God revealed in both the Old and New Testament.

Songwriter, Chris Bowater stated, *"To be a competent conduit for God's piercing word, the power of that word must be personally felt in a person's heart.... Isaiah's lips as a prophet were destined to proclaim God's truth. That day, however, in the temple at worship, he was concerned about having 'defiled lips' as a worshiper. To serve God honourably, it was imperative that Isaiah be a clean instrument. The God of burning holiness Himself provided His cleansing from the sacrificial altar."*

Clearly, Isaiah was not forced into God's service. It was a voluntary act. Isaiah knew that the response of his will was itself the outcome of divine grace, the appreciative ready-response to God's forgiving grace. All of a sudden, Isaiah was confronted with the challenge of personal commitment from God Himself. *"Whom shall I send, and who will go for us?"* In response to the call of God's grace, the prophet made his subjective reply. *"Here am I; send me!"* This reply inspired Chris Bowater to compose the very moving 'Here I Am Wholly Available'.

Echoing Chris' words, the legendary Victorian nurse, Florence Nightingale (1820-1910) was once known to pray the following prayer in response to her call-to-service. *"Oh, God, you put into my heart this great desire to devote myself to the sick and sorrowful; I offer it to You. Do with it what is for Your service."*

By the end of the 20th century, Chris Bowater was much beloved in the United Kingdom for his worship-leading ministry. Now also a well-established singer-songwriter, he never realised when he commenced his worship-leading ministry in the early 1970s that over the decades to follow, he would be producing quality recording albums, books, and worship songs. To his great amazement, much of his God-directed creative writing accomplished incorporation in denominational church hymnals in diversified parts of the globe. Before the close of the last century, his widespread 'praise & worship' songs such as 'Reign In Me', 'Holy Spirit, We Welcome You', Jesus Shall Take The Highest Honour and 'Here I Am Wholly Available' proved him to be a songwriter of time-honored standing.

Chris was born on 2nd May 1947 in Birmingham, England, a year after the Allies' victory over Japan. His dear parents were enthusiastically caught up in Church-planting. Meanwhile, Zionist guerrillas were fighting for an Israeli homeland in Palestine. The Bowaters were pastoring whilst retaining their 'bread and butter' secular employment. Christian conversion came to Chris at a Youth for Christ meeting in Birmingham Town Hall in 1955 when he was eight years of age. Graduating from the Royal College of Music in London in 1968, the twenty-one-year-old by then had nurtured a distinct interest in song composition and music conducting. Chris says, *"During my student years, I seriously compromised my faith and commitment. Praise God that it was graciously restored before the end of my education years."*

With a postgraduate qualification in Education from Birmingham University in 1969, he became a schoolteacher and taught in Birmingham, Solihull and Lincoln. This valuable teaching experience honed his communication skills and strengthened his ability to integrate contemporary music with more traditional styles. Apart from his home church commitments, Chris saw himself as a facilitator in his international seminar and conference work. Desiring to remain sincere and relevant, he aimed his sanctified art at a wide-age group appeal.

Hitting the road, he traveled extensively as a performing artist, worship leader and conference speaker. However, he never strayed permanently from his home base in the enterprising New Life Christian Fellowship of Lincoln, England. At this large local church, he was an enthusiastic member of Pastor Stuart Bell's leadership team. In this local church context, Chris gained considerable experience over many years in the leadership of house groups and area congregations. He delighted also in his role as the 'Director of the School of Creative Ministries' that took him throughout the five continents. His distinctive song-compositions are translated into scores of foreign languages, a fact that gives him great pleasure and fulfilment.

With the dedicated support of Robert Lamont of the *Sovereign Lifestyle Music Publishers,* he constantly explored the vanguard of contemporary music, and also zealously honoured the best of the hymnal-heritage tradition. Consequently, his recording albums and compositions were always under-girded with strong classical, jazz and hymnology structures.

Happily married since 1970 to Lesley, they parented five children-Rachel, Daniel, and triplets, Mark, Hannah and Sarah. Rachel became a doctor and Daniel a professional studio engineer. A great sports lover, Chris and the whole family share an avid support for the Aston Villa Football Club located in the midlands of England.

On a supremely higher level, of course, Chris Bowater's real heart-felt support is of Christ Jesus and His Cause. His words sum up his servant-like spirit : *"Here am I; send me!"* Chris is happy to be called a 'Servant Of God'. It is a term applied in the Old Testament scriptures to the great patriarchs, Moses, Joshua, David, the prophets, and others. Especially the prophet, Isaiah, chiefly used it in prophecy, however, as a title for the Messiah.

Later the New Testament writers, under the influence of the Holy Spirit, applied Isaiah's prophesied 'Suffering Servant' passages directly to Christ Jesus. They declared clearly that the prophesied Servant's mission was fulfilled only in Christ by His election; His birth; His anointing; His ministry; His obedience; His new covenant; His vicarious death; His resurrection; His offer of salvation; His mission to the Gentiles; His glorification, and lastly in His intercession.

Here I am, wholly available; as for me, I will serve the Lord.
Here I am, wholly available; as for me, I will serve the Lord.

The fields are white unto harvest, but oh, the labourers are so few;
So Lord, I give myself to help the reaping, to gather precious souls unto You.

The time is right in the nation for works of power and authority;
God's looking for a people who are willing to be counted in His
glorious victory.

As salt are we ready to savour? In darkness are we ready to be
light?
God's seeking out a very special people to manifest His truth and
His might.

How Deep The Father's Love
Stuart Townend

"And Jesus said, 'A certain man had two sons: And the younger
of them said to his father,
'Father, give me the portion of goods that falleth to me'.
And he divided unto them his living.
And not many days after the younger son gathered all together,
and took his journey into a far country,
and there wasted his substance with riotous living.
 And when he had spent all, there arose a mighty famine in
that land; and he began to be in want. And he went and
joined himself to a citizen of that country;
 and he sent him into his fields to feed swine.
 And he would fain have filled his belly with the husks that
the swine did eat:
and no man gave unto him. And when he came to himself, he
said,
How many hired servants of my father's have bread enough
and to spare, and I perish with hunger! I will arise and go to
my father, and will say unto him,
 'Father, I have sinned against heaven, and before thee,
And am no more worthy to be called thy son: make me as one
of thy hired servants.'
 And he arose, and came to his father.

But when he was yet a great way off, his father saw him,
and had compassion, and ran, and fell on his neck, and kissed
him.
And the son said unto him, 'Father, I have sinned against
heaven,
and in thy sight, and am no more worthy to be called thy
son.'
But the father said to his servants, 'Bring forth the best robe,
and put it on him;
and put a ring on his hand, and shoes on his feet:
And bring hither the fatted calf, and kill it; and let us eat,
and be merry:
For this my son was dead, and is alive again;
he was lost, and is found. And they began to be merry.
Luke 15:11-24

Songwriter, Stuart Townend is probably best known as a Stoneleigh International Bible Week worship leader. A major Christian event near Coventry in England, Stoneleigh drew over 20,000 visitors in its heyday from around the world. Not just a person merely of the big occasion, Stuart involved himself in worship situations in many other areas, great and small. At the start of the new Third Millennium AD, Stuart was making significant contributions to the life of many local churches with his worshipful song-creations. These included 'Lord How Majestic You Are', 'The Lord's My Shepherd' and 'How Deep the Father's Love'.

Amazingly, as he remembers, Stuart wrote nothing until he was twenty-two years old. *"I had a homework project to complete and had left it late. I picked the topic of worship and started to write. I had what I can only call a revelation and this led to my realizing there was a call on my life to write and lead worship. Until that moment, it had never crossed my mind."*

Stuart's beautiful song, 'How Deep The Father's Love' was inspired by Christ's parable of the Prodigal Son as well as the crucifixion of Christ. It could be said that that 'The Prodigal Son' (the usual title given to this parable) would be better entitled 'The Father's Love' or better still, 'How Deep The Father's Love'! Truly, this great parable speaks powerfully of 'the lost son' but it speaks even more eloquently of 'the depths of the father' love'. Conversely, the second part of the parable deals with the sour attitude of 'the elder brother'. Like the Pharisees of Christ's day, he could not comprehend the significance of the father's forgiveness. Stuart stated, *"The central figure, the father, remains constant in his love for both sons. By telling the story, Christ Jesus identified Himself with God in His loving attitude to the lost. He represented God in His earthly mission, the accomplishment of which should summon joy from those who shared the Father's compassion."*

Stuart well recalled hearing the story told in Sunday school and later expounded by his local pastor in sermon. The preacher explained, *"The 'share of the estate' that a younger son took possession of on the death of his father would be one-third, because the older son received two-thirds, a 'double portion'. If the possessions were given, as in this case, while the father lived, the heirs would have use of it. Sadly, the younger son squandered his wealth on wild living in a 'distant country' outside Jewish territory. Then widespread famine made employment and food even harder to get than usual. The wayward son found himself with the demeaning job of feeding pigs, unclean animals for the Jews. Fallen so low and now so insignificant, no one gave him anything. Starved, he even ate the pods, seeds of the carob tree used for pigs' food."*

The story continued to unfold....In the pigpen, coming to his senses, repentance was now at the heart of his words that he carefully prepared for his father. Hunger was his motivation in going home but it was specifically to his father that he wanted to return. Jesus' listeners knew that the loving father in the parable characterized the attitudes of God, the heavenly Father. The Prodigal planned to earn his room-and-board knowing that he had no right to return as a son. He had squandered his inheritance. But back home, the welcome was resplendent in love and grace.

Enraptured, the preacher moved his congregation as he continued, *"Christ portrayed the father as waiting for his son, perhaps daily scrutinizing the horizon hoping for his appearance. In the father's arms of compassion, the pitiable son received a warm embrace, a kiss, a robe, a ring, new sandals and to top it all a party! Christ illustrated the change between the son being once 'dead' but now 'alive' and once being 'lost' and now 'found'. These terms, the Bible applies to mankind's state before and after conversion to Christ."*

Stuart's splendid song, 'How Deep The Father's Love' commenced to crystallize in his tender heart. The Holy Spirit duly inspired poetic lyrics and a haunting Celtic-style melody as he put pen to paper.

Stuart was born on June 1st 1963 in Edinburgh, Scotland, the youngest of four children. The 'space race' between the USA and the USSR was at its height. It was the time when the Soviet Union put the first woman in space. In the more down-to-earth circuit of normal daily-living, Stuart's dear father, John Townend pastored in the Church of the Nazarene. Later, he became an Anglican minister in 1970 serving as the Vicar of Christ Church, Sowerby Bridge, West Yorkshire, England until his sad death in 1985. Stuart's mother, Catherine was until then a very busy vicar's wife. She resettled in Wheatley, Halifax, West Yorkshire.

Stuart states that his family always derived joy from music and one of his brothers, Ian, went on to become a member of the group Heartbeat. Stuart himself began to play the piano at the age of seven. He always had a fascination for the art, learning classical piano and forming a band with his two older brothers, Phil and Ian. Meanwhile, Stuart sharpened his songwriting pen doing reasonably well academically, with a growing interest in literature.

Stuart was still a child when the Townend family moved south to England from bonny Scotland. They settled first in Morley near Leeds. When Stuart was six-years-of- age they lived briefly in Kirkheaton near Huddersfield. From the age of seven to ten, they were domiciled in Sowerby Bridge. Brought up in a warm and secure Christian home, he came to a point of 'personal faith' in his early teens. It was while living in West Yorkshire that, at the age of thirteen, he made his Christian commitment. Then later at the age of eighteen, when helping to lead a children's camp in Hand Cross, West Sussex, he received a profound experience of the Holy Spirit.

During his teens, he attended Sowerby Bridge Grammar School. It became Sowerby Bridge High School while he was still there. He then went to Sussex University in Brighton to pursue 'American Studies'. He gained a literature degree qualification. During this time, staying in Brighton, he married pretty Caroline in 1988. Three children followed (Joseph, Emma and Eden). At home, he says that his likes are Indian food; playing with his kids; football; working with words; recording; and reading the newspaper in coffee bars. He also states his dislikes. They are olives; 'Marmite'; hesitant drivers and pop-music-by-numbers!

Stuart and Caroline joined and became actively involved in the 800-strong 'Church of Christ the King' located on England's south coast. A growing community of worship leaders arose in the church (Paul Oakley, Dave Fellingham, Phatfish and Kate Simmonds). Soon they enjoyed an international influence.

Stuart's personal musical influences, he described as 'very eclectic'. Growing up with Bob Dylan, David Bowie and Stevie Wonder, he later enjoyed Sting, Tom Waites, and what he describes as 'anything classy' in the pop world. Having overcome the hurdle of having to play them for piano exams, increasingly too, he enjoyed Bach and Mozart. He always loved Debussy's work. From the age of twenty-four, Stuart worked at 'Kingsway Music' in Eastbourne, England. He served firstly as the songbook manager and then went on to song-publishing manager, in-house record producer, and then head of the music division. Later going part-time, he concentrated his time as a songwriter, producer, worship-leader, conference-speaker. He headed-up the wider worship ministry of the 'Church of Christ the King'.

Stuart says, *"I slipped into Christian music by accident. While working with David Fellingham in his worship ministry, I arranged an album for him and began to work on various recording projects. Then I was offered a job at Kingsway. Then Dave was invited to lead worship at the Stoneleigh International Bible Week. So, I worked alongside him as music director, then as worship leader and producer of the live worship albums."*

Incidentally, Stuart's album production entitled 'Ruach' won the United Kingdom's Christian Booksellers Convention 'Album-of-the-Year' award. Stuart says that his 'biggest gig' was playing keyboards for Noel Richards. The event was a live BBC TV 'Songs of Praise' programme from the Millennium Stadium in Cardiff, Wales on January 2nd 2000. It was a packed house of around 65,000 people! He recalls, *"It was always a great privilege to lead worship at*

Stoneleigh. But I still get excited when I see any congregation worshipping with a song or hymn I've written…although I try not to show it! Having enjoyed leading worship at big worship events in the UK, USA and Canada, I really get a kick too out of teaching in seminars."

Known and respected by musicians and worship leaders throughout Great Britain and beyond, Stuart, by 2002, released two solo albums 'Say the Word' (1997) and 'Personal Worship with Stuart Townend' (1999). As the main driving force behind the UK's 'Worship Together Pack', of which he is the editor, Stuart had a major national impact on many developments in worship in churches. 'Worship Together' provided worship resources, information, training, and new songs through a quarterly pack, magazine and major seminars' program. Stuart explained, *"I see 'Worship Together' as a major way of resourcing the local church, not only with present resource needs like new songs, but also with yet unknown resources to come in the future. It is my passion for 'Kingsway' to make these resources, specifically tailored for the local church."*

How deep the Father's love for us, how vast beyond all measure,
That He should give His only Son to make a wretch His treasure.
How great the pain of searing loss –The Father turns His face away,
As wounds which mar the Chosen One bring many sons to glory.

Behold the man upon a cross, my sin upon His shoulders;
Ashamed, I hear my mocking voice call out among the scoffers.
It was my sin that held Him there until it was accomplished;
His dying breath has brought me life – I know that it is finished.

I will not boast in anything, no gifts, no power, no wisdom;
But I will boast in Jesus Christ, His death and resurrection.
Why should I gain from His reward? I cannot give an answer;
But this I know with all my heart – His wounds have paid my ransom.

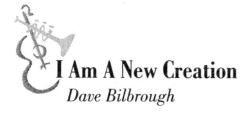

I Am A New Creation
Dave Bilbrough

*'So from now on we regard no one from a worldly point of
view.*
*Though we once regarded Christ in this way, we do so no
longer.*
Therefore, if anyone is in Christ, he is a new creation;
the old has gone, the new has come!'
II Corinthians 5:16-17

William Booth (1829-1912), the colourful founder of the Salvation
Army spoke with great conviction about his Christian conversion
that rendered him 'a new creation in Christ Jesus'. *"I remember as
if it were yesterday. The rolling away from my heart of the guilty
burden, and the going forth to serve my God and my generation!"*

'I Am A New Creation' composed by Dave Bilbrough also speaks
eloquently of this experience of being 'a new creation in Christ Jesus'.
Bright and cheery, known as the effervescent 'Bard of Romford',
Dave at the start of the 21st century was ranked among 'the Best of
British'. Since the 1970s, he consistently contributed quality material
such as 'Abba Father', 'Let There Be Love Shared Among Us' and
'I Am A New Creation' into the UK's expanding 'crucible- of-
revival'. Dave's Christian testimony and repertoire even caught the
attention of the British comedian, Spike Milligan who once phoned
Dave and encouraged him with inquiries and light-hearted
banter.

In 2001 Dave recorded 'live' under the auspices of Gerald Coates' Emmanuel Church Centre. The Centre was located in fashionable Westminster in London, England's capital. The resulting congregational worship album of new songs exuded a high degree of prophetic, cutting-edge, modern hymnody. The offering underlined Dave's continued key-role as one of England's foremost worship leaders.

Dave still describes himself in human terms as just 'a plain regular guy'. Yet spiritually-speaking, he heartily believes the scriptural assessment that, as a Christian, he is 'a new creation'. He believes that 'the old life has gone' and 'the new life has come'!

Dave stated, *"Although the word 'regeneration' is used only twice in the New Testament, many synonymous passages indicate its basic meaning. The related terms are 'born again', 'born of God', 'quickened' and renewed'. This 'regeneration experience' has as its basic idea the notion of being 'born again'. This theological term is used to describe the change that Christ makes in a believer. It is also called regeneration. It's the spiritual transformation wrought in one's heart by which one is empowered to respond to God in faith. All this is the wonderful work of the Holy Spirit of God and starts when one is born again'!"*

For several decades of the late 20th century, the name Dave Bilbrough was positively prominent as a ground-breaker in the burgeoning new fields of contemporary British worship music. Facilitated by Pat, his skillful and attractive spouse, his imaginative hymns and choruses reinvigorated the often exhausted, hackneyed Christian music environment. The Christian populace generally warmed to his unfastidious lyrics and uncomplicated melodies that pronounced spiritual truths in simple poetry without using pompous terms.

Romford, Essex was a place for 'post-World War II' over-spill of urban population just outside London's deprived East End. It was not one of the places that one would expect to find one of the most prolific of the 20th century's gospel songwriters! Certainly, Dave Bilbrough ranks as one of the proverbial 'diamonds-in-the-rough'. Under 'Kingsway Music's' enterprising producers such as John

Menlove, John Pantry and John Pac, he matured as a talented gospel songwriter and performer.

Dave said that it seemed that as a youngster, he could boast little promise. He was from a humble musical family of working-class stock. Up to fourteen years of age, he had little to do with churches of any description. Then, as he says, out-of-the-blue he was enticed to visit the local church youth group by his sister Anne who was a practicing Christian. *"I admit that I only attended,"* Dave openly admitted, *"because of my fondness for table tennis and in the hope of meeting some nice pretty girls. But in the midst of this first experience of Christian fellowship something much deeper was stirred in my heart!"*

Worldwide, pop-music was metamorphosing, focusing on philosophical searches of all kinds from Donovan to Barry McGuire to the Beatles to Simon and Garfunkel. 'Thinking man's music' caught Dave's attention. He remembered, *"I had been given a Paul Simon Songbook about the time that I visited the church youth club. I really related to his simple songs because they posed the kind of questions for which I wanted answers too! At the youth club epilogue, I can remember someone saying that Jesus was either the greatest liar on earth or, a nutcase... Or else, He was who He said He was, and there was truth in what He was saying!!"*

That sensational remark induced an already questioning Dave to thoughtfully deliberate for himself the issue of who Jesus was. About a year later, making his mind-up, he became a Christian. His song, 'I Am A New Creation' described this regeneration experience in his life, an act of God through the immediate agency of the Holy Spirit.

Dave said that this new Holy Spirit operation in him originated a new dimension of moral life. He said *"It was nothing less than a spiritual resurrection from old life to new life in Christ. My new life was not merely a neutral state arising out of the forgiveness of my sin. It was a positive implant of Christ's righteousness making me a believer spiritually alive."*

In theological terms, Dave Bilbrough was born of God, made a new creation and given a new life of divine nature! From reading the scriptures, Dave understood that the universal corruption of human nature required new birth by the mercy of God. He said, *"From this experience comes likeness to God, a greater knowledge of God, and a hatred of sin...It is evidenced by personal faith in Christ, personal righteousness and brotherly love!"*

With this new-born faith came an overwhelming desire for Dave to express himself musically. So jumping in with two feet, he decided to learn to play the acoustic guitar. At his Romford home, he discovered a dusty instrument hidden in the dim cupboard under the stairs where his father had stashed it away. It needed much attention but Dave was zealous. It was duly repaired and given a fresh coat of black paint to make it look like the one Elvis Presley played! Now Dave set himself the uphill task of teaching himself the basic chords. It hurt at first, his fingers getting red and raw. In spite of that, he endured advancing through the rudimentary chords, eventually plucking-up the courage to take it to the midweek Baptist Church Bible studies.

To his great delight, Dave's seventeen-years-old peers loved his guitar-playing, especially the girls! That galvanized him even more. Sitting on the carpet, he led the self-conscious gathering in songs, week by week. But he often felt that the worship-time was stilted and prayers were left to those few people who could wax eloquently and poetically. There was a gaping hole between the poetic flowery words of the Victorian hymns stored in sturdy hymnals and the simple direct language used by ordinary people from Romford! Dave realised that he needed to capture a cutting-edge of relevance. *"I longed for us (in the songs we were singing and the way we prayed and testified) to express ourselves more naturally and simply!"*

One day, Dave's good buddy, Nick Butterworth caught his attention, arousing his vision with a challenging question. Grinning at Dave, looking him squarely in the eye, Nick spoke in all seriousness. *"Dave, you're playing that old battered guitar pretty good nowadays! Why don't you try your hand at writing some new songs for us to sing?"*

"Are you kidding mate!!" was Dave's quick-fire, self-conscious, laughing retort. But at bedtime he tossed-and-turned in his sleep contemplating whether he could try his hand at songwriting. He remembered, *"Soon after, some undeniable major inspiration*

came to me while attending a music festival where I first heard Karen Lafferty's 'Seek Ye First The Kingdom of God' sung by Chuck Girard"

Listening to the song, Dave thought to himself, *"Man that's great! That's the kind of Christian music that me and my mates can relate to!"*

After the music festival, that night back-home in his small bedroom in Romford with his trusty guitar, Dave experimented with rhyme-and-melody as embryos of songs started to gestate. Times were changing in Dave's life too. He perceived that most of his teenage acquaintances were marrying and suddenly, he was aware of 'being left behind'. Low in spirit, Dave remembered the trying time well. *"I felt inadequate and needing the intimacy that personal faith brings! Days were tough, but I knew this was a 'pruning-time' in my life... Through it all, my desire to know the Lord more grew deeper!"*

Dave started to dig deeper in his Bible study. He checked over the Apostle Paul's letter to the Church at Corinth. In 2 Corinthians 5:16-17, Paul acquainted readers with the outcomes of Christ's death and his own personal dedication to 'live for Christ' alone. Dave noted, *"Subsequent to his dramatic Damascus Road conversion, life for Paul was never the same. He acquired deeply-held convictions about his own death and life. Firstly, Paul abstained from making shallow personal judgments fixed on 'external appearances'. He made it now his custom to view others, not in terms of 'nationality' (the old life) but in terms of 'spiritual standing' (the new life). The Jew-Gentile boundary was less consequential for him than the 'Christian' and 'unbeliever' differentiation. As far as he was concerned, all Gentile believers were to be regarded as 'new creations' and his 'brothers in Christ'. Likewise, his unbelieving fellow compatriots were classified as being 'without Christ'. Besides, his passionate yet reckless pre-conversion assessment of Jesus of Nazareth though sincere was sincerely wrong!"*

Like the Apostle Paul, Dave now knew without doubt that Jesus was the Christ. He was not a deluded messianic pretender whose followers were to be annihilated. Joining the Apostle Paul in his teaching, Dave Bilbrough in his uptempo song, 'I Am A New

Creation', totally repudiates the humanistic understanding of Christianity being totally false and irrelevant. Dave, like all true Christian believers, now formally accepted that Christ was the divinely appointed Messiah who brought 'new life' to His followers.

I am a new creation, no more in condemnation,
Here in the grace of God I stand.
My heart is over-flowing, my love just keeps on growing,
Here in the grace of God I stand.

And I will praise You Lord, Yes, I will praise You Lord,
And I will sing of all that You have done.

A joy that knows no limit, a lightness in my spirit,
Here in the grace of God I stand.

I Have Returned
Marijohn Wilkin

> " *Seek ye the LORD while He may be found, call ye upon
> him while He is near:
> Let the wicked forsake his way,
> and the unrighteous man his thoughts:
> and let him return unto the LORD,
> and he will have mercy upon him;
> and to our God, for he will abundantly pardon.* "
> Isaiah 55:7

The famous literary critic and author, Clive Staples Lewis (C. S. Lewis) (1898-1963) described repentance as *"not something God demands of you before He will take you back. It is simply a description of what going back to him is like!"*

C. S. Lewis' words dovetail well with one of the most requested songs to come from the pen of Marijohn Wilkin, 'I Have Returned'. A prolific, professional songwriter from Kemp, Texas, her song 'I Have Returned' has a haunting chorus that is really a statement from experience. Indeed, 'I Have Returned' is a wonderful, clear statement of repentance. The song states that her repentance, the process of changing her mind, brought her back to God. Such human repentance, she says, is always a change for the better, a conscious turning from self or disobedience or sin or idolatry to the living God.

As a child in Texas, Marijohn often heard preachers in church and on the radio declare that in the New Testament 'repentance and faith' are the two sides of the same coin. They said that it was a response to God's grace. Christ Jesus preached the need for the Jews to repent and required His apostles and disciples to preach repentance to all, both Jews and Gentiles. Repentance was thus for all believers to be not only a profound 'change of mind' but also a change in the direction of life. The positive side of repentance for Marijohn Wilkin was her conversion and re-dedication, an actual return to seek grace from God through Christ.

When Marijohn graduated from high school, she attended two Texas Baptist schools, one in Waco and one in Abilene. She told me: *"Evidently, Christianity was a way of life. As I look back, I'm truly amazed how tuned I was into the Spirit as a young person. I didn't know any other way of life. It was something that I can't say was forced on me. If a child is brought up by extremely spiritual as opposed to religiously emotional parents then faith is more like an evolutionary thing rather than emotional. But as I grew older and more independent, I grew away from the Lord. I figured that there were a lot of things that I should do for myself. I lost my spiritual roots."*

Her drift away from God lasted the best part of three decades. Her song in the mid-1970s, 'I Have Returned' testified to others that she returned to the Lord that she once abandoned. Now in Him were forgiveness, strength, peace, destiny and power to get through each passing day and give a clear purpose for living. Perhaps after all, it is not such a surprise that such a moving song should come from her struggles.

As war clouds thundered across the 1940s' sky, Marijohn began to lose her spiritual roots. Sadly, she was a war widow at the young age of just twenty-one years. Her young, beloved husband, was an Allied pilot shot down in North Africa in World War II. As a prisoner-of-war along with other Allied prisoners, he perished in a German submarine. The enemy vessel was transporting the prisoners back to Northern Europe across the Mediterranean Sea. The sub-craft was pounded by Allied warplanes not realising that it conveyed prisoners-of-war. Without a doubt, the sad news of her husband's demise laid waste to the young wife's life.

Now a young war widow, she said she began to shroud her emotions, becoming 'pseudo-sophisticated' and fragile. She asserted that it was her personal way of keeping herself from torment. In addition, she well nigh had an oppressive compulsion to be a 'giver' to everybody. She began lavishly giving away her time, cash and hospitality in a frantic bid to evade the anguish of her war-torn existence. But in due time the pressure was too profuse. She broke-down in tears wondering, *"My God, where is the individual to help me?"*

Deeply depressed and disheartened, Marijohn endeavored to salvage her life by launching her professional life as a schoolteacher. As the years revolved by, she encountered a love of songwriting. Absorbing herself in the new hobby, she sought to change her vocational course. Soon her beloved hobby became her full-time profession. Moving to Nashville, Tennessee, she began a career in one of Music City's well-known songwriting houses. In the years that followed she wrote over 300 songs for a series of artists (ranging from Johnny Cash to Joan Baez to Stonewall Jackson to Burl Ives to George Hamilton IV). Her hit-pop-song-'PT 109' by Jimmy Dean was about John F. Kennedy's wartime naval exploits and featured in a Hollywood movie of the same name.

At the right time, she quit from the music publisher to set up as a publisher in her own right. However, the administrative burdens and tensions took up much of her time and stole joy from Marijohn's songwriting creativity. Invariably, she fought against this lack of fulfillment in her work by even more work. She fashioned her own vocal harmony band that she called The Marijohn Singers. Highly talented, they performed across the USA, recorded for CBS and secured a three-year stint on the renowned 'Grand Ole Opry' TV Show beamed from coast-to-coast.

In her deep distress, her thoughts gyrated as her gray matter turned back-to-infancy. She recalled how she was lovingly nurtured in an eminently stable, secure and spiritual home. She had forsaken the spiritual verities of her Christian past that in childhood she took for granted. As she put it to me, *"My Christian background was nothing over emotionally. It was just a way of life as a child! It was to me just like breathing!"*

Now amid the mounting distress, it was time for her to repent and return to the God of her parents, the God of Abraham, Isaac and Jacob. In retrospect, she felt that this coming again to personal faith was an evolutionary process that she needed to urgently progress.

The memories are sweet and sour. *"One night, I came to the total end of myself. For the first time in my life, I knelt down and cried and cried and cried! I could see that night a solid wall before me and could visualise it finally breaking loose! This was like my own freedom breaking through! Until then, I was a prisoner behind the wall of my own self protection!"*

This hysterical breakthrough was the dawn of Marijohn's reconciliation to God although it took a few more years of searching and spiritual exploration first. Faith was not to fully ripen until she endured the sad demises of firstly a dear professional co-worker and then three months later, her beloved mother. In time Marijohn found herself tenderly caring for her next-of-kin, her 88-years-old Uncle who was sinking towards death from a terminal medical condition. For the first time in twelve years, Marijohn left Nashville for her home state of Texas for six weeks to nurse and care for him. It was his uncomplaining Christian testimony and behaviour in his ebbing days that so engaged her attention that she rededicated her life to God.

Written about the same time as 'I Have Returned', her 'Dove Award' hit song 'One Day At A Time' was co-written with a young movie actor and singer-songwriter, Kris Kristofferson. The lyrics of 'I Have Returned' and 'One Day At A Time' both mirror the frankness that Marijohn enjoyed with the Lord in her Christian life. Indeed, it was this candor that caused it to be recorded in the first instance! Kris Kristofferson came to Johnny Cash's studio and listened as she re-mixed her album. As Kris heard the songs played back, he turned his head away and wept. After it was all over, he looked at Marijohn and said that he was afraid that she had contrived a bunch of Gospel songs! But he said that, after hearing 'I Have Returned', he had admitted that he found her songs totally honest!

With a newly discovered faith, I asked Marijohn what her hopes and aspirations for the future are. Her eyes sparkled as she replied with a smile and a slight Texas drawl in her sophisticated deep voice.

*"Paul, I have no more knowledge about the future than you have.
So, I wrote these words on an airplane: 'I know not what the future
holds. Lord I have no way of knowing. But I know the One who
holds my future, and I've no fear in where I'm going!'"*

*I have returned to the God of my childhood,
To the same simple faith as a child I once knew;
Like the prodigal son I longed for my loved ones,
For the comforts of home and the God I outgrew.*

*I have returned to the God of my childhood,
Bethlehem's Babe, the prophets' Messiah;
He's Jesus to me, Eternal destiny
Praise His Name, I have returned.*

*I have returned to the God of my mother,
With unfailing faith for the child of her heart;
She said bring them up in the way that you want them,
Thank God when they're grown they'll never depart.*

*I have returned to the God of my mother,
I learned at her knee, He's the lily of the valley;
He's Jesus to me, eternal destiny;
Praise His Name, I have returned.*

*I have returned to the God of my father,
The most God-like man a child could know;
I just heard a shout from the angels in Glory,
Praising the Lord a child has come home.*

*I have returned to the God of my father,
Creator of Heaven and earth, God of the universe;
He's Jesus to me, eternal destiny
Praise His Name, I have returned.*

I have returned to the Yahweh of Judah,
On my knees I did fall where the wall now stands;
This lesson I learned as I've worked my way homeward,
The Saviour of all is a comfort to man.

I have returned to the Father of Abraham,
The shepherd of Moses, who called Him the 'Great I Am';
He's Jesus to me, Eternal Deity;
Praise His Name, I have returned.

I Have Returned (Marijohn Wilkin)

I Wish We'd All Been Ready

Larry Norman

"For as in the days that were before the flood
they were eating and drinking, marrying and giving in
marriage,
until the day that Noe entered into the ark,
And knew not until the flood came, and took them all away;
so shall also the coming of the Son of man be.
Then shall two be in the field; the one shall be taken, and
the other left.
Two women shall be grinding at the mill; the one shall be
taken, and the other left.
Watch therefore: for ye know not what hour your Lord doth
come.
But know this, that if the goodman of the house had known
in what watch the thief would come,
he would have watched, and would not have suffered his
house to be broken up.
Therefore be ye also ready: for in such an hour as ye think
not the Son of man cometh.
Matthew 24:38-44

Songwriter, Larry Norman passionately believed Christ's urgent
words in Matthew 24 that stressed the unexpected spontaneity of
His Second Coming. When it happens, Christ said, that it would be

a dramatic event evidenced by the sudden cleavage of two sets of people. The first set described by Christ would be two men dutifully working in a field; one is taken, the other left. The second set is two women working their mill as usual; one is taken, the other left.

In New Testament days, two women squatting opposite each other with the mill between them normally operated a hand-mill. Each individual in turn pulled the stone around 180 degrees. In Biblical days, the two would usually be sisters, mother and daughter, or two household slaves. Yet no matter how close their relationship, at the Second Coming, one is taken, the other left. Such dramatic imagery became the theme for Larry Norman's plaintive song, 'I Wish We'd All Been Ready'. 'Being Ready' is a necessity too when one's time inevitably comes to die.

In November 2001, Larry Norman was in the hospital with a serious heart condition. He knew that any surgical procedure that doctors would perform on him carried a certain amount of risk that could result in his death. Indeed, he even experienced a heart attack while in the hospital. Doctors performed an angioplasty to open up one of the arteries feeding his heart that was constricted. Unfortunately, this procedure was unsuccessful in restoring normal blood flow to Larry's heart. Thus his doctors scheduled for him to undergo heart bypass surgery.

Earlier, in discussion with Larry when he was fit and healthy, I asked him about his early days and he replied thoughtfully with his typical frown. *"I was born in San Francisco and raised in what one would call the missionary district where all the winos are. It was a sick and desperate all black neighbourhood. I really don't know how I got there, but I found myself in an all coloured neighbourhood! So, I didn't go out to play because I saw no point. Sometimes I got beat up because I stood out a little, so I stayed indoors and listened to the radio that back then was very rich in imagination. Then it became a continuous Top 30. Back then I listened to Sparky and I began to really love the songs of the Broadway musicals."*

About this time, Larry started to play piano and a ukulele that belonged to his father. Then as soon as he obtained a guitar, in his own words, he set the house rocking! Larry recalled, *"I didn't know what the music industry was! I just started writing rock 'n' roll when*

I was nine years old. My Christianity and music all happened at the same time. I went to Church but it was destroying me because the people all yelled and screamed from the pulpit. In Sunday school, they baby-talked me! I lived outside the church and was kind of on my own. But I'm glad Jesus came to me then and pulled me out of what might have been an unhappy childhood."

Originally, Larry was a member of Capitol Records' mainstream secular rock-band 'People' who recorded the 1960s hit 'I Love You'. After People broke up, he recorded four seminal albums of Christian rock between 1968 and 1976. His music was an unlikely mix of love songs, the gospel message, and wry commentary on American culture. Larry also took general education courses as he had an interest in journalism, with a desire to run a newspaper. For a while he worked at the Hollywood free paper but music was always more important. However, he told me that his first job after leaving school and running away from home was washing dishes. He stated, *"I would have rather starved than do something silly that has no productivity. So, I stuck at my music and within a year signed with Capital that was part of EMI and we had a hit."*

Larry Norman was arguably the 'Father of Jesus Rock', one of a host of people in Southern California making music from a Christian perspective. Such Christian music was then known as 'Jesus music'. By the 1970s, many teenagers living in North America and Europe were first introduced to the music and lyrics at youth groups and retreats. Youth could identify with Larry's long blond hair and rock music with a message. With the positive influence of Larry's music many were drawn to faith in Christ Jesus and were reminded in the lyrics of his songs that they were *"only visiting this planet"*.

Larry Norman recorded the milestone album 'Upon This Rock' with Capital Records in 1969. It contained songs such as 'Sweet, Sweet Song of Salvation' (also recorded at the time by Pat Boone), 'Forget Your Hexagram', 'Nothing Really Changes' and the now classic, 'I Wish We'd All Been Ready'. Larry always said that his music was aimed primarily at the disenfranchised, not the church crowd. 'I Wish We'd All Been Ready', however, became standard repertoire for many artistes from Connie Smith to Tennessee Ernie Ford. *"I want,"* Larry said, *"to declare the reality of God, but without being forced to say it in the same old way! I think all Christians should be evangelists so I want to obey Jesus too. I think everybody should be a full-time Christian even if they work on cars or sell insurance. You can turn all into a witness if you let Jesus show you the way."*

Critics of pop music of the day declared that Larry cut a masterpiece in 1972 when he recorded the album entitled 'Only Visiting This Planet' for MGM/Verve. It was an intriguing album that was produced by the legendary George Martin of Beatles fame. When I asked Larry to name his favourite song, he said, *"I think 'The Outlaw' on 'Only Visiting This Planet'. It's about Jesus - 'Some say He was an Outlaw. Some say He was a poet. Some say He was a sorcerer. He raised people from the dead, did tricks with fish and bread. Some say He was a revolutionary. But I say He was the Son of God!'"*

In 1988 this LP was voted the number one 'Best Contemporary Christian Album of All Time' by the staff of the USA's 'Contemporary Christian Music' magazine. The album included a reprise of 'I Wish We'd All Been Ready', but also entered new territory with the evangelistic challenge, 'Why Don't You Look Into Jesus' and a timely reminder for the church called 'Without Love You Are Nothing'. This album also contained, 'Why Should The Devil Have All The Good Music?' which became the anthem of many contemporary Christian musicians including Sir Cliff Richard. During this period, Larry was heralded by 'Time' and 'Billboard' magazines for his creative ability and received personal accolades from people like Sir Paul McCartney. On tour, he played the California's Hollywood Bowl, Australia's Sydney Opera House and repeatedly sold out The Royal Albert Hall in London, England. The Gospel Music Association at the Ryman Auditorium in Nashville inducted later Larry into the 'Gospel Music Hall of Fame'.

In June 1988, Larry continued to make music as an artist and producer for his 'Solid Rock' record label in Oregon. At the time, 'Contemporary Christian Music' magazine stated, *"It has been nearly twenty years since the release of Larry Norman's 'Upon This Rock', the album generally credited with giving birth to Christian rock. To one degree or another, thousands of albums have tried to follow in his footsteps. Most, of course, fail..."*

Larry told me about his hopes for the future. *"It is to continue to grow in Jesus and mature to enjoy old age and to watch Christian Music widen and broaden so that anyone listening to Jesus records can worship."*

Asked about his unusual gospel-singing ministry, he replied, *"I think my ministry is the same as anyone has. It is to find a hole and fill it!"*

And now, little children, abide in Him;
that, when He shall appear, we may have confidence,
and not be ashamed before Him at His coming.
I John 2:28

# I'll Fly Away
Albert Brumley

"For the Lord Himself shall descend from heaven with a shout,
with the voice of the archangel, and with the trump of God:
and the dead in Christ shall rise first:
Then we which are alive and remain shall be caught up
together with them in the clouds,
to meet the Lord in the air: and so shall we ever be with the
Lord.
Wherefore comfort one another with these words."
(1 Thessalonians 4:16-18)

Songwriter, Albert Brumley was elected to the 'Gospel Music Hall of Fame' in 1972. Known for his humility and 'down-to-earth' disposition, he often read the Apostle Paul's prophetic revelation in 1 Thessalonians 4:16-18 that foretells what will happen at Christ's return to planet Earth. Albert was excited to read that believing, born-again Christians who are still alive at Christ's return will fly to meet Christ in-the-air. Just before, 'the-dead-in-Christ' are resurrected from their resting places whether on land or sea, and they fly also. Albert deeply believed that Christ Jesus' teaching about our not knowing 'the day or hour' of His coming, surely should put all believers on a 'be ready' state of alert…Ready to fly!

Albert's Bible study informed him that the Apostle Paul was setting an example of expectancy for the church of all ages. Proper

Christian anticipation includes the imminent return of Christ. *"Christians"*, he said, *"should be ready to fly at a moment's notice! His coming will be sudden and unexpected, an 'any-moment' possibility."*

From the outset of the expansion of radio in the early 1930s, the USA abounded with passionate radio preachers. Frequently, their dramatic sermons on the Second Coming of Christ stirred Albert Brumley. Preachers stated that no divinely revealed prophecies remained to be given but will be fulfilled before that event. Without setting a date, the Apostle Paul hoped that it would transpire in his own lifetime. After hearing a member of the clergy preach on the Second Coming of Christ, England's Queen Victoria (1819-1901) made a startling declaration. *"I wish that He would come during my lifetime so that I could take my crown and lay it at His feet."*

To his readers, the Thessalonian believers and others, the Apostle Paul taught his converts much about this next greatest event on Earth in the prophetic calendar. He said that for them it was their being gathered-up to fly to Christ in-the-air. This 'flying away', he taught, will be a cosmic and datable event in world history, as valid for the 21st century as it was for the 1st. Just as God intervened in history through his Son's first coming, so he will do at His return!

Albert Brumley's song, 'I'll Fly Away' clearly covers the principle association of those who are alive (and anticipating Christ's momentary return) and their relation to 'those who have fallen asleep'. The former group 'will certainly not precede' the latter. This strong assertion assuages all believers' alarms about their dead loved ones. Indeed, Christ Himself will descend from heaven where He has been since ascending to the Father's right hand. In so doing, He will dispatch a resounding decree that will awaken those who have fallen asleep! With this command will be the voice of the archangel Michael and the trumpet call. Instantaneously, 'the-dead-in-Christ' will rise. Far from being exempt, they will be main candidates in the first act of the Lord's return.

Albert wrote 'I'll Fly Away' because he knew that this comforting message brings great cheer to countless Christians. Suddenly, after that resurrection (Paul likens it to a blinking-of-the-eye) the living Christians fly up for the meeting with Christ Jesus in the sky. In this expeditious sequence, the living believers will undergo an immediate change from mortality to immortality, after which they will be insusceptible to death. Contemplating the horrendous loss of life that wars bring, US President, Abraham Lincoln (1809-1865) declared, *"Surely God would not have created such a being as man…to exist only for a day! No, no, man was made for eternity!"*

Both resurrected and transformed believers will ascend, be enshrouded in the clouds of the sky, and meet the Lord somewhere in the interspace between earth and heaven. Bible teachers state that the whereabouts of that encounter in-the-air is subordinate in light of the concluding outcome. The Apostle Paul's words, 'be with the Lord forever' denote the attainment of a kinship begun at the new birth. It far surpasses any other esteem of time and eternity. These words of assurance, says Paul, give believers bedrock for them to console and cheer each other.

Rural poet, Albert Edward Brumley was country-born on 29th October 1905 in Le Flore County, Oklahoma. The newspapers-of-the-day announced that after a High Court action over its trademark, aspirin was to go on sale for the relief of pain. There was no such pain relief for Mrs. Brumley as she delivered her son. His enterprising farming parents raised corn and cotton on their agrarian property.

As he grew, music started to command his attention. He stated that he was always *"wild about lyrics and music"*. In his teens he enthusiastically attended a community singing school in his home town of Rock Island, Oklahoma. His love for music deepened as he engaged himself in further study under the auspices of gospel music notables such as J. R. Baxter Jr., Virgil and Frank Stamps of the Stamps Quartet, Homer Rodeheaver (writer of 'Then Jesus Came') and E.M. Bartlett (writer of 'Victory In Jesus').

At the height of the Great Depression in 1931, Albert married the lady who he said was *"the love of my life"*. He originally met Goldie Edith Schell in Powell, Missouri while teaching a singing school. Despite the economic struggles of the day, they parented five sons and one daughter. One son, Tom Brumley became a famed West Coast steel guitarist. He spent many successful years with country-hitmaker, Buck Owens as a member of his band, the Buckaroos.

Proud of her spouse's talent, Goldie Edith encouraged Albert to send his songs to a city publisher. *"Honey, your songs are great! Any publisher -worth his salt- would agree with me and should publish them. Send them off and see what reaction you get!"*

Albert Brumley's legacy is an opulent heritage of true classics from his pen including 'I'll Fly Away', 'River Of Memories', 'I'll Meet You In The Morning', 'Turn Your Radio On', 'Jesus Hold My Hand' and many more. High-selling recordings of these Brumley songs were plentiful throughout the last century from Ray Stevens, the Statler Brothers, Pat Boone, Jim Reeves, Tennessee Ernie Ford and many others. The Chuck Wagon Gang and the Statesmen devoted entire albums to Albert Brumley material. Albert died in 1977 having lived a full and active life.

"Speaking of Albert E. Brumley", James Blackwood (of the Blackwood Brothers) remarked at the end of the 20th century, *"I think one of the marks of a truly great man is humility and this was clearly evident whenever you met Albert E. Brumley. He was completely unassuming, always reluctant to be in the limelight. He was shy to receive the honours that he so bountifully deserved! Mr. Brumley was the second living man to be voted into the Gospel Music Hall of Fame, an honour definitely richly his due!"*

In Albert's local church, singing always played a prominent part in worship and community life as it did in the national life of the ancient Hebrews and the early church. Indeed, soon after the Garden of Eden, the first song in the Bible was sung by Lamech in Genesis 4:23-24. Albert came to realise that throughout their history, it was not uncommon for the Jews to compose songs celebrating special victories or religious experiences such as the crossing of the Red Sea. He noted too that the Psalter (or the Psalms) was designated 'The Song Book of Israel' and contained many kinds of songs. Then in the New Testament, the Apostle Paul urged all believers to sing. Albert too, in his song 'Turn Your Radio On' urged all believers to sing and tune into the songs of Mount Zion. God's people still sing as they have in every generation. The difference nowadays is, as Albert's song 'Turn Your Radio On' illustrates, the sound is broadcast widely on the airwaves on every modern form of media technology.

In a moment, in the twinkling of an eye, at the last trump: for the trumpet shall sound,

and the dead shall be raised incorruptible, and we shall be changed.

For this corruptible must put on incorruption, and this mortal must put on immortality.

So when this corruptible shall have put on incorruption,

and this mortal shall have put on immortality,

then shall be brought to pass the saying that is written,

Death is swallowed up in victory. O death, where is thy sting? O grave, where is thy victory?

I Corinthians 15:52-55

In Heavenly Armour
(The Battle Belongs To the Lord)
Jamie Owens Collins

"Finally, my brethren, be strong in the Lord, and in the power of his might.
Put on the whole armour of God, that ye may be able to stand against the wiles of the devil.
For we wrestle not against flesh and blood, but against principalities, against powers,
against the rulers of the darkness of this world, against spiritual wickedness in high places.
Wherefore take unto you the whole armour of God,
that ye may be able to withstand in the evil day, and having done all, to stand.
Stand therefore, having your loins girt about with truth, and having on the breastplate of righteousness;
And your feet shod with the preparation of the gospel of peace;
Above all, taking the shield of faith,
wherewith ye shall be able to quench all the fiery darts of the wicked.
And take the helmet of salvation, and the sword of the Spirit, which is the word of God." (Ephesians 6:10-17)

Pretty and petite, Jamie Owens the composer of 'In Heavenly Armour' (otherwise known as 'The Victory Song') was born a bonny baby in 1955 to the delighted songwriting husband-and-wife duo, Jimmy and Carol Owens. Surrounded by music, its pull on Jamie was to be expected. She says that after cautiously emerging from singing in her bedroom, it was not long before little Miss Jamie Owens became one of the top female Christian singers in the USA while still in her mid-teens. The mid-1970s were years of Christian music expansion and Jamie found herself in the thick of things.

At the tender age of fifteen, her loving parents persuaded her into the public limelight. She became as a lead singer in their Christian musicals. 'Come Together' quickly followed their entertaining musical, 'Show Me'. By 1973 Jamie was very experienced in studio recording. Her first album of 'Jesus People music' entitled 'Laughter In Your Soul' (backed by the new trio, 'Second Chapter Of Acts') possessed early promise and maturity. Excitedly at the time she said, *"I want to share with you the deep joy I am finding as I grow to know and love the Lord Jesus more fully. I invite you to take a drink of the living water. It'll do you good. Go swim in the river of peace, you really should. This is a time of a fresh moving of the Holy Spirit among His people. I offer my songs in the love of Jesus with prayers that He will refresh and strengthen the listeners. May the Prince of Peace establish His kingdom in hearts."*

'Laughter In Your Soul' became a top seller particularly in the United Kingdom and other parts of Europe. She displayed her developing songwriting skills further with the release of her album 'Growing Pains' in 1975. Then, after her marriage to Dan Collins in the following year, they conspired to release another album entitled 'Love Eyes' (on the 'Sparrow' label) that Dan produced. Marriage joyfully brought her the new roles of being a wife and mother. She stated, *"I see God's love displayed in new dimensions."*

She was always a keen Bible student and progressed from Sunday School to church. From being a youngster to a teenager and into an adult, along with the rest of her Christian friends, the increasingly attractive Jamie thrilled to the scripture. On Sundays in church, she remembered her pastor's story-telling teaching on the Christian's armour as listed by the Apostle Paul in Ephesians 6:10-17. Paul's address to the church in Ephesus was ever so challenging. It provoked a vivid mental picture of the Roman soldiers of the First Century.

Jamie's pastor, Jack Hayford expounded Ephesians 6:10-17 on many occasions. He said that the Apostle Paul delivered a powerful carillon-call-to-arms to all believers. This particularly captured the attention of young converts. Pastor Jack said that this call to 'Christian warfare' was an outer visible-manifestation of the faith while the unseen, inward-growth of the Early Church continued. *"The Apostle passionately believed that the 'Body of Christ' (the Church) is compelled to be united, built-up and geared for the inescapable combat with evil. Indeed, every believer is required to be prepared to fight the good fight. A charge and commission to all Christian soldiers, Paul echoed his words to the Church at Corinth, 'Be on your guard; stand firm in the faith; be men of courage; be strong!'"*

As a mature and experienced in the 21st century, songwriter Jamie Owens Collins says, *"We can take for granted that our victory is already guaranteed through what Christ completed by His death and resurrection. Christ the Lord was and is the Mighty Victor who vanquished all the hosts of sin. We, as Christians, are identified with His conquest! Even though our victory is secure, it has to be won through battle. All the resources that we as Christian soldiers need are drawn from Christ and His mighty power. As Christian soldiers we're protected from head to foot with spiritual armour made up of various pieces, both defensive and offensive!"*

Jamie understood that in scripture, 'to stand' was a military term for holding on to one's position. The soldier's equipment enabled him to fend off enemy attacks. Before any offensive action can be launched, one's own ground must be maintained.

Paul's fourfold use of the word 'against' stresses the determined hostility confronting the Christian soldier. Jamie's pastor would passionately preach, *"The commander-in-chief of the opposing forces is the devil himself, the sworn enemy of the church. Consequently, a believer's struggle is not merely against human foes but against supernatural forces, cosmic powers. Until the end of this age these demonic forces, already defeated by Christ on the cross, exercise a certain limited authority. But Christians can fight against such pernicious influences!"*

Because this spiritual warfare is inevitable, Jamie believed that all Christians should take advantage of the full armour of God. *"When the battle is at its fiercest, we soldiers of Christ will still be able to hold our line even against the most determined attack."*

The song 'In Heavenly Armour Bright' was an integral part of the musical, 'The Victor' which was presented and orchestrated by Jamie's parents, Jimmy & Carol Owens in 1984. Produced by Jamie's husband, Dan Collins, it included not only Jamie's song but songs by other writers too including Don Francisco, Scott Wesley Brown, Annie Herring, Michael & Stormie Omartian as well Jimmy and Carol Owens compositions.

The inspiration for the musical came when the Owens were discussing issues with friends. All confessed to spiritually going through dry times. *"We knew of course"*, Carol said, *"that this was to be expected because of the pressures of the world. We agreed that what we needed to see were victories in our lives. The scripture teaches us that by ourselves victory is impossible unless we have The Victor inside. So to help people open up to the person of Jesus (who is the only Victor over the world) Jimmy and I conceived this musical. Its theme is 'Christ in you - the Hope of Glory'. Our daughter Jamie wrote the song 'The Victor', a fine song, which we've used in other musicals and which Keith Green used also to such good effect. Of course there would be no victory without a battle. 'In Heavenly Armour Bright' or 'The Battle Belongs to the Lord' (as it is sometimes called) is not only a cute song but is a spiritual truth from our daughter Jamie put into inspiring song with an Israeli style melody."*

Jamie's song, 'In Heavenly Armour Bright' and, indeed the entire 'The Victor' musical, stressed that in Ephesians 6 several items of the soldier's armour appear listed must be put-on before taking the field. First, the spiritual belt tied tightly around the waist indicating 'preparation-for-action'. A soldier slackens his belt only when off duty. Truth is said to be the soldier's belt because Christians have accepted the truth of revelation and are now indwelt by the risen Lord, who is Himself the truth.

Then the spiritual bronze-breastplate covered the body from the neck to the thighs. Isaiah stated that God Himself put on righteousness like a breastplate. Christians should not seek protection in any works of their own but only in what Christ did for them and in them. Once the breastplate has been fitted into position, the soldier puts on his spiritually-strong army boots ensuring good grip. The military successes depend on armies being well shod for long, speedy marches over rough terrain. Believers who have already been reconciled to God are afforded a sure foothold in the spiritual campaign in which they enter into conflict.

Then the Christian soldier is to take up the shield of faith held in front of him for protection. For the Christian this protective shield is faith itself. Such a shield extinguishes all the incendiary devices flung by the devil. The spiritual helmet covering the head is the helmet of salvation. The final weapon is the sword-of-the-Spirit (The Word Of God), the Christian's only weapon of offence. Inspired by the Holy Spirit, Christians can drive away Satan every time. In the American Civil War, Confederate General Robert E. Lee (1807-1870) declared, *"I know in whose Powerful Hands I am, and on Him I rely, and feel that in all our lives we are upheld and sustained by daily Providence, and that Providence requires us to use the means he has put under our control."*

Jamie summed up her musical ministry very articulately as she focused on two issues. She said, *"Firstly, I want to thank God for all that He's given me. Secondly, I want to share with people my learning relationship with Jesus. That the Lord loves them as much as He loves me!"*

In heavenly armour we'll enter the land, the battle belongs to the Lord.
No weapon that's fashioned against us will stand, the battle belongs to the Lord.

And we sing glory, honour, power and strength to the Lord.
We sing glory, honour, power and strength to the Lord!

When the power of darkness comes in like a flood, the battle belongs to the Lord.

He's raised up a standard, the power of His blood; the battle belongs to the Lord.

When your enemy presses in hard, do not fear, the battle belongs to the Lord.
Take courage, my friend, your redemption is near, the battle belongs to the Lord.

In Times Like These
Ruth Caye Jones

"This know also, that in the last days perilous times shall come.
For men shall be lovers of their own selves, covetous, boasters,
proud, blasphemers, disobedient to parents, unthankful, unholy,
Without natural affection, trucebreakers, false accusers,
incontinent, fierce, despisers of those that are good,
Traitors, heady, highminded, lovers of pleasures more than lovers of God;
Having a form of godliness, but denying the power thereof: from such turn away.
… Ever learning, and never able to come to the knowledge of the truth. …
men of corrupt minds, reprobate concerning the faith.
…Yea, and all that will live godly in Christ Jesus shall suffer persecution.
But evil men and seducers shall wax worse and worse, deceiving, and being deceived."
II Timothy 3:1-13

Ruth Caye Jones, the modest writer of the uplifting hymn 'In Times Like These', was born in 1902, a momentous year that saw the USA's purchase of the Panama Canal for $40 million and a new King (Edward VII) crowned in England.

Ruth Caye Jones's great song composition, 'In Times Like These' was written in the solitude of her family home located in the Dormont area of Pittsburgh, Pennsylvania. Ruth composed 'In Times Like These' at a time in her life when world events were dangerous. It was Ruth's passionate belief that only an adequate trust in her trustworthy Lord would see her through the adverse experience. Stealing an hour early in the day from her housekeeping duties, she nestled into an easychair with a cup of coffee.

Ruth read a book about Mary Slessor (1848-1915), the Scottish missionary to West Africa. Ruth was intrigued how, almost single-handedly. Mary had ended the human sacrifices of the native tribes of the region amid great dangers from 'wild man and beast'. Ruth laughed to herself as she read how earlier as a teenager in Scotland, Mary confessed that she was often 'faithless' and therefore 'fearful' of all sorts of things. Indeed, she even feared to cross a local farmer's field with a cow in it. Now full of faith as a missionary in the African hinterland, she faced 'wild man and beast' fearlessly. Wide-eyed as she read on, Ruth was flabbergasted to read what Mary then wrote in her book. *"I did not used to believe the story of Daniel in the Lions' Den until I had to take some of these awful marches. Then I knew it was true, and that it was written for my comfort. Many a time I walked along praying, 'Oh, God of Daniel, shut their mouths!'...and He did!"*

Coffee-time ended, the chores of the day, such as the laundry and the ironing and the cooking, beckoned the busy housewife. Initially, feeling good after reading the book, she expeditiously did her family laundry. Yet she was troubled soon in spirit as she ironed the clothes. Moving the iron, she listened attentively to the World War II radio-newscast report on the latest progress of the Allied armies fighting in Europe, Africa and the Pacific. The news was serious and she initially became overwhelmed with the dire state of the world. It was then that in contrast the Holy Spirit's comforting presence took charge. She was vividly reminded of the love, the power and the greatness of the God of her salvation! Divine inspiration brought forth a new song. In the middle of her ironing chore, the challenging and faith-filled lyrics and melody of 'In Times Like These' came easily to Ruth. Pulling out a well-used, dog-eared, writing-paper-pad from her apron (that she normally used to jot down her reminders of groceries to be picked up from the local market), she scribbled down the inspired musical work.

Later in the afternoon she surprised her son, Bert when he returned from school after study. His mother declared, *"The Lord's given me a new song today, Bert! I can't wait to sing it to you! It came to me listening to the radio news while I was ironing!"*

Settling into a chair, placing his schoolbooks onto the kitchen table, he was duly impressed by his mother's unaccompanied, misty-eyed rendition. *"Wow, Mom! Did you really write that yourself?...It's wonderful!"*

Bert could barely wait to announce to the others in the family as they arrived home, the news of his mother's powerful new song. Later on after their tasty meal, gathering the whole of the interested family around the upright piano, movingly she sang and played the song through properly for the first time. Before it concluded, the haze in her eyes turned to flowing tears of emotion.

Ruth copyrighted the new song in 1944 about the same time that the Allied armies invaded Adolf Hitler's 'Fortress Europe' with the Normandy landings. The awe-struck Jones family all sensed that a special divine anointing was on Mrs. Jones new composition. However, little they knew how God would use her song in years to come. In the rest of the century, it became widely known via George Beverly Shea in the Billy Graham missions and on his RCA recordings.

Many years later, Ruth said one of the thrills of her life was when she was invited by George Beverly Shea to sit on the Billy Graham crusade platform in Columbus, Ohio. She was understandably nervous when in typical Shea style, before singing her song, Bev introduced her to the vast crowd who applauded her accordingly. She modestly blushed at the legitimate acclaim but, as Bev said, it was 'well deserved'.

George Beverly Shea famously recorded 'In Times Like These' with his long-term friends, Tedd Smith (piano-celeste) and Don Hustad (pipe organ) as the title-song on an 'RCA Victor' album released in 1962. Fortunately that year, the world breathed a sigh of relief as the USA and the USSR, the two super-powers stepped back from the brink of nuclear war over the soviet missiles based in Cuba. For several weeks before, 'eye-ball to eye-ball', President John F. Kennedy had successfully called the Russian leader, Khrushchev's bluff. Eventually, much to the distaste of Cuba's leader, Fidel Castro, Khrushchev agreed to dismantle the missile sites. Kennedy, in turn, promised not to invade Cuba.

In the studio to record 'In Times Like These' with Bev Shea, pianist Tedd, a fellow Canadian was clear about his Christian music motivation. Slim and quiet in disposition, he stated, *"The ministry I have as a musician has one motive - to constantly praise and honour our Lord Jesus Christ through my musical instrument. No matter what the mood - be it happy, solemn, or meditative, it is because of Him and for Him that I will praise Him."*

Also in the studio was Don Hustad, the organist on the 'In Times Like These' project. He was a former professor of the Southern Baptist Seminary in Louisiana. An accomplished arranger, prior to joining the Graham Team, he was also chairman of the Department of Sacred Music at the Chicago's Moody Bible Institute. He received wide acclaim as the conductor of the Institute's famed Moody Chorale. He played organ for many years with the Graham Team.

Although written in World War II, 'In Times Like These' was tailor-made for the 'Cold War' years that followed. During these times, the Billy Graham evangelism team took many a community hostage with their engaging and unashamed gospel message. Old and young became deeply challenged. The Team Missions contributed famously to the revitalisation-of-faith among hundreds of thousands and perhaps millions. They also contributed greatly to the continuation of gospel music into a new generation. As many Christian believers were progressively feeling that the times were the Last Days, 'In Times Like These' pointed particularly to the Rock of Ages (Christ Jesus). During the most fearful of times, life still has to be faced-up-to squarely. At a time in 20th century history when many people feared facing life's troubles, Mrs. Eleanor Roosevelt (1884-1962) the wife of the American president made an interesting statement. *"I could not at any age be content to take my place in a corner by the fireside and simply look on. Life was meant to be lived. One must never, for whatever reason, turn one's back on life!"*

Billy Graham often preached about 'the last days', an expression, used first by many prophets in the Old Testament. The Apostle Peter's quoted 'the last days' in his sermon on the day of Pentecost. He clearly referred to the whole messianic age because he declared that the prophecy was being fulfilled that very day. Some believers insist that 'in the last days' can rightly be applied to the last days of this age, just before the Second Coming of Christ. 'In Times Like These' by Ruth Caye Jones simply says that the characteristics of insecurity are becoming increasingly intensive and extensive as the end approaches. Indeed, the Apostle Paul declared in II Timothy 3:1-13 that the last days will see troublesome and dangerous times.

In these verses we find a list of vices that will characterize people in the last days. Billy Graham often said that these conditions always existed in some measure but are more marked in the 20th century. *"Who would deny that people are nowadays selfish, greedy, boasters, proud, abusive and that young people are disobedient to their parents?"*

The unhappy list of sins continues in II Timothy 3 with ungrateful, unholy, without love, unforgiving, slanderous, without self-control, brutal, treacherous, rash, conceited and lovers of pleasure rather than lovers of God. Yet in Paul's description, the people in the Last Days are religious, having a form of godliness but denying God's power. The Apostle Paul told his reader, the young Timothy to turn away from such hypocrites. Seventeen hundred years later, the famous American evangelist, Charles Grandison Finney (1792-1875) made a profound declaration. *"Sin is the most expensive thing in the universe, pardoned or unforgiven — pardoned, its cost falls on the atoning sacrifice, unforgiven, it must forever lie upon the impenitent soul."*

God, who at sundry times and in divers manners
spake in time past unto the fathers by the prophets,
Hath in these last days spoken unto us by His Son,
whom He hath appointed heir of all things, by whom also He made the worlds.
Hebrews 1:1-2

It Took A Miracle

John Peterson

*"In the beginning God created the heaven and the earth.
And the earth was without form, and void; and darkness
was upon the face of the deep.
And the spirit of God moved upon the face of the waters.
And God said, Let there be light: and there was light.
And God saw the light, that it was good: and God divided
the light from the darkness.
And God called the light Day, and the darkness he called
Night.
And the evening and the morning were the first day... And
God said,
Let there be lights in the firmament of the heaven to divide
the day from the night;
and let them be for signs, and for seasons, and for days,
and years:
And let them be for lights in the firmament of the heaven to
give light upon the earth: and it was so. And God made two
great lights; the greater light to rule the day,
and the lesser light to rule the night: he made the stars
also.
And God set them in the firmament of the heaven to give
light upon the earth,
And to rule over the day and over the night, and to divide
the light from the darkness: and God saw that it was good.*

And the evening and the morning were the fourth day.
Genesis 1:1-5, 14-19

English philosopher, Francis Bacon (1561-1626) in his essay on atheism rightly stated, *"God never wrought miracles to convince atheism, because His ordinary works convince it!"* Twelve hundred years earlier, also on the subject of miracles, Augustine (354-430) the distinguished Christian Bishop and theologian of Hippo in North Africa declared this: *"I have never any difficulty in believing in miracles, since I experienced the miracle of a change in my own heart."*

Early in the Third Millennium, the renowned Anglican minister of All Souls Church in West London, England, Richard Bewes recalled to me his meeting with Gospel soloist, George Beverly Shea in the American capital just weeks after the Islamic terrorist attacks on New York City's World Trade Center Twin Towers, the Pentagon, and a passenger plane in Pittsburgh. Indeed, it was just before Christmas 2001 and the war was raging against terrorism in Afghanistan. Meanwhile in Washington DC, there was an especially auspicious event taking place. It was the conferring of an honorary Knighthood on Billy Graham, by the British Ambassador, Sir Christopher Meyer on behalf of the Queen Elizabeth II.

Doctor Billy's witty but sincere and humble response to the ambassador's speech tickled the audience's funny-bone that day. Speaking of the Billy Graham Team's many UK experiences since 1946, Billy broached the subject of accents. *"We often had difficulty with accents especially when we were in Scotland or Yorkshire. George Beverly Shea was in London for our meetings in 1954, and he was singing 'It took a miracle to put the stars in space'. But one person, a member of the press, misheard the word and wrote that it seemed awfully arrogant that an American would say, 'It took America to put the stars in space!'"*

Billy was speaking of the song, 'It Took A Miracle' by John Peterson. A striking song about the miracle of creation, the lyrics expounded the doctrine clearly presented in key passages of scripture. The Bible teaches that the entire universe, including all matter, had a beginning and that it came into existence through the decision of the Eternal God. Some teachers hold that there is a long gap between verses 1 and 2 of the first book of Genesis. They say that God's perfect creation came into chaos through a great catastrophe. God then refashioned creation as we see it now.

Scholars differ too over the duration of the creative days of Genesis 1. Some say that the Hebrew word for 'day' may mean 'a period of light between two periods of darkness', some say 'a period of light together with the preceding period of darkness', and yet others say it is 'a long period of time'. But a miracle is a miracle. So whatever the interpretation, Creation is described as a distinct act of God.

Many have observed the inspirational quality and the diverse applications of the song 'It Took A Miracle' by John Peterson. It is considered by some to be a 'hymn of creation-praise' and, more particularly by others, 'a hymn of salvation praise'. The truth is whatever the application, the Lord is still the object of praise. Therefore, the praise is not merely an expression of joy in creation alone but in the joy of salvation too. The song looks at God as the good Creator, Ruler, and Sustainer of the world but also the Saviour of our souls.

As the Creator, the scriptures teach that God firmly incorporated two spheres of rule: heaven and earth. He established the celestial bodies in the firmament and gave them the rule over day and night and He appointed the human race to govern the earth. The heavenly bodies all have their commissioned place. In reference to the boundless space of space, the disposition and the importance of the heavenly bodies, the Psalmist asked, *"What is man?"* Human beings are by nature earthlings, and yet they are, as John Peterson's lyrics declare the particular objects of God's love. Amazingly, the Creator has invested love, glory and honour on mankind.

Throughout the second half of the 20th century, John W. Peterson was a prolific songwriter with thousands of gospel songs published as well as many sacred cantatas. A hit song of sorts, 'It Took A Miracle" was popularly recorded in the early 1950's by the crooning hit-maker, Eddy Arnold, Kate Smith and by the Blackwood Brothers, among others. John's other best-known songs are the beloved 'Surely Goodness and Mercy', 'Shepherd of Love', 'Over The Sunset

Mountains' and 'Heaven Came Down' (variously recorded by Doug Oldham, the Statler Brothers, Jimmie Davis, Sandy Patti, Billy Graham choirs and many others).

One of America's foremost contemporary composers, John W. Peterson was born on 1st November 1921. In the same week, America's World War I 'Unknown Soldier' arrived in his homeland from Europe for burial in Washington DC's Arlington Cemetery. Clearly the scars of the war were still sore even in the Swedish community of Lindsborg, Kansas. John was the youngest of seven children in a Swedish-American family. Sadly, his father died when he was only four years old.

John became a Christian at the age of twelve and was greatly influenced in his Christian walk by his grandfather, Charles Nelson. Charles was the first to realise the outstanding creative gift that God had given his grandson and predicted that John would one day use that talent to the glory of God. A handsome youth, John was an all-round musician playing piano and guitar as well as singing, writing his first song whilst still in High School. He sold his first composition in 1940 at the age of nineteen.

With the onslaught of hostilities, John was drafted and served in the United States Army Air Force as a pilot during World War II. Duty called in due time and he was ordered to fly dangerous lonely missions over the 'China Hump' in the Himalayas. The exploits of these brave pilots on these hairy, desolate missions were lauded with the making of a John Wayne adventure movie at the time. Especially on night missions, flying over those majestic peaks brought home to John W. Peterson the greatness and awesome character of the Creator God who put the stars in space! Those hazardous flights became the inspiration to many of his songs including 'Over The Sunset Mountains' and 'It Took A Miracle'.

Raised in a Christian environment and always keen to follow His Lord and Saviour, John's straightforward Christian declaration earned him the nickname of 'deacon' during his Air Force days. Every morning at his bunk-bed, he would be ridiculed but perhaps privately admired by his service buddies for reading his New Testament. After peace was finally declared, he studied at the famed Moody Bible Institute in Chicago, Illinois and then entered the American

Conservatory of Music, again in Chicago where he pursued his musical education.

John Peterson's post-WWII association with the renowned publishing house, 'Singspiration Music' was an extensive one. Ultimately, he was promoted to the executive editor position. He also continued to conduct as guest conductor at performances of his own numerous choral works in churches and auditoriums around the USA. His choral cantatas such as 'Night of Miracles', 'Easter Song' and others become firm favourites over the decades among choirs all over the world, selling millions of copies! Muriel Shepherd, leader of the London Emmanuel Choir, told me how 'Night of Miracles' was a perennial Christmas favourite of hers and the Choir's vast audiences.

John Peterson's great song inspired by the Creator's great love, speaks confidently of God's fidelity and great love of men and women. Speaking of this wondrous love of God, England's outstanding politician and social reformer, Lord Anthony Ashley Cooper Shaftesbury (1801-1885) said these impactive words to his mortally-ill, dying son, *"Human love is capable of great things. What then must be the depth and height and intensity of divine love? Know nothing, think of nothing but Jesus Christ and Him crucified!"*

My Father is omnipotent, and that you can't deny;
A God of might and miracles - 'Tis written in the sky.

It took a miracle to put the stars in place;
It took a miracle to hand the world in space.
But when He saved my soul, Cleansed and made me whole,
It took a miracle of love and grace.

Though here His glory has been show, we still can't fully see
The wonders of His might, His throne - 'Twill take eternity.

The Bible tells us of His power, and wisdom all way through,
And every little bird and flower are testimonies, too.

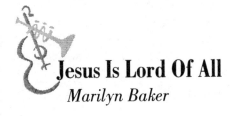

Jesus Is Lord Of All
Marilyn Baker

"Then Peter opened his mouth, and said,
 'Of a truth I perceive that God is no respecter of persons:
 But in every nation He that feareth Him,
 and worketh righteousness, is accepted with Him.
 The word, which God sent unto the children of Israel,
 preaching peace by Jesus Christ: (He is Lord of all),".
Acts 10:34-36

Although spoken in somewhat broken Greek, the Apostle Peter's wonderful sermon was in house of the Roman Centurion, Cornelius. The experienced preacher clearly stated that the Nazarene that he had personally-known, Christ Jesus was without doubt God, "He is Lord of all"!

Taking great delight in the chance to preach, the middle-aged fisherman from Galilee turned preacher had a radiant face as he held his foreign audience spellbound. Peter tutored much about the Jews' promised Messiah and Jesus' birth and earthly ministry in the Holy Land, because they were Gentiles who knew little. Even though these foreigners knew something about Jesus of Nazareth from living in Palestine, they required more details of Jesus' life and work than a Palestinian Jewish audience would.

That day the Apostle's sermon (recorded by Doctor Luke in the 'Acts of the Apostles') is prefaced by the significant words, *"Opening his mouth, Peter said"* because in Luke's eyes, Peter was making a weighty utterance. Indeed, he was sweeping away centuries of racial prejudice. His sermon stated that God does not show racial favoritism because, as Marilyn Baker's song affirmed 'Jesus Is Lord Of All'. He lovingly accepts men from every nation who fear Him and do what is right. This truth was plain in Israel's history and at times was expressed well by her prophets. But Peter's sermon was absolutely clear clarification. Peter declared that it was indeed the message that God sent to the people of Israel, telling the good news of peace through Jesus Christ, who is Lord of all.

This divine revelation that 'Jesus Is Lord Of All' is a message from God proclaimed in the Gospel to the people of Israel initially. Then it was related to the outside Gentile world in terms intelligible to the Gentiles. The expression, 'Jesus Is Lord Of All' clearly stated that Christ was 'Lord of all' to both Jews and Gentiles. This phrase 'Lord of all', scholars tell us, was a pagan title for deity, but it was re-baptized by the early Christians to become an appropriate attribute of Christ Jesus. Cleverly taken up in her song- 'Jesus Is Lord Of All', Marilyn Baker used this theological title to describe Christ.

Handicapped-by-blindness, Marilyn says she was born into a very virtuous household. An only child, her parents guaranteed that she had 'the whole shebang' that she wanted materially. Born prematurely and her dear mother being quite old when she had her, the medical team had to give Marilyn oxygen at birth. Unfortunately, she was given too much and this irrevocably damaged her eyes resulting in blindness. At the age of five years, she was sent to a boarding school. Such an arrangement in those days was normal for such blind children. Overwhelmingly grieved, she could only visit her devoted parents at weekends in South Birmingham.

Home visits grew very scarce when at the age of eleven years, she was posted to a different school, Chorleywood College in Hertfordshire. There sadly, so she could now only make social calls to her parents once a month. She remembered, *"Whereas I was top of the class at Junior School, I was just one of many at the Secondary School! So I found myself pretty much as the bottom of the class!"*

A further result of the oxygen accident at birth also affected Marilyn's sense of direction. *"All my friends seemed to be able to find their way around school buildings. I was always the slowest making me very unhappy and would often play the fool. I tried doing things to make people like me, but deep down I had a deep sense of insecurity!"*

Often lonely and insecure, matters got worse when at the age of fourteen her grandmother died. Sadly, it was an event that deeply shocked her, as she said, she loved her grandmother about as much as she did her mother. As often happens, the tragedy of death caused her to start thinking deeply about whether 'Jesus Is Lord Of All'. In her despair she started to pose many questions: *"Well, what is life all about then? When death comes is that the end? Is it really true that Jesus Is Lord Of All?"*

Providentially, around the corresponding time, a school Christian Union started up in Chorleywood College and she was asked her to join. Soon after, one of her girlfriends in her class-form approached questioning Marilyn with an attractive idea. *"Marilyn, I would like you to meet a couple of friends who take me out on Sundays for tea and things! They said that they'd like to meet you. Perhaps we could make a date with them sometime for a trip out?"*

Marilyn enjoyed the company of these new friends. She felt that the dear couple were different from any people she had met before. As Marilyn recalled with a grin, *"They called themselves 'Christians' and I had never met a person who actually said that before! They would often say that 'Jesus Is Lord Of All'! The couple's family life was different too, and the atmosphere was different in their house. But to be honest, there were certain things I was not too mad about. For instance, you could not play non-religious records on a Sunday! But there was this love in their lives that really spoke to me. I went along to their church a few times!"*

Later, Marilyn found a book in Braille in the school chapel called 'The Transforming Friendship' by the famous pre-WWII Methodist teacher, Leslie Weatherhead. Enthusiastically, Marilyn said, *"I read it. It talked about Jesus in such a personal way. It mentioned the fact that He is alive and wants to be involved in our everyday lives as a friend. I'd always assumed that He had died 2,000 years ago and maybe He had risen from the dead. But I'd never really understood that He is alive! Mindful of my wrong behaviour at school,*

I became fearful that I might have to give account of my actions to God. One night, I just prayed that this Jesus would be my Saviour. I just prayed that He'd forgive me, and be my friend! Bit by bit my relationship with Him grew and I developed a keenness for the Bible, reading it every minute I could!"

Newly inspired, Marilyn started attending St. Andrews-the local evangelical Church of England Church and the Brethren Assembly with the friends who took her out on Sundays. After some soul-searching, it was there she was joyfully baptised by immersion when she was eighteen years of age. She was deeply appreciative of her new friends, as she recalled, *"These friends proved to be my spiritual parents, helping me with all sorts of questions and doubts!"*

After finally leaving school, Marilyn attended the Royal College of Music to study oboe and piano. *"I knew I was musical but my harmony teacher said my melodies were boring! I knew that was true. So I just said, 'Lord, if You want me to write I want You to give me a new ability and I want to dedicate my musical talent to you!'...I wrote a song after that, a song of joy called, 'He's My Saviour, My Friend, And My Lord'."*

Marilyn never thought of writing any more. *"I don't know why, I just didn't!... Three years later, I met a friend called Carol who shared her house with me. She didn't have any musical training but possessed a very pleasant voice. So I started to write songs for her. Then I was asked by my minister to share in the evening service. I played the piano while Carol sang!"*

Progressively, Marilyn continued to write songs and made a custom-recording that the local singing pastor of the Elim Church heard. The Reverend Len Magee, realising her gifting should be used, arranged an interview with London's Pilgrim Records' bossman, David Payne. Soon after, Marilyn was delighted that the result was her first album. Meanwhile, she was employed at Watford Girl's Grammar School in North London, teaching oboe. She also taught part-time at her old school, Chorleywood College. Loving her job, she did not considering a full-time music ministry at all!

In 1982, record company boss, David Payne suggested that Marilyn seek God's guidance on her future. After three weeks of praying, she said that God left her in no doubt that He wanted her to give up her job, which she did! Two days later she received a phone call from a recording company in New Zealand asking her to tour that autumn!

Marilyn Baker's musical ministry touched many people, something that always gladdened her heart. She stated, *"We all have our ups and downs in life and I am no exception! So a lot of my songs reflect this! It's wonderful when people come up to me and say, 'We heard your record when we were going through a really down-patch and we found that through it the love of God really came through to us!'"*

Marilyn said that she proved that 'Jesus Is Lord Of All' even the Lord of her disability. Of course, being blind caused her some difficulties especially as it resulted, she said, in her sometimes not feeling accepted as a natural person. *"I feel it is very important for me and other handicapped people to feel loved for who we are!"*

Marilyn said that many times, well meaning people would pray for her to be physically healed of blindness. But she says she accepts God's will in her life saying He accepted her as she was! She says, *"We are all individuals in God's sight! I am thankful that the Lord knows without exception what He's doing with every person!"*

Augustine (354-430 AD) the distinguished Christian Bishop and theologian of Hippo in North Africa declared, *"Jesus Christ will be Lord of ALL or He will not be Lord at all!"*

Jesus is Lord of all, Satan is under His feet, Jesus is reigning on high
And all power is given to Him in heaven and earth.

We are joined to Him, Satan is under our feet, we are seated on high
And all authority is given to us through Him.

One day we'll be like Him, perfect in every way, chosen to be His bride,
Ruling and reigning with Him for evermore.

Jesus Stand Among Us

Graham Kendrick

> *"Then the same day at evening, being the first day of the week,*
> *when the doors were shut where the disciples were assembled for fear of the Jews,*
> *came Jesus and stood in the midst, and saith unto them, 'Peace be unto you.'*
> *And when He had so said, He showed unto them His hands and His side.*
> *Then were the disciples glad, when they saw the Lord.*
> *Then said Jesus to them again,*
> *'Peace be unto you: as my Father hath sent me, even so send I you.*
> *And when He had said this, he breathed on them, and saith unto them, 'Receive ye the Holy Ghost:*
> *Whosesoever sins ye remit, they are remitted unto them and whosesoever sins ye retain, they are retained.*
> *John 20:19-23*

Graham Kendrick, as a musician and composer, is a name that epitomised the best of the British contemporary Christian music scene of the latter 20th century. Someone once said that he writes the songs that make the whole church sing. So what is the secret of his success? Graham is typically modest. *"I don't have any formal musical training and often envy people who do! I've learned mainly by trial and error. I take the 'hit and miss' route. I try it this way and I try it that way. I try the hoping-for-happy accidents' approach. It's probably not the most efficient way of writing songs! But now and again it works!"*

His insightful lyrics have been translated into numerous languages. His devotional songs are sung daily by millions of worshippers around the globe. Crossing international and denominational barriers, his beloved songs have been used from countless small church events to major festivals. These include 'Promise Keepers' rallies, Billy Graham crusades and a four million-strong open-air meeting in the Philippines capital Manila. Graham received a 'Gospel Music Association' Dove Award in 1995 for his international work. In 2000 he received an honorary doctorate in divinity from West London's Brunel University in recognition of his contribution to the worship life of the church.

Graham Kendrick was born in Northamptonshire County in England in 1950. Since the age of fifteen years when he first announced to his surprised parents that he wanted to be a songwriter, Graham achieved the adulation and approval of old-and-young with his theological musical applications. A teacher by trade, he launched out as a singer-songwriter in 1972. Trained not in formal music schools but in the crucible of evangelistic coffee bars, Graham excelled at putting Christian truth into the contemporary folk-rock music styles of the time. Later, he shifted the performing artist's skills of storytelling and memorable tunes into a worship setting. It proved to be a powerful mix. The resulting compositions travelled far and wide. Graham became recognised as a follower in the footsteps of the great hymn-writers of the past. They, like Graham were at the cutting-edge of their culture's art, using contemporary music in worship. He said, *"Surprisingly, many of the hymns we venerate today as quality music were originally sung to popular tavern tunes!"*

Surprisingly Graham chose to quietly slip out of what he said was the lonely and unfulfilling world of Christian showbiz. He said that the prevalent disease of Christian showbiz was caused by spiritual starvation. Seeking more meaningful involvement in the local Body of Christ, he widened his ministry accordingly preferring as he says *"to minister rather than perform"*.

In the mid-1970s, he became burdened about young Christians who wanted to use their musical ability for God's glory but were becoming lost along-the-way due to lack of fellowship, teaching and belonging. With the 'Kingsway' record company and 'Thankyou Music', he helped organise popular retreats for musicians who were serious about their calling. Many musicians testified during those days that bearded Graham's ministry heavily influenced their lives and prompted their involvement in organisations like the 'British Youth For Christ', 'Continental Ministries', 'Operation Mobilisation' and 'Youth With A Mission'.

In the latter 1970s, Graham Kendrick became more and more active in partnership with the head of British Youth for Christ, Clive Calver. Years later, Clive went on to successfully head-up the English Evangelical Alliance before Joel Edwards was appointed for his term. About the same time, Graham became associated with the preacher-teacher, Roger Forster. He headed up an enterprising and inspiring group of churches in the south London area known as Ichthus Fellowships. Initially, Roger had been nurtured in the progressive Honour Oak Christian Fellowship that sponsored the visit from China of Watchman Nee to the UK in the 1930s. At the Ichthus Fellowships, Graham was pleased to see believers worshipping, enjoying the 'presence of God' and using his songs. He said, *"Songs are just vessels that can be filled up with the 'presence of God' and poured out into people's lives."*

A catalyst and co-founder, Graham gave his substantial support in 1968 to the worldwide phenomenon known as the 'March For Jesus'. MfJ began in the humble surroundings of central London's Soho. It grew into a massive interdenominational prayer, praise and proclamation event that involved a total of around 55 million people. Over its years it became a globally co-ordinated event. Across the world, hundreds of thousands of Christians in city streets demonstrated their faith by taking part in the International March For Jesus. It was a demonstration that delighted Graham who declared, *"Today the sounds-of-praise are filling streets all over the world overflowing from the hearts of people of many nations. And there is one name on all our lips, the name of Jesus Christ! As Christians unite across the continents and islands to march together, the world will have to ask why we are marching and where we are going. We will tell them we are marching for Jesus, we are marching with Jesus, and we are marching to Jesus. As the world of 'not yet' believers looks on, they see the radiance on our faces, the reflected glory of the One on whom we are all gazing. They hear our joyful praises in the songs we are singing. They are touched by His love and long for His embrace. As our procession-of-worship moves majestically towards the throne, we call others to come with us. We long to present them as an offering to the Lamb that He might receive the rich and full reward of His suffering."*

There is no denying that Graham Kendrick always had a winning way with lyrics and melodies. Indeed, his fame extended to the 'Who's Who' publication in the UK. From his initial exposure in Britain's massive 'Spring Harvest' meetings in the latter decades of the 20th century, his worship songs spread around the world. His many modern hymns ably demonstrated that his song-lyrics theologically took a stand that was superior to most of his peers. Graham admits to starting with the advantage of being a preacher's kid!

Raised in Putney Baptist church in southwest London, England, he was well apprenticed by his father. The Reverend Kendrick senior was the local Baptist minister who also taught himself piano and accordion. On Sundays at suppertime after church services, the family and friends would gather to sing their favourite hymns and choruses around the piano. Graham was always somewhat shy but along with his brother and sister began piano lessons. He recalled, *"I had an ear for music and was able to learn the little exercises from the teacher."* He struggled, however, he said, with what he described as the *"funny little musical dots on paper"* and eventually was dropped by the frustrated piano-teacher.

Years later, inspired by songs on the radio, Graham tried his hand at the old dusty guitar that he founded stashed away in a cupboard by his father. Slowly he conquered the beast and although he was short on formal musical teaching, chords and tunes started to emerge by practice. Indeed, creative juices started to flow freely as new tunes came to him as he cycled his newspaper delivery route around the streets of Putney. In the 1960s, the three Kendrick siblings and friends aspired to become a band that they featured in local coffee-bar venues concocted for evangelistic purposes among young people. Asked what were his song-writing influences, Graham laughingly replied. *"Firstly, the Baptist hymn book and then secondly, the Beatles!"*

Reverend Kendrick (Graham's father) ensured that the family members were soaked in solid Bible knowledge from an early age. Graham said it enabled him to re-tell many of the familiar scriptural incidents through the eyes of the people there. *"I do so, calling on all the tools that I as a poet have at my disposal - imagery, symbolism and so on. The thing that inspires me is stepping into the shoes of these people. However, I must point out that the source of my inspiration is the living Jesus Christ. As I get to know Him better I hope my songs will picture Him more clearly, not as a picture recalled from the past, but as He is. He is on the throne living in resplendent glory in and among those who belong to His Kingdom on earth!"*

In the era of the 1970s fashionable shaggy-hair, jeans and mini skirts, Graham cut his performing and song-writing teeth. His lack of formal music training was never a disadvantage. Those who were trained were branded as being old-fashioned. Graham's early song 'Jesus Stand Among Us' was inspired by Christ's appearance to His disciples in the evening of the first day of the Resurrection. Apostle John cites this appearance to the collective group of Christ's followers. Christ appeared in order to allay their fears. They had narrowly escaped arrest with Him in Gethsemane. Realizing that as the disciples of the One who was regarded as a dangerous agitator, they would be under suspicion. They probably consulted together on how best to withdraw from the city without attracting the notice of the temple police or the Roman authorities. The doors were locked for fear that the Jews would send an arresting detachment for them as they had for Jesus.

As Graham's song, 'Jesus Stand Among Us' implied, an appearance of Christ Jesus in the room of any local church results in both amazement and fear. The implication is clear in the story: locked doors did not impede Jesus. His resurrection body has properties different from the body of flesh; yet it was not ethereal. There was a definite continuity between the physical body of Jesus' earthly career and the new body since His hands and side still showed the scars that identified Him. His greeting of *"Peace be unto you!"* and the assurance of Christ's identity calmed their fears and demonstrated by unmistakable proof that He was alive again. They were overjoyed, not only to see Him again, but also to realize that He was undefeated by death and that His claims were validated.

Christ's repetition of the common greeting *"Peace"* reassured the disciples of His real presence. Not only did His appearance renew their devotion and their hopes, but it also renewed their commission as disciples. Had there been no Resurrection, there would have been little motive for them to undertake a mission in His name. But since He had risen, the old commitment was even more compelling. He said, *"As the Father has sent me, I am sending you!"*

Graham Kendrick passionately believed that Christ entered into the world to fulfill the Father's purpose—to speak His words, to do His works, and to lay down His life for the salvation of humans. Today He expects His followers in every local church to continue His work. In His absence, they deliver His message, do greater works than He did, giving their lives in His service. They would have all the privileges, all the protection, and all the responsibilities that He had during His ministry. The beautiful words of the risen Christ Jesus emphasized that the Holy Spirit was not bestowed on the church as an ornament. He was to empower an effective application of the work of Christ to the entire human race.

Graham lived in southeast London for many years, where he served on the leadership team of Ichthus Christian Fellowship. He and his wife, Jill - who helps run their company 'Make Way Music'- raised four daughters. Graham's co-worker, Roger Forster was a strong advocate of the teaching that for all church ministry Jesus provided the Holy Spirit. Indeed, the Spirit continues to empower the commission given to the church to proclaim the forgiveness-of-sins in Christ's name. The Spirit-and-the-Word are linked together for the gospel ministry. This was initially announced two thousand years ago at Pentecost, the historic fulfillment of God's promise. The descent of the Spirit on the church at Pentecost brought the following proclamation by the Apostle Peter to his hearers. *"Repent and be baptized, every one of you, in the name of Jesus Christ so that your sins may be forgiven."*

Graham stated, *"God still has the same agenda. He's building His temple out of 'living stones' that He wants to fill. Out of this temple He calls the nations to worship. His agenda involves the preaching of the gospel to the ends of the Earth and then comes the end of the Age of grace."*

The initial scene of Graham Kendick's song 'Jesus Stand Among Us' was old Jerusalem 2000 years ago. The Upper Room drama was the perfect picture of Christ in every generation meeting with the local church! *"Wherever believers find themselves in the Body of Christ, they have a part to play. I see my task as helping the church to worship! Much of worship is about singing God's truth back to Him and to one another. We should guard against everything being too individualistic and subjective, based on personal opinion and experience. Sometimes a song's content is so very personal it does not transfer into suitability for a congregation. But God's truth is always objective. A quality worship song combines objective truth, scriptural truth and a worshiper's personal response to that truth!"*

At the height of his songwriting abilities, Graham said that he felt the urgency to not only preach the gospel but to encourage other Christians, particularly the young, to do likewise. He said, *"Many of us feel that we are in the last few years of grace. That's why many of my recordings major on the end times and our Christian responsibilities to a lost and dying world. Before we know it the day will have ended and the night will have come!"*

Jesus, stand among us at the meeting of our lives;
Be our sweet agreement at the meeting of our eyes.
O Jesus, we love You, so we gather here;
Join our hearts in unity and take away our fear.

So to You we're gathering out of each and every land;
Christ the love between us at the joining of our hands.
O Jesus, we love You, so we gather here;
Join our hearts in unity and take away our fear.

Jesus, stand among us at the breaking of the bread;
Join us as one body as we worship You, our Head.
O Jesus, we love You, so we gather here;
Join our hearts in unity and take away our fear.

King Of Kings (He Came To Earth)
John Pantry

"And I saw heaven opened, and behold a white horse;
and He that sat upon him was called Faithful and True,
and in righteousness He doth judge and make war.
His eyes were as a flame of fire, and on his head were many
crowns;
and He had a name written, that no man knew, but He
himself.
And he was clothed with a vesture dipped in blood:
and his name is called The Word of God.
And the armies which were in heaven followed Him upon
white horses,
clothed in fine linen, white and clean.
And out of his mouth goeth a sharp sword, that with it He
should smite the nations:
and He shall rule them with a rod of iron:
and he treadeth the winepress of the fierceness and wrath of
Almighty God.
And he hath on his vesture and on his thigh a name written,
KING OF KINGS, AND LORD OF LORDS!"
Revelation 19:11-16

When I asked British singer-songwriter, John Pantry about his song,
'King of Kings, He Came To Earth', he replied, *"There's really not*

much of a story behind it, I'm afraid! However, it came from the realisation that Christ Jesus was the Lord of every atom in the universe. Moreover, He became finite and vulnerable in order that I could appreciate God, have my sins forgiven and enter into an eternal relationship with the Father. It's a song that speaks about the Lordship of Christ!"

Handsome, gentle-voiced and a deep thinker, Englishman John Pantry had a varied career structure ranging from record producer to radio DJ. Born northwest of London, in Harrow, Middlesex, he developed an early interest in music as a member of his local church choir. He recalls with a smile, *"They tried to get me to learn to read music! But like most other kids, I didn't try very hard at it, something I was to regret afterwards! But, nevertheless, later in life, I taught myself to read music!"*

An avid Bible reader, John stated, *"The Apostle John's words in Revelation 19:11-16 are important for understanding the Lordship of and Kingship of Christ."* Interestingly, John noted that Old Testament writers speaking of the Lordship of and Sovereignty of the coming Messiah, used the word 'King' while New Testament writers used the word 'Lord' of Christ Jesus. Jesus said of Himself that the Son of Man is Lord even of the Sabbath. Bible students like John find profitable reflection in studying the various forms of expression used by the authors of the New Testament in which they attribute Lordship to our Saviour.

In his great vision of the 'Return of Christ' and the 'Consummation of This Age of Grace', the Apostle John describes the great appearing of Christ. It was prophetically an event to which the New Testament bore frequent and unified witness. The Apostle John's great vision of Christ looked alternately back to the Old Testament and to John's previous references in the book of Revelation. Awe-struck, the Apostle saw a vision of a white horse (representing conquest and victory) with a Divine Rider (representing faithfulness and truth). The Rider stands in contrast to the forces of the Antichrist of the Last Days with their empty promises and lies. In spite of the fact that John used Old Testament language descriptive of a warrior-Messiah, he does not depict Christ The Rider as a great military warrior battling against earth's sovereigns. Rather, the kind of warfare

Christ engages-in is more like the 'execution of justice' than military conflict. He who is the faithful and true Witness will one day judge the rebellious nations.

As the Apostle's revelation unfolds it becomes clear that Christ's power is so great that His Name is known only by Himself. His 'secret Name' may be one that will not be revealed until Christ's return. Interestingly, 'knowledge of a name' is in antiquity associated with the power of an ancient god. When his name becomes known, then his power is shared with those to whom the disclosure is made. Bible students such as John Pantry note the possible conclusion that arises. Since two names of Christ are revealed in this vision (the 'Word of God' and 'King Of Kings And Lord Of Lords'), it may be concluded that the exclusive power of Christ over all creation will on that day to be shared with His faithful followers.

The imagery in this verse traditionally is related to a passage understood messianically by the Jews and one that the Apostle John used in portraying God's wrath. The Old Testament's Isaiah pictured a Mighty-Warrior who slaughtered His enemies. Their life-blood splashes on His clothing as He tramples them down in His anger, just as the juice of grapes splashes on the wine-treader in the winepress. But in the book of Revelation, Christ's blood-dipped red-robe is red not from His enemies' blood but from His own. Christ comes from heaven with His robe already dipped in blood before any battle is mentioned. Interestingly, the sword with which Christ strikes down the nations comes from His mouth and is not in His hand, incompatible with battle imagery.

The adjectives 'true and faithful', applied to Christ, are likewise identified with the Word of God. Thus Christ Jesus in His earthly life bore reliable and consistent witness in all His words and actions to the purposes of God. He was completely obedient. In Him the will of God found full expression. Indeed, the Word of God and the person of Christ are one.

After leaving school, John Pantry decided that he would like to get into the UK's booming recording business of the 1960s in London's busy West End. Fortunately, he became a trainee to the internationally respected IBC Studios in central London's Portland Place where he trained for two and a half years.

Soon he was engineering on albums for an impressive array of musicians such as the Bee Gees, The Who, the New Seekers, the Small Faces, the Kinks and Manfred Mann. Alongside his obvious engineering and recording talent, he was also becoming recognised as a very proficient songwriter. Whilst he was working in the studios, John recorded a few demo discs of his compositions. Soon he was having singles recorded by several household names of the time including Billy J. Kramer and the Fortunes.

John then recorded his own single-the James Taylor song-'Something In The Way She Moves' that became a hit in the USA. He then won a recording contract with 'Phillips Records' who, seeing his potential, released his first album appropriately entitled 'John Pantry' in 1973. Unfortunately, the success he felt that he deserved did not materialise. Meanwhile, John also ran his own company that made TV advertising jingles for products such as 'Harp lager', 'Shredded Wheat' cereal and 'Jacob's Cracker Biscuits'. At one time, he had several jingles running on television all at the same time!

Once again he began writing and producing for other artistes. Among these assignments was a Christian group called Parchment whose inspiring 'Light Up The Fire' song (which John produced) seemed to capture the savour of the British Christian scene of that time. The single received considerable radio airplay as it was chosen for the BBC's national DJ play-list. Through his increasing contact with Christian musicians, John was led into a personal relationship with Jesus Christ. This in turn bought him into contact with Christian artistes via Geoff Shearn's Kingsway Music who wanted him to produce their albums from such as Adrian Snell, Graham Kendrick, Dave Pope and many others on England's south coast.

John remembered, *"When I became a Christian, it seemed that a high proportion of my secular work just seemed to fold up! It wasn't that I stopped taking that kind of business, it's just that the phones stopped ringing as far as those clients were concerned."*

Circumstances were on the change and it was a very difficult time for John, a situation he found hard to understand. Suddenly, he was finding that he needed to rely on what he called his 'Christian work' to survive! Work in Christian music in the UK at that time was extremely difficult to procure but it started to flow for John.

Looking back, John stated that he realised that God did know best because as a 'Baby-Christian', he would not have been able to resist the unchristian influences that the secular world had to offer. Later when stronger in the faith, John was able to resume his secular work.

After working as Kingsway Music's record producer for a number of years with numerous record productions completed, John spent a year in California producing albums for 'Maranatha Music' before he produced his first solo Christian album- 'Empty Handed'- on the UK's Kingsway label in 1978. Joining John in the USA were his wife, Jackie, and children Joanne and Benjamin.

Returning to the UK, John began to tour as a Christian artist himself and in the early 1980s, John became a director of 'Ears and Eyes' a Christian record production company with fellow directors Kevin Hoy and New Zealander, Chris Norton. The company ran from 1984-1989.

In 1989 John was accepted for the Anglican ministry and the following year began studying at Oak Hill College to become an Anglican minister and was ordained accordingly in 1994. He also worked for the 'Scripture Union' writing Bible Notes and organised seminars, workshops and missions to churches, schools and prisons, as well as performing at his own gospel concerts. In 1996, a further feather-in-his-cap was achieved when his soft-spoken voice became well known across the London radio airways. He secured the resident morning DJ role on London's 'Premier' Christian radio station.

In the vision of Revelation 19:11-16, the soldiers, like their leader, are riding white horses of victory and their clothing is bright and clean linen, identical to the Bride (the Church)'s attire. In vision, these human victors accompanying Christ are both resurrected and raptured or the company of the martyrs. The Apostle writes that the Lamb will overcome the beast and the ten kings because He is Lord of lords and King of kings; and with Him will be His called, chosen and faithful followers! In his beautiful song, John Pantry ably describes Jesus as the absolute Lord and King, full of the divine power and authority. Indeed, the name of Christ (as Lord of lords and King of kings) in vision is one that all can read. It is displayed on His most exposed part of His cloak, the part that covers His thigh. The Name, on that great day, cannot escape notice.

He came to earth, not to be served, but gave His life to be a
ransom for many;
The Son of God, the Son of man, He shared our pain and bore
our sins in His body.

King of kings and Lord of lords, I lift my voice in praise;
Such amazing love, but I do believe This King has died for me.

And so I stand, a broken soul, to see the pain that I have brought
to Jesus;
And yet each heart will be consoled, to be made new, the joy of
all believers.

And from now on, through all my days, I vow to live each moment
here for Jesus;
Not looking back, but giving praise for all my Lord has done for
this believer.

Living He Loved Me
(One Day When Heaven Was Filled With His Praises)
J. Wilbur Chapman & Charles H. Marsh

*"And the grace of our Lord was exceeding abundant
with faith and love which is in Christ Jesus.
This is a faithful saying, and worthy of all acceptation,
that Christ Jesus came into the world to save sinners; of whom
I am chief.
Howbeit for this cause I obtained mercy,
that in me first Jesus Christ might show forth all longsuffering,
for a pattern to them which should hereafter believe on Him
to life everlasting.
Now unto the King eternal, immortal, invisible,
the only wise God, be honour and glory for ever and ever.
Amen."*
I Timothy 1: 14-17

The songwriting-preacher, Dr. J. Wilbur Chapman (1859-1918) was fully aware how in scripture the Apostle Paul typically had a habit of breaking out spontaneously into praise. J. Wilbur wrote the testimony story-song to reflect the heart-felt theology of the Apostle Paul in singable rhyme.

"Initially", said J. Wilbur Chapman, *"Saul (later to be known as the Apostle Paul) was a wicked, cruel blasphemer. Great was his opposition to the Christian movement expressed in the First Century Church and he literally cursed the name of Jesus. After his*

conversion, he changed his name to Paul. He had realized that his previous behaviour was blasphemy, because Jesus was truly divine!"

The young Saul, as a savage persecutor in his zeal to protect Judaism, believed that he must obliterate Christianity by insults and extreme violence. In spite of these sins, by God's grace, Paul was shown mercy because he 'acted in ignorance' as well as unbelief. He was genuine in believing that he was aiding God through his vehemence against the Early Church. But it was more than mercy that Paul secured from God. He also received 'the grace" of God' poured out on him, 'along with faith and love that are in Christ Jesus'. Paul could personally identify with the sentiments of J. Wilbur Chapman's lyrics, *"Living, He loved me. Dying He saved me. Buried, he carried my sins far away. Rising, He justified freely forever! One day He's coming , O glorious day!"*

Wilbur Chapman was born on June 17th 1859 in Richmond, Indiana, the son of Alexander and Lorinda Chapman. Throughout his days, Wilbur was well known for his staid demeanor. He obtained his ministerial training at Lake Forrest University and Lane Theological Seminary. As well as his pastoral duties, Wilbur began to hold revival meetings and during the ten years after Dwight Moody's death, conducted large revival meetings in such major cities as Boston, New York and Philadelphia. He was accompanied in his meetings for several years by the renowned evangelistic singer Charles M. Alexander.

Wilbur Chapman's zeal for evangelism also saw him travel around the world taking the Good News of the Gospel to everyone who would hear. He organised and conducted many Bible conferences and was the first director of the Winona Lake Chautauqua and Bible Conference in Indiana. It was at this Conference that Dr. Chapman met the musician, Charles Howard Marsh.

In 1895 Wilbur stopped his evangelistic travels, settling down to take up a pastorate in Philadelphia, and in 1901 was made head of a special committee of the Presbyterian Church to stimulate evangelistic interest in the USA. At the time, he took Billy Sunday on as an assistant, sending him out as 'advance man' for the various meetings across the country, thus starting Billy Sunday's evangelistic career. Chapman's method of holding a meeting was known as 'simultaneous revivalism' and apparently Billy Sunday and other evangelists continued this form. Just weeks after the Allied victory over Germany in World War II, Wilbur Chapman died in Jamaica, Long Island, New York on Christmas Day, December 25th 1918. Ironically, the two biggest secular hit-songs of the Christmas period in that year were 'After You've Gone' and 'Till We Meet Again'. But neither would achieve the longevity of the Wilbur Chapman hymnal classic, 'Living, He Loved Me' even though it seemed to be involved in many games of 'musical chairs' regarding copyrights and publishers and such.

Two decades earlier, Charles Howard Marsh had been invited to be the organist and accompanist at the Conference for the three summer months that it was to run. Just out of high school, the young Charles, was paid $100 a month do a job that he said that he loved. He was born in Magnolia, Iowa on April 8th 1886. His English parents had recently emigrated to America where his father, George took on the pastorship of the Congregational Church in Magnolia, Iowa. Charles Marsh's gifted piano playing had been recognised in his high school years. Then in 1908, Wilbur Chapman invited him to accompany him to a Bible conference that he was conducting at Stony Brook, Long Island. It was there at Stony Brook that Wilbur gave Charles the poem 'One Day When Heaven as Filled With His Praises' that Charles then set to music and copyrighted in his name. He later sold the publishing rights to Dr. Parley E. Zartman (Dr. Wilbur Chapman's assistant).

Charles Marsh then left his association with Wilbur Chapman to go to college. After his studies, he took up teaching and taught at the University of Redlands and the Bible Institute of Los Angeles. In 1924 he moved to France to study organ at the Fontainebleau Conservatory with Charles-Marie Widor and Henri Libert. He then moved on to Paris to further study piano, organ, composition and orchestration . Returning to America he became president of the European School of Music and Art in Fort Wayne, Indiana. He also served as organist and choirmaster of the First Presbyterian Church.

Moving to Florida in 1932, he was the university organist at the University of Florida, Gainesville and organist-choirmaster of the

First Baptist Church. In 1935 he moved to California to take up the position of district supervisor of the Federal Music Project, San Diego, California and as organist-choirmaster for the St. James-by-the-Sea Episcopal Church, La Jolla, California. He was a Fellow of the American Guild of Organists where he was also well known for his poetry and painting. His creativity in music was evidenced in the large volume of solo songs, instrumental works and anthem literature he produced .

Charles M. Alexander, who had apparently obtained the publishing rights from the Hope Publishing Company of Chicago, then copyrighted the song, 'One Day When Heaven as Filled With His Praises'. The Rodeheaver Publishing Company then bought the song from Charles Alexander. But when it came up for renewal, it then reverted to the original composer Charles Marsh.

Charles published eight books and a number of hymn texts including 'Jesus! What A Friend For Sinners' and, of course, 'One Day When Heaven Was Filled With His Praises'. He died in La Jolla, California in April 12th 1956 at a time when the USA was just beginning to feel the cold winds of racial disquiet blowing, initially in the streets of Montgomery, Alabama as buses were ordered to desegregate. Ironically, the Chapman-Marsh hymnal composition 'One Day When Heaven Was Filled With His Praises' was already a favourite of all races even in areas of racial upset.

Two thousand years earlier, the Apostle Paul faced great racial and religious intolerance in the Holy Land. Although a great Apostle historically, Paul claims that of all sinners he was the worst or chief especially in the area of racial and religious fanaticism . He felt this way by virtue of him persecuting Christ's followers so vigorously. As far as decency was concerned, young Saul was raised a strict Pharisee, living a life that was blameless before the Jewish law. Although a chief sinner, Christ's 'unlimited patience' was wonderfully displayed to Paul as an example to all who would believe in Jesus and thus receive eternal life. Paul's life was a stalwart demonstration of what divine grace can do in a surrendered life. To the end, his testimony remained the sentiments of J. Wilbur Chapman's lyrics :

"Living, He loved me. Dying He saved me. Buried, he carried my sins far away.
Rising, He justified freely forever! One day He's coming, O glorious day!"

One day when heaven was filled with His praises. One day when sin was as black as could be,
Jesus came forth to be born of a virgin, dwelt amongst men, my example is He!

Living, He loved me; dying, He saved me; buried, He carried my sins far away,
Rising, He justified freely for ever: one day He's coming: O glorious day.

One day they led Him up Calvary's mountain, one day they nailed Him to die on the tree:
Suffering anguish, despised and rejected; bearing our sins, my Redeemer is He!

One day they left Him alone in the garden, one day He rested, from suffering free;
Angels came down o'er His tomb to keep vigil; hope of the hopeless, my Saviour is He!

One day the grave could conceal Him no longer, one day the stone rolled away from the door;
Then He arose, over death He had conquered; now is ascended, my Lord evermore!

One day the trumpet will sound with His coming, one day the skies with His glory will shine;
Wonderful day, my beloved ones bringing; glorious Saviour, this Jesus is mine!

J. Wilber Chapman

O Happy Day
Edwin Hawkins

'Happy is he that hath the God of Jacob for his help,
whose hope is in the LORD his God:
Which made heaven, and earth, the sea,
and all that therein is: which keepeth truth for ever:
Which executeth judgment for the oppressed: which giveth
food to the hungry.
The LORD looseth the prisoners:
The LORD openeth the eyes of the blind:
the LORD raiseth them that are bowed down:
the LORD loveth the righteous:
Psalm 146:5-8

Singer-Songwriter, Edwin Hawkins agreed with the psalmist King David when he declared, *"Happy is he that hath the God of Jacob for his help!"*

Edwin knew that the subject of man's ageless 'quest for happiness' is an oft repeated theme in scripture. Indeed in the Bible, a divine contrast is often made between the 'happiness of the wicked' and the 'happiness of the righteous'. The 'happiness of the wicked' is said to be: limited-to-this-life, short, uncertain and vain. 'Happiness of the wicked' is, the scripture says, derived from the wicked person's wealth, power and pleasures, all of which lead to sorrow. However, the 'happiness of the righteous' is said to be: *in-the-Lord, in His*

abundance, in good works, in hope, in obedience and in peace.
Indeed, the 'happiness of the righteous' is said by the Bible to
endure in sunshine or storm.

Edwin Hawkins had come through sunshine and storm. 'Oh,
Happy Day', his uplifting black-gospel song about happiness first
exploded onto the music scene back in 1969. It was an enormous
pop hit, a re-working of the old Baptist hymn's chorus-refrain, 'Oh,
Happy Day When Jesus Washed My Sins Away'. Other great
recordings of the song followed from Glen Campbell, Roy Clarke
and many others.

The original hymn started its life in England. Penned by
clergyman, Philip Doddridge (1702-1751), it was published in 1755
without the chorus-refrain. The chorus-refrain, authored by Edward
Rimbault, was added in 1854 when published in the 'Wesleyan Sacred
Harp' songbook in Boston.

Following Edwin's hit of the 'Oh, Happy Day' chorus-refrain,
his lively music continued to be enjoyed throughout the world in the
remainder of the 20th Century. Edwin appeared with his musical
message at many venues as diverse as New York's Madison Square
Garden and Las Vegas' Caesar's Palace. Often at such places, he
made history by mixing gospel with orchestral classical music,
performing with various symphonies across the USA and Europe.
He was rewarded with three 'Grammy Awards' for his recording
skills.

Edwin Hawkins said that his deep commitment to gospel music
began back in his early childhood. In those early days, he cut his
proverbial performing teeth at a young age, starting his singing career
by vocalizing with his family under the aptly-titled name of the
'Hawkins Family.'

At the age of five years, Edwin said that he personally experienced
faith and found that God had given him the ability to play piano
without any formal training. Taking up the electronic organ at the
age of sixteen years, he became a choir director after vocal experience
over many years in numerous churches in the San Francisco Bay
Area. By then, most of his life was spent residing in Oakland,
California.

In 1969 at his 'Ephesian Church of God' in Oakland while 'tent-making' as a teenage interior decorator, Edwin became involved with his community choir. Proudly, they called themselves the Northern California State Youth Choir. Amazingly, they were chosen to represent Northern California at an influential and prestigious Youth Congress to be held in Washington DC. To raise funds for the expensive trip, an album was planned accordingly for the Choir.

'Oh Happy Day' was first recorded by Edwin with the Northern California State Youth Choir on a two-track tape recorder in the local church. Interestingly, the recorder was up for sale in the church but had not yet gone. Evidently, demand was slow coming.

Demand for the album, however, was quick as the first five hundred tapes were efficiently sold-out so very soon. Thus another thousand tapes were hurriedly produced that sold likewise. The fame of 'Oh Happy Day' spread even further when radio station, KSAN, an underground rock broadcaster, picked up on the single-record. Soon 'Oh Happy Day' started getting even more radio airplay in faraway places like San Francisco and New York. It was then that Edwin's Christian music career took a dramatic turn upwards.

By Easter of that year, record labels nationwide were seeking out the rights to the 'Oh Happy Day' master recording for wider nationwide distribution. 'Buddha Records', a label that many people said was an unbecoming logo-title for a Christian song, acquired 'Oh Happy Day' for national release. Before long, the spirited record crossed all musical genre boundaries, establishing Edwin Hawkins and his choir - by then known as The Edwin Hawkins Singers - as new leaders in the contemporary black gospel music scene.

The Edwin Hawkins Singers' 56 vocalists and 22 chaperones were flown swiftly to New York City for performances at Madison Square Garden followed by the Yankee Stadium at an Isley Brothers' anniversary concert. More rock and pop venues followed. Edwin recalled, *"Coming from Christian roots, we prayed for confirmation that pop-venue dates were right for us...I believe that the answer was yes as music ministry is like a preaching ministry... I believe that a preacher should go anywhere where he has opportunity to preach and reach souls . The same goes for Christian music!"*

Although they met with some criticism from concerned conservative-Christian quarters, Edwin still felt that it was right for him and his Edwin Hawkins Singers' choir to extend their witness to even more secular venues such as Las Vegas. It was not long before other hits followed. Among them was 'Every Man Wants To Be Free', an award winner in 1970. Following the release of a further two gospel LP's, Edwin said that he took a break in his recording career to devote time to his family church and community choir performance work.

In 1978 he returned to the gospel music field renewed in spirit. Edwin explained that he had a new vision to spread his Christian music even further. It seemed revolutionary when he said that he wanted to see his choir perform with a symphony orchestra. Boldly, he contacted the head of the Oakland Symphony Orchestra. Simultaneously, the Oakland Symphony Orchestra had also been seeking ways to involve the local community in its work and so there came a merger of symphony music and gospel music in no time at all!

Edwin and the Edwin Hawkins Singers headlined the opening night of the Oakland Symphony's pop series. The venue was sold out. The house was packed to the rafters and it was said that the Choir stopped the show with the clear testimony song, 'Oh Happy Day'. When the next season arrived, the performance was filmed and aired nationwide on television by America's 'Public Broadcasting System' with the title 'Edwin Hawkins: Gospel at the Symphony'. There followed joint performances in Washington DC's 'Kennedy Center' and another performance with the Kansas City Philharmonic Orchestra. In 1979, ten years after 'Oh Happy Day' hit charts worldwide, the Edwin Hawkins Singers appeared at the 'John F. Kennedy Performing Arts' venue with the National Symphony Orchestra. Edwin stated, *"God opened this new door to reach a totally different segment of society with the gospel's good news. The new crowds were not church-oriented but symphony folks who may not darken the door of a church."*

Skilled in many ways, in addition to recording and performing, Edwin founded the 'Edwin Hawkins Music and Arts Seminars' that drew people (particularly the young) from around the USA for training in the music arts by established artists in various fields. Edwin declared that his emphasis during these seminars was to teach that God specially created every individual person with diverse personal giftings. The Seminars emphasised that Christian believers especially should use their God-given talents for Christ's glory and honour and to minister to others.

Incidentally, Edwin was thrilled when given the chance to record a tribute LP to the late Tommy Dorsey. This was not the famed big-band, jazz musician of World War II fame, but Thomas Dorsey, the legendary 'father of black gospel music' (writer of 'Peace In The Valley', 'Take My Hand Precious Lord' and many more black-gospel classics. As a treat, on this special project, the 85 year old Thomas Dorsey himself joined with Edwin.

Overjoyed with any opportunities to sing and testify, Edwin said that he was particularly delighted with two invitations. The first was to appear as a guest soloist with his 'Oh Happy Day' hit at the Billy Graham Reno Crusade. Secondly, this was followed in 1981 at the star-studded 'Presidential Inaugural Celebration' entitled 'With Love'. Indeed, it was generally well known in Washington DC that the Edwin Hawkins Singers 'Oh Happy Day' hit was a personal favourite with President and Mrs. Jimmy Carter.

O Happy Day, O Happy Day when Jesus washed my sins away. He taught me how to watch and pray, and live rejoicing every day.
Happy Day, Happy Day when Jesus washed my sins away.

Philip Doddridge

O Lord You're Beautiful
Keith Green

> *"One thing have I desired of the LORD, that will I seek after;*
> *that I may dwell in the house of the LORD all the days of*
> *my life,*
> *to behold the beauty of the LORD, and to inquire in his*
> *temple.*
> *For in the time of trouble He shall hide me in His pavilion:*
> *in the secret of his tabernacle shall He hide me;*
> *He shall set me up upon a rock.*
> *And now shall mine head be lifted up above mine enemies*
> *round about me:*
> *therefore will I offer in his tabernacle sacrifices of joy;*
> *I will sing, yea, I will sing praises unto the LORD.*
> *Psalm 27:4-6*

Songwriter, Keith Green was said to diligently and passionately pray for the continual worshipful experience of God's presence. Just like the psalmist (of Psalm 27:4-6) who longed for God's presence in His temple, he too expressed the zealous intensity of seeking after God himself. Keith like the ancient psalmist desired to dwell in the temple of God for the rest of his life and to gaze on the Lord's beauty and to seek after Him. This 'beauty of the Lord', said Keith Green was displayed best in grace, Christ's unmerited favour toward His mankind. 'O Lord You're Beautiful' was his heart-felt expression of wonder as he meditated on God's wonderful grace.

Not immune of course, from life's storms, like the psalmist, Keith Green by his example sought to 'seek the Lord in his times of trouble', whenever the difficulties may occur. Keith believed passionately that God is in Christ Jesus. He saw Him as the Rock of Ages, a very present help in times of trouble, for those who place trust in Him. In worship, Keith anticipated finding protection for himself and his family in God's presence. He said, *"We have the assurance that the believer is in God's protective hands. This Divine protection is like the protection of being placed high upon the high Rock of Ages!"*

Reading the scriptures caused Keith to be more and more confident of God's care and help in trouble. He read how the psalmist anticipated victory over those who troubled God's people. He vowed to sacrifice to the Lord to express his devotion, while singing a hymn to his God. Doubtless, he saw the psalmist proclaim the mighty acts of God's redemption in his shouts-of-joy and song, in anticipation of victory. His articulate expressions of loyalty to God arose from the psalmist's trusting heart.

If anyone could be qualified to write an informed book of experience about subjects such as the occult, drugs, therapies, philosophies and the age-long search for the reality it was, Keith Green! Born in 1953 in Sheeps Head, New York into a musical family from busy Brooklyn, New York, he was surrounded from the start by the sound of show-biz music. His dear mother sang with the big bands of the day and his grandfather wrote for musical star of the Thirties, Eddie Cantor. A young achiever, at the age of two Keith began appearing in television commercials. He played the ukulele at three years of age, the piano at six years and started writing songs by the time he was eight! It seemed he was born not only with good looks but with perfect pitch also. Taught three-chord rock n' roll on the piano by his grandfather, he wrote about 40 songs by the age of eleven. That year he signed a five contract with the major Decca Records and become the youngest ever member of ASCAP (the American Society of Composers and Publishers). The family moved to Southern California's San Fernando Valley and groomed young

Keith for show-biz stardom. In 1964 he stared in the famous theatre musical, 'The Sound Of Music'. 'Time' magazine described Keith's voice as 'trembling with conviction' and his rising talent as 'prepubescent dream-boat'!

His parents were Jewish, yet for some reason, he was brought up as a Christian Scientist. Despite having a natural pride in his Jewish background, he found both religions to be inadequate in his search for reality. Rebelling along with many of his peers, by 1967 Keith ran away from home and found solace in the drugs and free-love culture. *"Throughout the Sixties and Seventies of my youth"*, he said, *"I shunned the conventions of the establishment. In the culture of materialism, I become acutely aware of my spiritual need for something deeper in this life!"*

Working in hippie songwriters' bars, he spent his search writing songs about how "there must be something more to life than this!" His hatred of churches and all things 'happy-clappy' led him to unwisely decide that of all the possible spiritual options, Jesus would be his absolutely last consideration! He experienced and experimented with a host of Asian religions and gurus, and with astrology and self-hypnosis. It was not until all his other philosophical experiments into spiritual fulfilment left him and no other options remained. Buying a necklace on which hung a Cross, in desperation he knelt down and prayed. *"Oh, Jesus I'm praying to you, asking you if you're real to make yourself known to me!"*....And as Keith later simply wrote, *"He did!"*

"In two years", Keith said, *"I was pleased to call myself, a follower of Jesus...I was totally delivered from the occult, drugs and the whole desire to make it in the world! In early 1973, Christ even brought me a beautiful wife, Melody!"*

They married on the morning of Christmas Day 1973. Melody said that it was until two years later that true conversion came under the helpful ministry of Pastor Kenn Gullikson, founder of the Vineyard Christian Fellowships. For Keith and Melody, there followed several years of intensive Bible study, discipleship and evangelism. Anyone invited to the Green household was seen as a potential candidate for evangelism! They opened their lives up to runaways, misfits and unmarried mothers.

Throughout the Seventies, Keith Green probably did more to theologically challenge America's gospel music scene than anyone else! With his acute hatred for all things un-Godly, he initially shunned the Christian music industry as it was, for being wishy-washy and weak, accusing those involved for doing it for personal motives such as gain and fame. He refused to charge for admission to his concerts, giving away his recordings for free!

Keith acknowledged that *"Christian music, at best, is a very poor and weak instrument of the gospel. Potentially it can communicate the truth of God; the joy of the Lord; one's Christian experiences; and even warnings of judgement!"* But he also realised that if Christian music did not remain commercially pure, it would cease to do the job God had intended. He was aware that young impressionable Christian kids might unwisely put their favourite Christian singers on a pedestal, replacing their favourite pop idols. *"There is a fine line between idolising the person and real appreciation or admiration!"* Keith's aim of pointing people's attention heavenward was aptly expressed in his song, 'O Lord You're Beautiful'.

He and his wife Melody chose to give up their home and live in a community of Christians, forming in 1977 what was to become 'Last Days Ministries', pooling their money and dividing it between the community group or giving it to the needy. 'Last Days Ministries' eventually grew into a full time evangelistic organisation which ran a Christian training school for young people, producing millions of tracts for distribution and producing a free newsletter-magazine which featured articles from such people as George Verwer, Brother Andrew, Leonard Ravenhill, Winkie Pratney and David Wilkerson along with those by Keith and Melody themselves.

During his short lifetime, Keith was described as a prophet who upset the gospel music establishment, exposing faults like pride, fame, greed, arrogance and routine where there should have been God-led humility and grace. Undoubtedly he 'put noses out of joint' with his no-nonsense communications. Wholeheartedly, he pursued high motives, above all- the desire to love God and introduce others to the Christ who had revolutionised his life. His active life was cut dramatically short in July 1982. At the age of 29 , Keith tragically perished in a wreckage of a small private plane. Yet even after his death and into the new millennium, Keith's call to discipleship, missionary service and passionate worship still rings out loud and clear in his story and songs! 'O Lord You're Beautiful' speaks of the earnestness of his worshipful love and commitment to His Lord and His purposes. As he traveled, Keith often expressed how disheartened he was to see so many modern affluent Christians settling into lives devoid of missionary drive and passionate worship. He said that it was a serious situation that displayed a lack of true love for God, His gospel, and the lost souls in darkness. Such complacency would not lead to holy and sanctified lives.

Oh Lord, You're beautiful, Your face is all I seek,
For when Your eyes are on this child, Your grace abounds to me.
Oh Lord, please light the fire that once burned bright and clear,
Replace the lamp of my first love That burns with holy fear!
I want to take Your word And shine it all around,
But first help me just to live it Lord! And when I'm doing well,
Help me to never seek a crown, For my reward is giving glory to
You.
Oh Lord, You're beautiful, Your face is all I seek,
For when Your eyes are on this child, Your grace abounds to me.

Room At The Cross
Ira Stanphill

But now in Christ Jesus ye who sometimes were far off
are made nigh by the blood of Christ.
For He is our peace, who hath made both one,
and hath broken down the middle wall of partition between
us;
Having abolished in His flesh the enmity,
even the law of commandments contained in ordinances;
for to make in Himself of twain one new man, so making
peace;
And that He might reconcile both unto God in one body by
the Cross,
having slain the enmity thereby:
And came and preached peace to you which were afar off,
and to them that were nigh.
For through Him we both have access by one Spirit unto the
Father._ Ephesians 2:13-18

Christ's *'old rugged Cross'* was the spiritual inspiration behind this beautiful invitation song, 'Room At The Cross'. Written by Ira Forest Stanphill who was white-haired in latter life, 'Room At The Cross' was often used by evangelical preachers as an altar-call appeal-chorus. It became regularly used by the stocky, no-nonsense, Texas-based-minister, John Hagee. The well known TV preacher stated,

"How the Apostle Paul as a Roman came to glory in the Cross is one of the absurdities of history! At the time, anyone crucified was an object of scorn. To Paul as a pious Hebrew, anyone hanged or crucified was cursed! But in fact his opinion was changed when the Apostle realised that the Cross held the Crucified Messiah, the Christ of God!"

Songwriter, Ira Stanphill understood that fact well. He knew too that in its Biblical use of the words, *'the Cross'* included not merely a wooden instrument of torture, but it was a symbolic representation of *God's redemption of all mankind*. Throughout history, execution by crucifixion was one of the most cruel and barbarous forms of death known to man. Routinely, it was practiced, especially in times of war, by the Phoenicians, Carthaginians, Egyptians, and later by the Romans. It was so severely dreaded that even in the pre-Christian era, the 'cares and troubles of life' were often proverbially compared to 'a cross'. Two thousand years ago, the geographical location of Christ's crucifixion was a hill called Golgotha or Calvary just outside Jerusalem's Old City Wall on the public road.

Ira Stanphill loved to study the Bible. In scripture, he discovered that the Apostle Paul declared that the 'preaching of *the Cross'* seemed like laughable divine folly, in sharp contrast to earthly wisdom. Consequently, in Ephesians 2:13-18, he rationally presented to his readers that the 'preaching of *the Cross'* was still God's medium of reconciliation. Paul taught that there is room at *the Cross* for all believers. There, all can receive 'peace with God' through *the Cross*. By the shedding of Christ's precious blood, the dire penalties of the Law are removed from the believer via faith in the *Christ of the Cross*. Ira fell in love with the message of *the Cross* and 'Room At The Cross' was lovingly conceived by divine revelation in an unusual way.

While preaching in a revival service in Kansas City, Missouri, Ira (as was his custom) asked his congregation to submit proposals for consideration as song titles. 'Room At The Cross' was the title that grabbed his attention out of the fifty or so submitted to him that day. Taken with the thought of there being sufficient 'Room At The Cross' for all, he penned the song as the choir performed their special song that morning.

Successfully and memorably recorded in the 1950s by Rosie Rozell and the Statesmen Quartet of Atlanta, 'Room At The Cross' was recorded again in the mid-1960s by George Beverly Shea and the Anita Kerr Singers on the Grammy Award winning album entitled 'Southland Favourites' on RCA Victor. Kate Smith, Tennessee Ernie Ford and hundreds of others later recorded it. Ira wrote several other beloved classics including 'Mansion Over the Hilltop' (later recorded famously by Elvis Presley and others), 'Suppertime' (recorded by Ricky Van Shelton, Johnny Cash, Jimmie Davis, Faron Young, Vernon Oxford and Jim Reeves) and 'He Washed My Eyes With Tears' (recorded by George Beverly Shea). It is likely that these great recording artistes learnt many of their Stanphill songs from Blackwood Brothers' recordings.

Ira recounted an incident that occurred in the 1950s at the time of the Cold War that followed the hostilities of World War II. During an eventful and much blessed tent revival-meeting in Western Germany (conducted by the 'Assemblies of God' evangelist, Willard Cantelone and 'Word Records' gospel-soloist Al Garr), a drama took place. One of Ira's songs, 'Room At The Cross' was being sung in German as an appealing altar-call. It could have proved very dangerous when a rough-looking local man entered the meeting secretly toting a gun. No one knew that he was planning to commit suicide that evening with a bullet. Instead, Al Garr quietly sang Room At The Cross' as the chorus-invitation melody. The man wondrously came under the conviction of the Holy Spirit. Thus convinced, captivated and challenged by Ira's song and the sermon, the man went forward to the plain-wooden altar at preacher Willard's open invitation. The repentant sinner surrendered to the claims of Christ on his ruined life, was converted and miraculously made new. That was not the end of the story as later the man became a minister of the gospel crediting Ira's song, 'Room At The Cross' as being the catalyst that brought him to faith!

A 'man-of-the-west', he was born on February 14th 1914, a few weeks before the outbreak of World War I in Europe. His humble birthplace was in Bellview, New Mexico. At the time, US marines were preparing to fight in Mexico. Meanwhile, not far away, Ira's parents homesteaded in the New Mexico area following a harrowing covered wagon-train journey from Arkansas.

At the age of eight years, the family moved on to Coffeyville, Kansas. Later after Junior College, from 1930 to 1934, the sweet-voiced Ira sang on a daily radio programme on station KGGF. Two years later, he became an evangelist and then pastored churches in West Palm Beach, Florida and Lancaster, Pennsylvania. In 1966 he moved on to pastor the Rockwood Park 'Assembly of God' Church in Fort Worth, Texas.

A poet from the start, as he became spiritually mature, he honed his talent. Surprisingly, he did not write his first song until the age of seventeen, composing over 600 in his full life. From 1938 to 1967 he administrated his own publishing firm under the 'Hymntime' banner before selling his rights to the Zondervan Publishing House.

"I knew Ira well!" James Blackwood recalled his dear, white-haired friend with heart-warming nostalgia. *"I had the wonderful privilege of doing some joint concerts with him. Hilton Griswold (our Blackwood Brothers' pianist from 1940-50) worked with Ira's son (Larry), a pastor of a large church in Juliet, Illinois. Hilton syndicated a TV show to about twenty-five stations, taping the show in Chicago in Channel 38's Christian studio and later in Milwaukee. I guested several times with Ira. We also did some Sunday evening services.*

Ira and Gloria, his wife, were also with me on a Gaither Homecoming video taping in the early Nineties and we were booked for more. Sadly, he suffered a heart attack and died. But Gloria sang a song with me on the next video as a dear tribute to my brother in Christ! Several of Ira's songs were performed on that video taping day including, at my suggestion to Bill Gaither, 'Unworthy' by John McDuff of the McDuff Brothers. It was so moving. I had previously recorded the song on an RCA solo album."

On the subject of *the Cross*, Charles Haddon Spurgeon (1834-1892), the famous English Baptist preacher stated, *"There are some sciences that may be learned by the head, but the science of Christ crucified can only be learned by the heart!"*

Now there stood by the cross of Jesus His mother,
and His mother's sister, Mary the wife of Cleophas, and Mary
Magdalene.
When Jesus therefore saw His mother, and the disciple standing
by, whom He loved,
He saith unto His mother, 'Woman, behold thy son!'
Then saith He to the disciple, 'Behold thy mother!'
And from that hour that disciple took her unto his own home.
John 19:25-26

Search Me O God
James Edwin Orr

"Search me, O God, and know my heart:
try me, and know my thoughts:
And see if there be any wicked way in me,
and lead me in the way everlasting."
Psalm 139:23-24

It is said that 'heart-songs' are the greatest songs of all. The ancient Chinese philosopher and ethical teacher, Confucius (551-479 BC) was right when he declared, *"To put the world in order, we must first put the nation in order; to put the nation in order, we must first put the family in order; to put the family in order, we must cultivate our personal life; and to cultivate our personal life, we must first set our hearts right."*

James Edwin Orr was born on 15th January 1912 in Belfast, Northern Ireland, the often troubled province of the United Kingdom. It was a time of political unrest. Over 30,000 people attended protest rallies in Ulster against the British government's proposals to give Ireland Home Rule. Preceded by drums playing in the rain, they came in farm carts, traps, and charabancs to Omagh to hear the Ulster MP Sir Edward Carson declare, *"If we cannot remain as we are, we will take the matter into our own hands."*

Feelings in Ulster against Home Rule continued to run so high that Liberals were said to be unable to book a hall for a meeting planned for February of 1912 at which Winston Churchill (First Lord

Of The Admiralty) was due to present the British government's case for reform. James Edwin Orr was raised in the midst of all this political passion and uncertainty but heard the call-of-God to personal repentance as a young man, making peace with God. Later feeling the missionary zeal, Edwin felt constrained to take the gospel into the world as an evangelist, leaving his native homeland in 1933. It was a year in which hearts not controlled by the Spirit of God ran wild. The words of ancient scripture rang out in truth, *"The heart is deceitful above all things and desperately wicked. Who can know it?"*

That same troubled year of 1933 in Europe, impassioned political unrest was brewing again in Ireland, civil war was active in Spain, and the Nazi party came to greater power in Germany as Hitler took over as the Chancellor of the German Reich. Consequently, the Jewish people of Germany were hounded and herded into concentration camps. Then Germany and Japan stormed out of the League of Nations. The world was plunging headlong towards World War II.

In 1939, the same year that the United Kingdom declared war on Nazi Germany, Edwin joined the People's Church of Toronto, Canada as assistant pastor of Dr. Oswald J. Smith. A year later, Edwin moved to the USA where he was ordained as a Baptist minister in New Jersey. Feeling the need to study for further qualifications, he later studied at Northwestern University where he obtained his Master of Arts in 1941. This was followed by further studies at Northern Baptist Seminary where Edwin graduated with a theology degree in 1943. There followed, for the thirty year old Ulsterman, a spell in the United States Air Force during World War II from 1942-46. Following his military service, Edwin gained a degree in philosophy from England's University of Oxford in 1948, but still feeling the missionary zeal, he felt constrained to continue to take the gospel into the world as a full-time evangelist. Again leaving the United Kingdom, his native homeland, he traveled worldwide, engaging in missionary work. He also served on the faculty of the 'School of World Missions' of the Fuller Theological Seminary in Pasadena, California.

Edwin wrote the heart-rending gospel song, 'Search Me O God' in 1936 in the midst of what he described as extraordinary revival meetings in New Zealand. He recalled, *"I was attending an Easter Conference in Ngaruawahia, New Zealand where God's Spirit was moving in a special way. And it was during this time that I heard the Maori song, 'The Song of Farewell' being sung by some young Maori ladies."*

Hearing the beautiful tune, Edwin was inspired to paraphrase the words of scripture. He said that he wrote the heart-warming words to the beautiful folk melody in five minutes whilst standing in the local Post Office! The song was first published in London by the publishers, 'Marshall, Morgan and Scott' in 1936 in a book about revivals entitled 'All Your Need'. Incidentally, the Maori tune (originally called 'Haere Ra') was also high-jacked in 1913 as 'Now Is The Hour' (by writers, Clement Scott, Kaihan and Dorothy Stewart) who made it an attractive secular love song that movie artists like Hollywood's Bing Crosby and Gene Autry, and even England's Lancashirelass, Gracie Fields made famous during and after World War II. Bing's version sold over a million, however, *"Search me, O God, and know my heart"*, Edwin's lyrics married to the Maori tune are likely to outlive other uses of the tune. It captures with empathy, the ever-contemporary *heart-of-a- believer's* plea for God to purify his heart. Use of the word 'heart' is very common in love-songs, gospel songs and hymns. Indeed, scripture uses the word 'heart' more than 900 times, yet almost never literally. Often the heart signified the innermost being of a human being. Just like today, the heart back in ancient times was regarded as the 'seat of the affections', 'the seat of the intellect' and 'the seat of the will'.

From his studies, James Edwin Orr was fully aware that Bible writers spoke of the heart being *changed; hardened; known to God; regenerated; renewed; pure; enlightened; established; refined; tried; tested; strengthened*, and so on. Indeed in the scriptures, all believers are encouraged to render to God 'heartfelt' virtues such as obedience, faith, trust, love, fidelity, zeal and much more. In the New Testament, Christ's followers are encouraged in scripture to be: *joyful, perfect, upright, clean, pure, sincere, repentant, devout, wise, tender, holy, compassionate and lowly in their hearts!*

Conversely, the scriptures also speak clearly of *the unbelieving heart and unregenerate heart as being full-of-iniquity; loving evil;*

a-fountain-of-evil; wayward; blind; double-minded; hard; deceitful; subtle; sensual; worldly; malicious, impenitent; diabolical; covetous; foolish, and under the wrath of God! It is therefore no wonder that the Psalmist appealed for God to determine his motives and his actions, especially in the context of Psalm 139:23-24.

This Psalmist's prayer-song inspired Edwin Orr to write the probing 'Search Me O God'. The psalm came out of a situation when evil people had accused the Psalmist. Instead of enjoining his defence to his antagonists, he raised up his speech in lamentation to God, who the Psalmist saw alone as the wholly-righteous Judge who is capable of fairly discerning his heart and thoughts. Like Edwin Orr, the Psalmist desired nothing less than adherence to God's will. He concluded his psalm by acknowledging that there are only two ways that an individual can follow: one leading to destruction and the other to life and fellowship with God.

Search me O God, and know my heart today; Try me O Lord and know my thoughts I pray;
See if there be some wicked way in me, Cleanse me from every sin and set me free.

I praise Thee, Lord, for cleansing me from sin; Fulfil Thy Word, and make me pure within;
Fill me with fire, where once I burned with shame Grant my desire to magnify Thy Name.

Lord, take my life, and make it wholly Thine; Fill my poor heart with Thy great love divine;
Take all my will, my passion, self and pride; I now surrender - Lord, in me abide.

Holy Ghost, revival comes from Thee; Send a revival - start the work in me:
Thy Word declares Thou wilt supply our need; For blessing now, O Lord, I humbly plead.

J. Edwin Orr © Maranatha Music Publishing/
Administered By Copycare, PO Box 77, Hailsham, BN273EF, UK
music@copycare.com / Used With Permission

Shout To The Lord

(My Jesus My Saviour)
Darlene Zschech

*O sing unto the LORD a new song: sing unto the LORD,
all the earth.*
*Sing unto the LORD, bless His name; show forth His
salvation from day to day.*
*Declare his glory among the heathen, His wonders among
all people.*
*For the LORD is great, and greatly to be praised: He is to
be feared above all gods.*
*For all the gods of the nations are idols: but the LORD
made the heavens.*
*Honour and majesty are before Him: strength and beauty
are in his sanctuary.*
*Give unto the LORD the glory due unto His name:
bring an offering, and come into his courts.*
*O worship the LORD in the beauty of holiness: fear before
Him, all the earth.*
*Say among the heathen that the LORD reigneth:
the world also shall be established that it shall not be moved:
He shall judge the people righteously.*
*Let the heavens rejoice, and let the earth be glad;
let the sea roar, and the fullness thereof.*
*Let the field be joyful, and all that is therein:
then shall all the trees of the wood rejoice*

Before the LORD: for He cometh, for He cometh to judge
the earth:
He shall judge the world with righteousness, and the people
with His truth. Psalm 96 : 1-13

Of course, Australia is famous for its kangaroos and koala bears but in the 21st century now can boast a gospel singer of true worldwide standing. Smiling and attractive Darlene Zschech attained worldwide recognition as a singer, songwriter and worship leader in the early years of the Third Millennium AD following years of instruction and preparation. She reached the summit of the Australian gospel music world as the lead vocalist, worship leader, and co-producer of Hillsong Music Australia's best selling albums. These live worship albums accomplished gold status. Best selling songs included 'Stone's Been Rolled Away', 'People Just Like Us', 'God Is In The House', 'Friends In High Places', 'All Things Are Possible', 'Touching Heaven, Changing Earth', 'By Your Side', 'For This Cause', 'You Are My World', 'Blessed' and, of course, 'Shout To The Lord'.

Darlene was born on the 8th September 1965 in Brisbane, Queensland, Australia. 'Shout To The Lord' was penned by her at time when as a child of God, she ran to her Lord, seeking Him in the midst of despondency. She experienced a renewal of faith, strength and peace as the lyrics and melody came to her. Later turning to her Bible, Darlene Zschech thumbed to Psalm 96. With her delight for God's Word shining forth clearly from her countenance, it seemed to her that she could see and hear the seas roaring and the mountains bowing down before their Creator, her beloved Lord. Scottish-born but Luton, England-based pastor, Sandy Duncan remembered how he felt the same emotions on hearing the song at England's mammoth Christian convention, Spring Harvest. When he died in the summer of 2002, his wife Wilma fondly recounted the experience at his funeral.

'Shout to the Lord', an impressive chorus written by Darlene was by 2002 sung by an estimated 25 to 30 million churchgoers every week around the world. The praise-song was the title track for the first live album co-produced with 'Integrity Music' featuring

Darlene as a prominent female worship leader. It took little time for the song to become universally popular. Predictably in 1997 and 1998, 'Shout To The Lord' was nominated as the 'Song of the Year' in the Gospel Music Association's Dove Awards. It was recorded by others too on dozens of different albums in diverse parts of the world. Late in 2000, Darlene was nominated as the 'Songwriter Of The Year' by the GMA. In addition to 'Shout To The Lord', Darlene also wrote many other praise-and-worship songs published by Hillsong Music of Australia. She also authored books on her passion for praise-and-worship, one of which was titled 'Extravagant Worship'.

Darlene stated that music was an essential part of her life since she was a child. Initially, she received a piano as a gift from her parents when she was only five years old. From the age of ten years she performed in a weekly children's television show, singing, dancing and hosting segments. Then as a teenager, Darlene persisted in music pursuits, fronting various local gospel bands in Brisbane, Queensland. She started writing songs when she was fifteen years of age. She then started on the session music scene in Sydney, working on advertising jingles for 'McDonalds', 'Special K' cereal, 'Kentucky Fried Chicken' and 'Diet Coke'.

Darlene recalled her 'hour-of-decision'. *"At the age of fifteen, my Dad (my beloved hero) who had been attending a church and had recommitted his broken life to Christ, took me to a youth group called 'Royal Rangers'. I attended for a few weeks, meeting people, making friends, tying knots, learning about camping, teamwork, the code of life and most importantly, the giver of life, Jesus Christ. My memories of an early evening are so clear ... the irresistible invitation to receive Jesus into my life and even though I had very little understanding of the significance of that moment I knew that this was a name I could trust. My longing to be made whole overtook my limited understanding. I with a couple of others got out of my seat and walked toward the leader who then led us into the most beautiful prayer I have every prayed. Some of the words were a blur, but some are etched in my love forever 'wash me, forgive me, come into my life'! Oh, the irresistible, unconditional, immeasurable love of Christ invaded my little insecure, out-of-control life and He took my hand in His and He has continued to hold it to this day. There has hardly been a day gone by from that day to this that the reality of receiving that incredible sense of love and peace in my heart has not taken my breath away."*

Since the mid 1980s, Darlene and her husband Mark performed a critical role in the leadership team of the Hillsong Church in Sydney. It was renowned to be Australia's largest church with an estimated congregation of over 12,000. The Hillsong Church prized its role in the promotion of contemporary praise-and-worship and achieved a reputation for excellence with its choirs and musicians. As its Worship Pastor, Darlene Zschech was the overseer of the Hillsong Church's 'Worship & Creative Arts Department' at the Hills and City congregations. While Darlene led worship every week for the internationally distributed Hillsong Television program (that reached eighty different countries across the globe), her husband, Mark was the Director of the Television Ministry.

Darlene was also the Associate Director of the Hillsong Conference that was the annual music and leadership conference of the church. In the 2001, over 12,000 full time delegates attended the conference at Sydney's Super-Dome at Olympic Park.

Darlene and Mark reside in Sydney with their three daughters, Amy, Chloe and Zoe. Darlene states that her desire in life is to lead folks into a closeness with God and encourage them realise their full potential in Him.

Since written in 1993, 'Shout to the Lord' has been translated from English into many foreign languages. Many Christians have testified that it is their favourite worship song. Consequently, hundreds of thousands of believers around the world sing it enthusiastically at church services, conferences, conventions, concerts, weddings and even funerals. Incidentally, the heavy-weight boxer, Evander Holyfield was captured in a global TV broadcast singing 'Shout to the Lord' in his dressing room just before his world championship fight against Mike Tyson in 1997.

Darlene says that she never dreamed that one day she would sit down and write a praise-and-worship song that will touch so many people in many nations. She is tickled when interrogated about the story-behind-the-song as she readily admitted that there was no grand story to recount. But she does recall the experience, however that inspired 'Shout to the Lord'. Somewhat depressed, she remembered that the song came to her on what could be described as one of the dark days of her life. It seemed as if everything was on top of her and that there seemed to be no way-out. In desperation, she said that she looked heavenward and sought the only One who could help, the Lord. Frantic for the peace of God, she remembered opening her Bible to Chapters 96-100 in the book of Psalms. Sitting at an old piano, she began plinking and plonking gently on the keyboard. Darlene beamed as she pictured the scene again in her memory. The old and very out-of-tune piano was the one received from her parents when she was five years old. Soon a song was born. 'Shout to the Lord' was overflowing from her worshipping heart. She says that she was not consciously thinking about writing a song, she was simply worshipping. Pouring-out her heart to God, within twenty minutes, the song 'Shout to the Lord' was penned. She sang it, over and over again, and it lifted her up from the depths of her depression. *"I was translated from the depths of despair to the heights of faith!"*

During the following week, the beautiful song kept ringing around in her head. It refused to leave her and it began to dawn on her that it might be a usable praise-and-worship song. Painfully timid and feeling somewhat self-conscious, she brought up the subject of 'Shout to the Lord' to her friends, Russell Fragar and Geoff Bullock. At the time, Geoff was the Music Pastor at the Hills Church. Sitting down at the piano, Darlene's palms were sweaty and she could barely play as she was so nervous. She kept starting and stopping, and apologizing each time. Indeed before they heard the song, she eventually made them stand with their backs to her, facing the wall while she played. Even when they turned around and acknowledged that they thought that it was splendid song, Darlene was persuaded that they were just being polite. Then when Pastor Brian Houston heard 'Shout to the Lord' for the first time, he prophesied confidently that the new song would be sung around the world because of the television exposure.

Indeed, the modest worship-leader is astonished and somewhat self-conscious of all the attention the song has received. Humble in nature, she speaks shyly about what she calls her God-given talents. She insists that she does not want any honour because she says that she knows it is not hers alone. She is keen to retain a purity-of-heart and an intimate love for God. She directs praise heavenward as she says it was Christ Jesus who has raised her up to became the accepted worship leader that she is today.

Darlene was amazed to discover that before she had even recorded the song, she began receiving letters from people all over the world who sung the song in their churches. One heart-warming letter she remembered came from Nigeria in Africa. A seven-year-old boy, thanked her for writing 'Shout To The Lord'. Soon it appeared on the recording of Hillsong Music Australia's *'People Just Like Us'* album in 1994 followed by translations into many languages including Hungarian, Danish, French, Italian, Mandarin, Japanese and Swedish, to name a few.

Like 'Shout To The Lord', Psalm 96 is a proclamation of personal relationship and universal praise that exalts the Majesty and Rule of the Lord over the earth. Darlene's powerful song exclaims the Lord's greatness, Him being worthy of praise because of His awe-inspiring nature. Christ Jesus alone is God even if the pagans may claim that their gods have power over the heavenly realms. The Lord is the sole claimant to having created the heavens and the earth, and His royal glory is evident in creation yet we can still call Him *'my Jesus'* and *'my Saviour'*. The evidences of His royal presence surround us.

My Jesus my Saviour, Lord there is none like You,
All of my days I want to praise the wonder of Your mighty love.
My comfort, my shelter, tower of refuge and strength.
Let every breath, all that I am, never cease to worship You.
Shout to the Lord, all the earth let us sing.
Power and majesty, praise to the King.
Mountains bow down and the seas will roar at the sound of Your name.
I sing for joy at the work of Your hands, forever I'll love You, forever I'll stand.
Nothing compares to the promise I have in You.

Standing On The Promises
Russell Kelso Carter

'Grace and peace be multiplied unto you
through the knowledge of God, and of Jesus our Lord,
According as His divine power hath given unto us all things
that pertain unto life and godliness,
through the knowledge of Him that hath called us to glory
and virtue:
Whereby are given unto us exceeding great and precious
promises:
that by these ye might be partakers of the divine nature,
having escaped the corruption that is in the world through
lust.'
II Peter 1: 2-4

Preaching to his London congregation on the subject of the 'exceeding great and precious promises of God', Charles Haddon Spurgeon (1834-1892) the famous Baptist minister declared, *"I beseech you do not treat God's promises as if they were curiosities for a museum; but use them as everyday sources of comfort. Every promise of scripture is a writing of God that may be placed before Him in reasonable request, 'Do Lord as Thou hast said.' The Creator will not cheat the creature who depends upon His truth; and far more the Heavenly Father will not break His own word to His own child."*

Also on the 'promises of God', here's two more interesting quotations from key personalities of the Faith. England's Hudson Taylor (1832-1905), the founding missionary of the China Inland Mission, testified, *"There is a living God; He has spoken in the Bible. He means what He says and will do all He has promised!"*

French theologian, John Calvin (1509-1564) in the 'Institutes of Christian Religion' declared, *"The main hinge on which faith turns is this: we must not imagine that the Lord's promises are true objectively but not in our experience. We must make them ours by embracing them in our hearts."*

'Standing on the Promises' was written and composed by Russell Kelso Carter. Inspired by the 'Second Epistle Of Peter', the hand-clapping gospel song majors (like the Epistle) on the subject of the Promises of God. Russell was born in Cantonsville, Baltimore, USA on 18th November 1849. He studied at Pennsylvania Military Academy in Chester and excelled himself as an academic and a sportsman. Indeed, he earned himself an envious reputation as an outstanding gymnast and baseball player. As a baseball pitcher, he was a star performer. He gave considerable time to his sports and yet he amazed himself by graduating in 1867 with a first class degree.

It was in the Pennsylvania Military Academy that he took up a position as an instructor, followed by professorships in chemistry and natural sciences in 1872, and civil engineering and higher mathematics in 1881. He proved that a man can balance study and sports in such a way that he can succeed in both.

Surprisingly, he also spent some time in 1873-76 raising sheep in California, returning to teaching afterwards. His pastoral care of sheep and the lessons he learned set him up for the next stage of his life. In 1887 he left the teaching profession to enter the Methodist Church as an ordained minister where he was well known in the Holiness movement, taking part in camp meetings. In jest, he always said that it was an exchange of sheep-rearing direction from animals to humans.

An accomplished author, Russell wrote several novels, along with books on mathematics, science and religion. He was also involved in the publication of a hymnbook entitled 'Hymns of the Christian Life' published in 1891. Co-edited by A. B. Simpson, Russell contributed fifty-two hymns to the book along with tunes and arrangements for other writers. He is also credited with writing the verses to 'Once I was far in Sin' that was published in the Salvation Army songbook 'Glad Hallelujahs' to which was added a chorus by James C. Bateman (1854-88).

Russell later left the ministry and teaching to study medicine, becoming a practicing physician in Baltimore. He was remembered as a great achiever in many fields not least in songwriting. 'Standing on the Promises' was first published in 'Songs Of Perfect Love' compiled by John R. Sweeney and Russell in 1866. The John J. Hood Publishing Company published it in Philadelphia. Russell died in Baltimore on 23rd August 1928 at a time when fifteen countries (including the UK and the USA) in Paris, France were vainly signing a 'Pact for the Renunciation of War'. Even the most commendable of mankind's pacts are sadly all doomed for failure, but God's promises go on forever.

The circumstances that motivated the Apostle Peter to write his 'Second Epistle Of Peter' are inferred from its contents. The immediate occasion was the author's understanding that his time on earth was short and that God's people were encountering many dangers. Just as sheep are prone to wander, so Christians are inclined to forget the basic promises of the faith. Local pastors (shepherds-of-the-flock) are given the gift of exhortation in the church as a means of correcting this tendency. Peter's epistle reminded 'the sheep' of the basis for their Christian faith. It was founded on the promises of God. Faith in Christ Jesus as the Messiah is not rooted in myths or clever stories; it is based on the 'sure revelation' from God.

When Jesus Christ came to Bethlehem in His first advent, God made certain promises that the Apostle Peter described as being very great and precious. The promises related to life today and in the new Messianic Age to be brought in when Christ returns. Astoundingly, these promises enable all Christians to participate in the divine nature of God. How does this participation come about? They come about in at least two ways. Firstly, the promises of God themselves have a refining and purifying value in the Christian believer's life. Secondly, conversion evokes an emphatic break with the corruption caused by evil desires. In coming to know God through Christ, believers escape the corruption of sin; and Christ renews and restores the image of God in them.

'Standing on the Promises' became very popular in the early part of the 20th century, a musical statement of faith in the promises of God. Yet surprisingly, in the Old Testament there was no Hebrew word corresponding to 'promise'; the words 'word', 'speak' and 'say' are used instead. In the New Testament, however, as Russell Kelso Carter discovered, the word 'promise' is often used, usually in the designated sense of God's plan to visit humankind redemptively in the person of His Son, the Messiah. This long-awaited promise was first granted in the book of Genesis in 3:15. It was reiterated to Abraham and given also to David when God promised that his house would continue on his throne. Similar promises and prophecies are found repeatedly in the Old Testament. In the New Testament all these promises have their fulfillment in Christ. Christ's personal promise of the Holy Spirit to His followers was fulfilled at Pentecost.

In Romans 4:13-16, the Apostle Paul makes crystal-clear that God's promises to Abraham's seed were intended not only for the Jewish people but also for all who have Abraham's faith. Indeed, Russell Kelso Carter stated his delight to learn that there are hundreds more promises of divine blessing made to believing Christians including the kingdom, eternal life, the Holy Spirit and Christ Jesus' Second Coming. More personal promises to believers also included 'response-to-prayer', 'blessings-upon-worshipers', 'consolation-in-grief', 'spiritual-enlightenment', 'God's-abiding-presence', 'forgiveness-for-sin', 'mastery-over-temptation' and many, many more!

Standing on the promises of Christ, my King! Thru' eternal ages let His praises ring;
"Glory in the highest!" I will shout and sing, standing on the promises of God.

Standing, standing, Standing on the promises of God, my
    Saviour;
Standing, standing, I'm standing on the promises of God.

Standing on the promises that cannot fail, when the howling storms of doubt and fear assail,
By the living Word of God I shall prevail, standing on the promises of God.

Standing on the promises, I now can see perfect, present cleansing in the blood for me;
Standing in the liberty where Christ makes free, Standing on the promises of God.

Standing on the promises of Christ, the Lord, bound to Him eternally by love's strong cord,
Overcoming daily with the Spirit's Sword, Standing on the promises of God.

Standing on the promises, I cannot fall, listening every moment to the Spirit's call,
Resting in my Saviour as my all in All, Standing on the promises of God.

Russell Kelso Carter

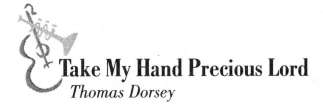

Take My Hand Precious Lord
Thomas Dorsey

Whither shall I go from Thy spirit?
or whither shall I flee from Thy presence?
If I ascend up into heaven, Thou art there:
if I make my bed in hell, behold, Thou art there.
If I take the wings of the morning, and dwell in the
uttermost parts of the sea;
Even there shall Thy hand lead me, and Thy right hand
shall hold me.
Psalm 139:7-10

Famously recorded in the 1950s by the Blackwood Brothers Quartet and then Elvis Presley, 'Take My Hand Precious Lord' has since become a time-honoured classic. The initial Blackwoods' version was beloved by Elvis when he was then an impressionable truck-driving teenager from Tupelo, Mississippi. Years later as a superstar, Elvis recorded the song himself using the Blackwoods' arrangement. Since then, the limelight that Elvis' version gave the modern spiritual, projected it so widely that it has become world-famous, traversing the globe!

The song was already a black-gospel favourite before the Elvis recording. At this time, the adolescent musical taste of 'rock 'n roll' (the phrase coined by the legendary radio DJ, Alan Freed) was certainly in vogue popularising the black 'rhythm and blues' music of the South. Amazingly, before the 'rock 'n roll' term was introduced, 'rhythm and blues' music was actually called 'race music'. Such demeaning racist terminology perplexed many and was indicative of unchristian attitudes.

On the contrary, Elvis's assorted song repertoire was never exclusively from the white domain. He progressively always plucked from diverse cultures, not least from the black circuit. Comfortably, he started with Negro spirituals and camp meeting songs of his 'Assemblies of God'-Blackwood Brothers upbringing. Astutely learning from the Blackwoods, he steadily progressed to Thomas Dorsey's 'Peace In The Valley' and 'Take My Hand Precious Lord'. Despite the politics and cultural differences, black Christian songs were generally well received in the white market place. Elvis helped many songs to cross over from the black music sphere into general usage actively extending the horizons of some fortunate black songwriters by freely exploiting their catchy material. Such a fortunate writer was Thomas Dorsey.

Always a paradox, many found Elvis to be very likeable and friendly, not at all eccentric or abrasive or rebellious! The sensational media hyped-up rumours of his non-existent anti-social stance. Some of the establishment displayed undue paranoia about his so-called outrageous charisma. They considered him and his music to be a threat to the morals of young America. His background and musical aspirations had clearly been deeply influenced by the Blackwood Brothers Quartet. His home church, as a young boy, was the First Assembly of God in Memphis, the same church the Blackwood Brothers attended at that time. Elvis regularly attended the teen Sunday school where a fellow classmate was Cecil Blackwood. Cecil, along with Jim Hamill, their church pastor's son, was starting a church gospel quartet called the Songfellows. Already it had received radio exposure. Elvis desperately wanted to join the group but initially no opening was available. That did not curtail him getting together with Cecil and the others for carefree 'sing along' times on songs such as 'Take My Hand Precious Lord'.

Elvis' first girlfriend, Dixie Locke told me that Elvis always revered and highly cherished the Faith and found expression in the gospel quartet scene. He regretted not going the gospel route although he seriously aspired, on several occasions, to join a major professional gospel group before other secular forces swept him up. Clearly, gospel music figured highly in his musical priorities in his teens and throughout his years. Indeed this love of Christian quartet music never left him. This is evidenced in the clear fact that throughout his immensely successful career, Elvis used gospel quartets as backing singers for both his secular recordings and stage work. Christian groups that worked with him included The Imperials (with Terry Blackwood, son of Doyle Blackwood as lead vocalist), J.D. Sumner and the Stamps Quartet, the Jordanaires, and the Sweet Inspirations.

The last time that Dixie saw Elvis was in Las Vegas. It was just weeks before he died. Dixie said that he expressed unhappiness and regret for not remaining more true to his Christian calling. At about the same time, Elvis sought counsel from the television evangelist Rex Humbard and his wife, Maude Aimee. Looking back over his uniquely successful career, it seems strange to contemplate the outstanding fact that the only Grammy Awards Elvis would ever receive would be for his gospel recordings!

In 2000 Dixie Locke and her husband were still faithfully attending the Assemblies of God Church in Memphis. Dixie served as the church secretary. She told me how all his life Elvis loved the scriptures. The word 'hand' is one of the most frequently used words in Scripture, occurring over 1,600 times. Besides its literal use, it figuratively stood for power. In ancient times, to put one's hand on the head meant blessing and signified ordination. Unlike pagan deities, the scriptures declared that the Lord's authoritative Hand extended to *"the heavens . . . the depths . . . the wings of the dawn . . . the sea"*. Indeed, the Lord's Hand protected His children wherever they were, in sunshine-and-storm, in plenty-and-poverty. Believers know that there is only light with God. His light brightens up the darkness so that the Psalmist can say affirmatively, *"The night will shine like the day, for darkness is as light to you!"*

'Take My Hand Precious Lord' penned by the renowned Chicago pastor, Thomas Dorsey (Georgia Tom) today enjoys a classic reputation. Originally in error, it was thought that 'Take My Hand Precious Lord' was a folk song of the public domain and has often been used in western movies as if it was around in the 1880s which it wasn't!

Thomas Dorsey was born on 1st July 1899 in Villa Rica, a small settlement about forty miles from Atlanta, Georgia. He was raised in the poverty of the rural Southland. Many white inhabitants of the defeated Confederacy resented and begrudged the freedom from slavery granted to his parents' generation following the American Civil War. When he left his severely deprived boyhood home, he settled in Chicago in 1916 and rubbed musical shoulders with some of the legendary blues and jazz artistes of his day such as Bessie Smith, Ethel Waters and Ma Rainey.

Morally, for many years (as a blues-entertainer known as Georgia Tom), he struggled between such adverse, unwholesome influences as drink, gambling and sex, and the benevolent pull of the Holy Spirit! In the latter 1920s, Thomas recorded extensively as a blues artist finding success with his composition, 'It's Tight Like That'. Finally in 1930, he began to compose and publish religious songs and testified that he surrendered to Heaven's claim on his wayward life. Joining singer Sallie Martin, he developed a new career with the Gospel Choral Union.

Years later, as the pastor of the Pilgrim Baptist Church in Chicago, he penned some three hundred songs. 'Take My Hand Precious Lord' came from his own heart-rending, personal experience of tragedy. In 1932, he booked to go to a church revival meeting in St. Louis. Upon his arrival, after an exhausting journey, he received devastating news about his spouse. Earlier, Nettie bearing their first child, had persuaded him to attend the revival. While still on the revival meeting platform, he was slowly and sensitively told of the death of Nettie during childbirth. His St. Louis friends heard the news via a telegram. Heartbroken, he immediately rushed to a telephone to confirm the sad news. His friend, Gus Evans offered to accompany him on the painful journey home. Together they drove north and homeward, arriving back only to receive yet another blow. Initially, the newborn baby seemed to be doing well but then surprisingly, he too died during the night. Thomas said, *"Funeral arrangements were hastily arranged and both mother and child were interred in the same coffin. I was very despondent for several days as I mourned. I was severely tempted by Satan to go back to the world's music. But the Lord held me up and strengthened me!"*

Greatly distressed, initially Thomas drove aimlessly around the streets of the big city. Then as he drove, he conceived under divine inspiration the basics of what was to become the now renowned prayer-in-song, 'Take My Hand Precious Lord'. Stopping at Madame Malone's College, he visited his friend, Professor Frye. Together they strolled though the peaceful greenery of the college campus. Finally, entering one of the empty music rooms Thomas parked himself beside the piano. As his hands gently caressed the ivories, a simple melody took shape as Thomas vocalised, *"Blessed Lord! Blessed Lord! Blessed Lord!"*

Professor Frye enquired, *"Why don't you turn it into precious Lord, Thomas?"*

There and then, *'Take My Hand Precious Lord'* crystallised and later he recorded it accordingly. The song stirred the interest of many including the Heavenly Gospel Singers who famously recorded it. Then it was translated into about 35 foreign languages over subsequent decades. The composition is accepted today as standard fare with plentiful recordings available in both black and white traditions. Still preaching and singing, Thomas Dorsey remained active into a remarkably old age appearing in a television film in his eighties. He died in 1965.

But Jesus took him by the hand, and lifted him up; and he arose. Mark 9:27

Take This Bread I Give To Thee
(Communion Song)
Barry McGuire

*For I have received of the Lord that which also I delivered
unto you,
That the Lord Jesus the same night in which He was
betrayed took bread:
And when He had given thanks, He brake it, and said,
Take, eat: this is my body, which is broken for you: this do
in remembrance of Me.
After the same manner also He took the cup, when He had
supped, saying,
This cup is the new testament in my blood:
this do ye, as oft as ye drink it, in remembrance of Me.
For as often as ye eat this bread, and drink this cup,
ye do show the Lord's death till He come.
1 Corinthians 11:23-26*

Folk-singing protester, Barry McGuire was born in 1935 in Oklahoma
but grew up in Southern California. His father was a construction
worker that meant that the location of the family home moved around
frequently. The consequence of so much relocation was that Barry
went to ten grammar schools and four high schools! At the age of
sixteen, he dropped out of school and joined the US Navy, lying
about his age to do so. He told me that the structured life of being
told what to do did not suit his rebellious nature and so he told the

truth about his age, thus bringing his short navy career to an end!

Until he was twenty years of age, he worked on fishing boats, quitting that life also to go into construction work at the age of twenty-five. It was the time of the 1960's folksong era and after listening to the music, Barry got the desire to learn to play the guitar. He remembered how he and his buddies would sit around in the backyard and sing songs. One time at a birthday party of a friend, Barry was introduced to a man who owned a night club. He asked Barry to sing in his club one-night-a-week and he would give him $20 a night.

That first night, with the support of his friends, Barry entertained the customers and was duly paid $20 plus tips. Afterwards driving home that night with a pocketful-of-money, he hardly believed that people would actually pay to hear him sing! Consequently, Barry learned six or seven more songs on the guitar, singing these around the folk clubs in the area. If anyone requested a song, he would say he did not know it and ask them to teach it to him!

Within a year after he bought his first guitar, Barry became part of the up-and-coming group known as the New Christy Minstrels. Membership of the group took him all across the United States including a visit to the White House to perform before President Lyndon Johnson. The group also appeared weekly on the popular Andy Williams TV Show side by side with a young family group called the Osmonds. At the time Barry soon took up songwriting with some success. The group's million dollars hit-song 'Green, Green' was a McGuire composition. Soon he was making thousands of dollars a week in performance fees with people stopping him on the streets and in airports, asking him for his autograph.

Barry recalled, *"It was fun at the time because it was new. It was just like riding a roller coaster. It is fun the first four or five times you ride it, and then it's just a big drag. After you have gone over the same roller coaster about thirty times, you can hardly wait until the ride is over."*

In 1965 he recorded 'Eve Of Destruction' that can accurately be described as a statement of the times. It was a massive number one hit on both sides of the Atlantic with its pessimistic message. From there he went on to play the male lead in the controversial Broadway production of the musical 'Hair'. Barry said that the 'freedom-for-everyone' climate that prevailed at that particular time was soon to ensnare him and his friends into the drug culture. Indeed, his friends were definitely using and some were dying from drugs. He was himself heavily into the drug scene starting with cannabis, then amphetamines, barbiturates and then into the hard drugs.

Barry stated, *"The four years with the New Christy Minstrels were just like a dream. From one place to another, to another! You never really got to meet anybody; and when you did they looked at you from goggly eyes, thinking you were some kind of a super hero!...There was nothing real! It was just a big fantasy. My friend Paul and I used to talk about 'reality'.... What was real?...We started getting books on neurology, astronomy, biology and psychology. We would lie there stoned out of our heads and read and read and read. It got to the point where I couldn't perform anymore and I left the group in February of 1965."*

Paul went to San Francisco and discovered the effect of psychedelic drugs and introduced Barry into it too. Barry stated that the effect of the drugs caused him to believe that he was a god and he was totally free from any moral restraint. *"I used to think that drugs would give me a greater awareness of what life was all about, but within a few years I was using this greater awareness to rip others off. Without Christ I was an animal. I lived for myself....People encouraged me to get into transcendental meditation with the promise of relaxing me, giving me peace of mind. It does, but so do painkillers. Imagine someone giving a person a painkiller when both his legs have been lost when a train ran over them. The painkiller will make him feel better. It will give him peace of mind, but it hasn't fixed what's wrong with him. In reality, he's dying. Transcendental meditation and drugs only remove the symptoms, not the real source of the problem. I've seen the end result of all these different trips - all dead end into an open grave."*

Barry said that this downward spiral of drug abuse pulled him down for about ten years. It caused him to have a sense of real desperation and despair about himself and the world that he was living in. Then, suddenly, in a desperate search for the truth, he found Christ Jesus as a relevant help. Barry remembers the time well. *"Truthfully, I wasn't looking to become a Christian. In fact, I thought*

Christian morality was the hang-up of the human race. I wanted to be free from all those moral dogmas."

One day, Barry recalled, a street preacher *"pierced him with the living love of God"*. This person was a different kind of person than any Barry had previously encountered. *"He was a living person in a city of dead people. I hadn't seen a living person before. We were all dead. Biologically we were all live, but there was nothing going on inside of us. There was something going on inside him. He explained to me how Jesus was slaughtered by the lawlessness of humanity in order to absorb the ultimate death that selfishness brings. He explained that my debt had been paid. I wrestled with that piece of truth for eight months. I didn't want to be a Christian. I dug Jesus, but I didn't want to be like those other Christians. I said they were hypocrites. They were calling themselves by His name, and yet no one was like Him. But I knew later that no-one was there yet. We are all in different stages of growth. So when I looked at Him, I was captured. I couldn't get away. I died to death and came alive to life-in-Jesus. If I hadn't received Jesus as my Saviour then, I would do it today, all over again!"*

Barry's first gospel album entitled 'Seeds' was aimed particularly at street kids with whom he could personally empathize. Later his musical ministry became more worship-related and directed to building up a stronger relationship between Christians and their Father God. Barry felt that the Lord had told him that the priority of his ministry was firstly to his Father, then to his family, then to the Church and finally to the world. He explained the reason for that order. *"If my relationship with my Father is out of shape, how can I minister to my wife and child? If my family or home is disjointed, how can I effectively minister to the Body of Christ? Then if the Body is out-of-shape and pulling in different directions how can we reflect the love and oneness of Jesus to the World?"*

Barry felt that Christians need to be living examples of Christ, bringing light where there is darkness and life where there is death. *"In our society today, war is raging between the elements of life and death. We are being hypnotised into the belief that there is no death, that we don't really die. The serpent said the same thing to Eve in the garden, 'Ye shall not surely die' (Genesis 3:4).' ...We have a choice to either live for ourselves or live for God. If we live for God: we live. If we live for ourselves: we die!"*

When Barry became a Christian he became an avid Bible student. He conceived his song, 'Take This Bread I Give To Thee' to express the rightful way for Christians to understand communion. As he read, he discovered facts about the Early Church of the first century. Their communal meals (*agape* feasts) apparently conformed to the pattern of public sacred-feasting among the Jews and Greeks. Food was brought together for all to partake like a 'potluck supper'. The wealthy brought more and the hard-up less. However, as the Apostle Paul described it, cliques resulted and the food was dealt-out inequitably. The wealthy took the 'lion's share' and became overeaters while the poor remained hungry, bringing scorn on the Church of God and humiliation on the poor folk.

The Apostle Paul was clear that such behaviour did not agree with the spirit of the Lord's Supper as he had received it. Writing in 1 Corinthians 11:23-26. Paul said that he *"received from the Lord and passed on"* to them the true Christian tradition of the Lord's Supper. Celebrated in conjunction with the Jewish Passover, the Supper bread was unleavened. Christ Jesus gave thanks, as was the Jewish practice at a meal. In Barry's song, 'the breaking of the bread' was symbolic of Christ's tortured body given for others in sacrifice.

Barry thrilled to the truth that the contents of Lord's Supper cup symbolized the 'new covenant in Jesus' blood' that brought forgiveness. The new covenant secured God's agreement of salvation with His people. It fulfilled the covenant promises from God in the Old Testament shown by example in the sacrifices. Barry stated, *"At the Last Supper, Christ did not say how often believers should share 'the communion' but indicated that it was to be held periodically. As we eat and drink, we remember Him in death and look ahead to His second coming."*

Take this bread I give to you, and as you do, remember Me.
This bread is My body broken just for you. Take it, (take it) eat it, (eat it) each time you do;
Remember Me, remember Me.

Take this cup I fill for you, And as you do, remember Me.
This cup is the new covenant I'm making with you.
Take it, (take it) drink it, (drink it) each time you do;
Remember Me, remember Me.

Take this love I've given you, And as you do, remember Me.
Remember Me, remember Me.

The Glory Song
(When All My Labours And Trials Are O're)

Charles Hutchinson Gabriel

If ye then be risen with Christ, seek those things which are above,
  where Christ sitteth on the right hand of God.
Set your affection on things above, not on things on the earth.
For ye are dead, and your life is hid with Christ in God.
When Christ, who is our life, shall appear,
  then shall ye also appear with Him in glory.
Colossians 3 : 1-4

Written by Charles Hutchinson Gabriel, the majestic anthem of the coming resurrection day of the saints, 'The Glory Song' was first published in 1900 in Chicago by Ohio-born, Edwin Othello Excell (1851-1929) in 'Make His Praise Glorious'. It was a song that gained considerable popularity with congregations and gospel singers in the first couple of decades of the 20th century.

One such gospel singer was Charles M. Alexander who became famous for his heart-felt interpretation of 'The Glory Song'. As he sang out the lyrics heartily, 'When All My Labours And Trials Are O'er' emotions were stirred accordingly at his vast meetings and tears flowed. Charles Alexander was so well known for singing 'The Glory Song' that he was often mistakenly thought to be its writer.

The confusion was compounded as both the singer and the writer was called 'Charles'.

Born in 1867, Charles Alexander became the renowned song-leader and soloist for the preaching evangelist, J. Wilbur Chapman. Charles popularised 'The Glory Song' throughout North America and Europe and this song about heaven was often sung around parlour organs and pianos in homes. Charles' emotional approach with his crowds was to use simple joyful songs to set the mood for the preached-gospel-message. Years later this approach particularly inspired Cliff Barrows making lasting impressions on the Billy Graham Team.

Born in the 'Volunteer State' of Tennessee, Charles Alexander trained for church ministry at the famed Moody Bible Institute in Chicago. Nicknamed 'Charlie', his genial personality warmed-up audiences with smiles and charisma. Despite his jovial exterior, it was said that he was very earnest about the gospel message of Christ and sought new ways to seek those whom he described as lost. He and Wilbur Chapman's new evangelistic initiative in 1909 in Boston, Massachusetts was known as 'Simultaneous Evangelism'. They discovered that dividing the city into zones and evangelising with different teams at the same time, proved very effective. As Charles Hutchinson Gabriel's song said so poetically, *'when all his labours and trials were o'er'*, Charlie M. Alexander died in 1920. He faced this final experience- 'the last enemy'- positively. He firmly believed as 'The Glory Song' declared, he anticipated *'glory for me'*!

'The Glory Song's composer, Charles Hutchinson Gabriel was born on the hot day of August 18th 1856 in the rural environs of Wilton, Iowa. His father Isaac Gabriel took great pleasure in his new son. Although as he grew Charles was evidently a natural poet, out of necessity he diligently spent the first seventeen years of his life labouring on an Iowa farm. At an early age, music captured his impressionable heart and he was delighted when the family purchased a small reed organ for the living room of the home. It was not long before he was teaching himself to play; indeed soon he was so proficient that he was teaching others too. Incredibly at the young age of sixteen years, he began teaching 'singing schools', his fame and expertise as a song composer and teacher spread like wildfire throughout the community.

From 1890 to 1892, Charles was employed as the music director of the Grace Methodist Episcopal Church in San Francisco, California. Then moving again from one big city to another, in the latter 1890s he re-settled in Chicago, Illinois. During this period, he published several collections of sacred songs and authored several other books including 'Gospel Songs And Their Writers'. This was followed in 1912 by employment with the fledgling gospel music publishers, 'Homer Rodeheaver Publications'. This successful teaming lasted until Charles' death on September 15th 1932 in Los Angeles, California. At the time of his death, Los Angeles was the glittering venue for the world's biggest ever Olympics. Hollywood too was consolidating its claim to be the 'Entertainment Capital of the World' with new movie stars like child-actress, Shirley Temple and Johnny Weismuller as Tarzan. But the glories of the show business and sports worlds pitifully paled in the beams of the glories that Charles perceived in his classic song.

Equally talented as the Hollywood brigade with their lyrics and melodies, Charles Hutchinson Gabriel's enduring legacy includes some timeless gospel music classics: 'Higher Ground', 'He Lifted Me', My Saviour's Love', 'Send The Light', 'Since Jesus Came Into My Heart', 'So Precious Is Jesus', 'The Old Time Power', 'The Way Of The Cross Leads Home' and many more . Most of his lyrics were signed with his pseudonym 'Charlotte G. Homer'. He used his own initials but reversed the G and H. Positively, his output of sacred song compositions was most prolific. Amazingly at the time of his professional peak, the large tally that he produced included 35 gospel songbooks, 8 Sunday school songbooks, 7 songbooks for men's choirs, 6 songbooks for ladies' choirs, 10 kiddies' songbooks, 19 collections of anthems plus 23 cantatas.

Charles Gabriel always declared that he was greatly inspired by his preacher-friend, Ed Card (Superintendent of the Sunshine Rescue Mission, St. Louis. Missouri). Known as 'Old Glory Face', Ed usually concluded his passionate prayers with the joyous expression *"and that will be glory for me!"* A powerful communicator, Ed often quoted the Apostle Paul's profound exposition of the glorious cosmic significance of Jesus Christ' Second Advent in Colossians 3 : 1-4. *"If ye then be risen with Christ, seek those things which are above, where Christ sitteth on the right hand of God. Set your affection on things above, not on things on the earth. For ye are dead, and your life is hid with Christ in God. When Christ, who is our life, shall appear, then shall ye also appear with Him in glory.*

Ed would often remind his congregations that the Apostle Paul exhorted believers to give outward expression in daily-living to the deep inward experience that is theirs in Christ. *"Never forget"*, Ed declared, *"truly, the Christian life is a life 'hidden with Christ in God', but it is still a life lived out on earth! You good Christian-folk must therefore give attention not only to your 'inward experience with God' but also to your 'outward relations with your fellow human beings!"*

Charles Gabriel also often heard Ed Card standing in the pulpit declaring, *"Brethren, our Brother Paul urges us as Christians to seek heavenly things and set our minds supremely on them. As believers, our lives are now safeguarded and hidden with Christ in God. We belong to the invisible realm and when Christ appears, there will be a glorious materialization of all that we truly are! So brothers, as genuine Christians let's see everything against the background of eternity. Don't make earthly things such as wealth, fame, power and pleasure, a preoccupation! Such earthly goals in life are unworthy of us who have been raised with Christ and look forward to sharing in His eternal glory! Of this there is no doubt, one day, the world that persecutes believers will be blinded with the dazzling glory of His return!"*

Study of the scriptures reveals that *'Kabod'* (the Hebrew word translated glory) means the weight or worth of something. Hence, 'the glory of God' is 'the worthiness of God', the fullness of His attributes. Such glory is both physical and spiritual, as in the Christmas story, 'the glory of the Lord shone around' the shepherds on the Bethlehem hillsides. Several decades later, the Apostle John referred to the glory of the Father that Christ Jesus gave to His disciples. As for the saints on the coming resurrection day, their glory culminates in the changing of their bodies to the likeness of their glorified Lord. Indeed in the context of eternity, scripture sees the glorified saints as a great cloud of witnesses, righteous people now made perfect before the throne of God singing songs of worship, glorifying God!

When all my labours and trials are o'er, and I am safe on that beautiful shore,
    Just to be near the dear Lord I adore will thro' the ages be glory for me.

Oh that will be glory for me, Glory for me, glory for me!
    When by His grace I shall look on His face, that will be glory, be glory for me!

When, by the gift of His infinite grace, I am accorded in heaven a place,
    Just to be there and to look on His face will thru the ages be glory for me.

Friends will be there I have loved long ago; Joy like a river around me will flow.
    Yet, just a smile from my Saviour, I know, Will thru' the ages be glory for me.

Charles Hutchinson Gabriel

The Heart of Worship
(When The Music Fades)
Matt Redman

'*But the LORD said unto Samuel,*
 "Look not on his countenance, or on the height of his
 stature...
 for the LORD seeth not as man seeth;
 for man looketh on the outward appearance, but the LORD
 looketh on the heart."
 1 Samuel 16:7
 I will praise thee, O LORD, with my whole heart;
 I will show forth all thy marvellous works.
 I will be glad and rejoice in Thee:
 I will sing praise to Thy name, O Thou most High.
 Psalm 9:1

In the spring of 2002 in England, the British record company 'Survivor' was most pleased to proudly announce to the world that the 'Gospel Music Association' in Nashville, Tennessee rewarded Matt Redman with the 'International Award'. The presentation was of the award was received by in Matt's absence by 'Kingsway Communications' delighted Chief Executive Officer, John Paculabo, on his behalf. Richly deserved, Matt had developed into one of the young leaders at the helm of the contemporary worship movement in Great Britain, and was fast becoming one of the most popular songwriters and worship leaders of his generation.

That year, Matt and his family moved back to the United Kingdom after their six months of sabbatical leave in the United States. His return to England coincided with the release of Matt's new album 'Where angels fear to tread' in July 2002. He declared that his heart remained in the desire to lead people in times of worship, teaching and ministry. Matt, his wife Beth, daughter Maisey (and new baby on the way) decided to base themselves on England's south coast in Brighton, and serve in the Church of Christ the King (CCK).

America's premier contemporary Christian music journal, 'CCM Magazine' credited Matt Redman for 'narrowing the gap between worship and pop music'. Years before, it was the insightful youth worker, Mike Pilavachi, leader of the 'Soul Survivor' youth festival in England, who first perceived the latent talent in Matt. The risk was worth taking and Mike's predictions bore fruit. *"Mike was obviously putting his neck on the line, because I was young,"* says Matt. *"We had a few embarrassing moments where I was obviously out of my depth! But it was a good discipleship."*

Matt Redman's place and date-of-birth were Watford, England on 14th February 1974. He says that he come to faith growing-*up "talking to God, and loving going to Church"*. Then at aged ten, he went to a mission in London conducted by the famous evangelist from Argentina, Luis Palau and made his conversion "official"! He says that his signature song is 'The Heart of Worship' because it sums up a little of what worship is all about, and says something about the journey he is on finding out what truly pleases the heart of God. He first began conducting worship when he was a fresh-faced fourteen-year-old in his church youth group located 25 miles northwest of London. His youth club was part of Saint Andrews Church, Chorleywood, the local Anglican Church conveniently located just off a junction of the major M25 orbital road that skirts the metropolis.

As opportunities arose and the years passed, Matt became better known for conducting worship at the Soul Survivor gatherings. Indeed, the organisers of Soul Survivor saw Matt's potential and sought to involve him with from the start. The annual Soul Survivor youth festival, by 2002 was gathering over 15,000 teenagers every year for worship and teaching. Invitations soon started in flow into

Matt's mailbox. Consequently, he conducted worship seminars across the UK that included Spring Harvest, Greenbelt and Wembley Stadium. Foreign invitations followed and he traveled to Holland, Ireland, Norway, South Africa and the USA for meetings and concerts. The events varied in size but Matt recalled the thrill of leading worship at Passion's One-Day event that accommodated more than 40,000 youth and college students in Memphis, Tennessee.

When asked to describe the trust of his music, Matt said that he could tie himself down to having one theme. He said that undoubtedly, his focus is firstly on believers having a personal intimacy with God. However, he stated that, secondly, he is also very conscious of other Christian performers and their needs. Therefore, he is interested in encouraging other songwriters accordingly. This desire is evidenced in his active participation in a project called 'The People's Album' that was released on under the 'Survivor' banner. It was a project that was conceived to help new writers to get their songs recorded. Several consecutive CDs were issued in that series. Matt was delighted to play his part in giving other people similar opportunities to those that he said that he enjoyed as a budding songwriter. Matt stated, *"The People's Album' series with some brand new worship songs was made as a resource for the Church. It was also made to directly encourage new songwriters."*

Matt's growing repertoire of songs are now used far-and-wide across the globe and include in addition to 'The Heart Of Worship':- 'Once Again', 'I Will Offer', 'Let Everything That Has Breath', 'Better Is One Day' and 'Let My Words Be Few'. Experts-in-the-field have often stated that from the very beginning, Matt's music displayed maturity beyond his years. Despite these accolades, Matt states that he must remain humble and guard against complacency.

All artists have their influences and Matt is no exception citing the sway that 'Vineyard Music' men Andy Park and Eddie Espinosa, along with others such as Kevin Prosch and Martin Smith have had on him. Matt states that while conducting worship, he tends to curb his desire to chat between songs. Astutely, he declares that he does this not because he does not have anything worthwhile to say. Rather, once a congregation's focus is on God, he wants it to stay there! Matt's ongoing vision is to see people draw near to God in adoration and intimacy, and *"to see the church rise up, filled with plenty of raw, holy passion"*.

Matt delights in saying that he has received of testimonies from people who have come to faith in that way. *"Testimonies from people make what I do all worth while. I want to write songs that really help people engage with God more. Not just another song, but a song that will help people in terms of their life with God, where God might change them, or someone might even become a Christian through it."*

The United States of America opened up warmly to Matt's music. He spent a 6-month sabbatical in the USA in 2002. At the end of his sabbatical, he recorded another album, 'Where Angels Fear To Tread', with Jason Halbert and Dwayne Larring (co-founders and former producers of Sonicflood). It was an excellent collection of contemporary worship songs. It was recorded in a studio environment, where Matt felt free to express his worship with an extremely gifted group of musicians. For this project he also co-wrote songs with Chris Tomlin ('Wonderful Maker'), Tom Lane ('Where Angels Fear To Tread') and his wife, Beth ('Blessed Be Your Name'). The album was simultaneously released in the UK, Europe and the States in July 2002. At the time, Matt was very encouraged by the response to his book 'The Unquenchable Worshipper'. *"I see the book as an opportunity to share my heart of worship. I am well aware that worship music has become trendy. That both excites and worries me. It excites me because it seems to be something the Holy Spirit has been doing in the church. I come across so many young worship leaders and songwriters, and I'm amazed, the quality of material has just gone up and up. However, as the late John Wimber reminded us: the real test will not be in the writing and presenting of new and great music, it will be in the godliness of those who deliver it."*

Matt stated that he is very concerned that people do not just go running after new forms of music and better sounding albums, yet lose the heart of it. *"I saw a US worship album recently subtitled 'America's Ten Most Powerful Worship Songs'. Who told them that? God? It made me giggle, but it also made me concerned. That sort of marketing shows we easily lose the plot if we're not careful. The true sign of progress in this whole worship area will be more heart in our recordings, and not necessarily better music."*

When the music fades and all is stripped away, and I simply come,
  Longing just to bring something that's of worth that will bless Your heart.
  I'll bring You more than a song, for a song in itself is not what You have required.
  You search much deeper within through the way things appear,
  You're looking into my heart.
  I'm coming back to the heart of worship and it's all about You, it's all about You, Jesus.
  I'm sorry Lord for the thing I've made it but it's all about You, it's all about You, Jesus.

King of endless worth, no-one could express how much You deserve
  Though I'm weak and poor, all I have is Yours, every single breath.
  And I'll bring You more than a song, for a song in itself is not what You have required.
  You search much deeper within through the way things appear,
  You're looking into my heart.
  I'm coming back to the heart of worship and it's all about You, it's all about You, Jesus.
  I'm sorry Lord for the thing I've made it but it's all about You, it's all about You, Jesus.

The Lord Is Good
Paul & Susan Hansen

> *"...but be filled with the Spirit;*
> *Speaking to yourselves in psalms and hymns and spiritual*
> *songs,*
> *singing and making melody in your heart to the Lord;*
> *Giving thanks always for all things unto God*
> *and the Father in the name of our Lord Jesus Christ.*
> *Ephesians 5:19-20*
> *O give thanks unto the Lord; for He is good:*
> *for His mercy endureth forever."*
> *Psalms 106:1*

Husband and wife Christian songwriters, Paul and Susan Hansen passionately believe, as their chorus says, 'The Lord Is Good'! They also believe that one of the best ways to touch people's lives with the Gospel is through music. Paul stated, *"We're interested in people. That's why we're in the ministry. We know what it's like to be lonely and hurting. We also know what it's like to be touched with God's love and mercy; how it brings absolute peace to a troubled mind. And music has more of an influence on our lives than we might think."*

The Hansens' song, as if it were not already obvious, was inspired by the famous Biblical words of praise, *"O give thanks unto the Lord; for He is good: for His mercy endureth forever"* found in Psalms 106:1; 107:1; 118:1, 29 and 136:1.

Although the complete quote appears in the above references, that final and important phrase, *"for his mercy endureth forever"*, appears repeatedly through both Psalm 118, Psalm 136 and once again in the wonderfully hopeful Messianic prophecy found in Jeremiah 33:11. Paul Hansen says that he must give some well-deserved credit to his mother who quoted this scripture quite often while he was growing up.

Paul and Susan were born hundreds of miles apart, Paul on March 3rd 1946 in Bloomington, Illinois, and Susan on March 10th 1951 in Boston, Massachusetts. They met in Brandon, Vermont in 1972. At that time they were both searching for truth and fulfillment in the hippie life-style of the 1960s with its music, drugs, and occult philosophies. Paul had left college in 1967 to become a folk-singer and songwriter in New York City. He lived in Greenwich Village and played in the clubs there off-and-on for three years. Eventually, he moved to Atlanta, Georgia where he teamed up as a duo with the now successful songwriter Pat Alger playing locally and touring clubs and colleges in the southeastern United States. By this time, Paul said that he moved far away from his traditional Lutheran upbringing, venturing into astrology and eastern religions in search of peace-and-purpose.

Disillusioned after a year at Boston University, Susan moved to Vermont in 1971and was working at an institution for the mentally handicapped. She said that because she had not seen evidence of God's existence in the church where she grew up, she also began looking into eastern religions for the supernatural.

One day a couple from Atlanta moved into the apartment downstairs from where she was living. Soon after their arrival, there began a steady flow of visitors, the first of whom was Paul Hansen. Many of those people were musicians and songwriters. Susan had played guitar periodically since she was eight or nine years old, and during her time at Boston University had even written a few songs. Susan's new friends, including Paul, seemed to have 'a-lot-of-love to give', and they encouraged her to the point that her singing and songwriting began to blossom.

The couple's friendship grew slowly over the next couple of years. They found they had a mutual desire-for-truth and continued to explore the occult sciences, but following that line only brought increased confusion, poverty and shame. Even though they loved each other, they lacked stability until a turn of events brought God into their troubled, searching lives.

Paul became convinced that he and Susan should be married, and went to Atlanta to pursue an offer of a record deal in order to secure funds to start married life. But when he arrived, to his dismay, he found the deal was off. Paul's hopes were dashed. He was angry, out of money, and stranded. Then one day, in the midst of despair, he was sitting on the curb with his guitar under some dogwood trees in a residential area of Atlanta. He looked up the street to see a car slowly making its way to where he was. The car stopped, and the lady in it called out cheerfully, *"Hey, do you want to jam?"*

She pulled a harmonica out of the glove box, and got out of the car. Paul obliged and began dutifully playing some chords on his guitar as his new acquaintance played on her harmonica. Then she began talking to him about Jesus. The more the lady talked, the brighter her face became. A voice inside Paul said, *"This is God talking to you…Listen to what she says!"*

As the conversation progressed, the lady posed Paul a question that convicted him somewhat. *"Do your parents know where you are?"*

She made him promise her that he would telephone home. As soon as she left, he went inside, called his parents on the phone and a week later found himself on a bus to Iowa, where they were living at the time. It was in that setting of reconciliation that Paul asked Jesus Christ to come into his heart. He said that suddenly everything was all right - there was peace.

It was to be a year before Paul returned to Vermont to resolve the relationship with Susan. But once together, Paul started to share what he learned about Jesus with Susan. They began reading the Bible together. As they studied, their interest in astrology and the eastern cults diminished. Their excitement about the promises that they found in the Bible began to grow.

Traveling through Illinois, during a trip to Iowa to visit Paul's family, their car was pushed violently around by strong gusts-of-wind, making driving very difficult. Susan looked up at the sky, pondering on the hugeness of the universe in contrast to the tiny capsule in which they were riding. How insignificant she felt! As the wind continued to gust Susan found her heart constricted by fear. This fear of dying and death threatened to engulf her. She believed they were about to die. Suddenly, she remembered something that Paul had said about Jesus, how He came and changed his life. *"I had seen that change for myself and it was good!...As I considered the possibility of asking Jesus for help, I sensed that doing so would mean making a life-long decision to follow Him. It was only a matter of a few moments before I actually took that step. Immediately, the fear left, and a warm feeling of peace, joy, and relief flooded into my being. I knew that Jesus had come into my life and it was His strength that had driven out that fear of dying."*

Two months later, Paul and Susan were married. Throwing away all their books on the occult and eastern religious and replacing it with the Truth found in Jesus Christ in the Bible, the couple began to seek God's guidance for their lives.

In 1976 they moved to Tulsa, Oklahoma where they began studying for the ministry. They then worked for six years in their local church as counselors and music ministers. Paul was on staff as a graphic artist for two years, and for a year and a half both served at a nearby affiliate church as music ministers and children's pastors. Then for five years they traveled extensively in a full-time music ministry of their own - chiefly in the USA and UK. In 1988 Paul and Susan became Music and Media Directors of a church in San Francisco, California. They also served for several years in the music department of another church in Hayward, California before returning to their full-time traveling ministry. They have since been to France, India and Costa Rica.

In concert, the Hansens accompany themselves on guitar and bass guitar. Their desire to use music as a ministry tool remains uppermost in their hearts. *"Our motivation is to bring people into a real experience with Jesus Christ. We are not just Christians playing music, we play to communicate Christ. There is a calling on our lives to sing, to teach and to bring healing to all the nations. We're not interested in changing people's cultures, we simply want to watch God do miracles in their lives. We want to see them saved, healed,* refreshed, comforted and encouraged. The only way this can happen is if we tell them what the Bible says...The Bible is different from any other book. It has supernatural life in its very words. As people hear those words and receive them, God's power goes into them and changes them. That's why we put the Bible into our songs. We never get tired of singing them because they contain the life of God - life that is ever new."

Based in 2002 near Boston, Massachusetts, Paul and Susan sing and play in their unique and refreshing style. They state that they want to create an atmosphere that lifts people into a place where they can receive what they need from God. Through word and song, they continue to teach that indeed the Lord is Good!

The Lord is good. The Lord is good. His mercy endureth forever.
The Lord is good. The Lord is good. His mercy endureth forever.
Great is the Lord and greatly to be praised
Great is the Lord. Let holy hands be raised.

You're coming to the Lord if you're looking for the truth.
You thought it was the end; you said it was no use.
He wants to be your friend. He's turned you loose—
He's already gotten your release. He wants to set you in His heavenly peace.

He loves you as you are, no matter what you've done.
He's washed away the past so you don't have to run.
Just come into His arms: He's the One
You've been looking for so long. He's loving and He's strong.

The Lord is good. The Lord is good. His mercy endureth forever.
The Lord is good. The Lord is good. His mercy endureth forever.

Then Jesus Came
Oswald Jeffray Smith & Homer Rodeheaver

*As He went out of Jericho with His disciples and a great
number of people,
blind Bartimaeus, the son of Timaeus, sat by the highway
side begging.
And when he heard that it was Jesus of Nazareth,
he began to cry out, and say, 'Jesus, thou son of David,
have mercy on me.'
And many charged him that he should hold his peace: but
he cried the more a great deal,
'Thou son of David, have mercy on me.'
And Jesus stood still, and commanded him to be called.
And they call the blind man, saying unto him, 'Be of good
comfort, rise; He calleth thee.
And he, casting away his garment, rose, and came to Jesus.
And Jesus answered and said unto him, 'What wilt thou
that I should do unto thee?'
The blind man said unto Him, 'Lord, that I might receive
my sight. '
And Jesus said unto him, 'Go thy way; thy faith hath made
thee whole.'
And immediately he received his sight, and followed Jesus
in the way.
Mark 10:46-52*

Dr. Oswald J. Smith penned the moving ballad-styled lyrics of 'Then Jesus Came'. Born in 1889, he was a most accomplished hymn-writer and author. Also, he became known to 20th century Christendom as the beloved, world-renowned founder and (for more than thirty years) the pastor of the People's Church in Toronto, Canada. Beyond those years as the senior pastor, he then continued his ministry as the missionary pastor of this notable church. During his time of service, the People's Church was often acclaimed as 'the leading missionary church on the face of the globe'. Indeed, the People's Church contributed regularly millions of dollars to the cause of world evangelism. Recognised as a 'missionary world leader', before his death, Doctor Smith fulfilled his objective in visiting every continent on Earth in the promotion of missionary endeavors. While on such assignments as a preacher-teacher, he also conducted great evangelistic campaigns around the world.

In the mid 20th Century, Doctor Smith's song-writing partner was Homer Rodeheaver, a gospel singer of great renown. Homer himself often stated that he was in awe of Oswald Smith and called him *"the greatest living hymn-writer in the world today"*. More than 600 poems, hymns and gospel songs come from the Smith pen. For some of his classic songs, Oswald skillfully composed the tunes as well as the lyrics. In contrast, for some others, other notable songwriting musicians such as Alfred H. Ackley, B. D. Ackley, Redd Harper and, of course, Homer Rodeheaver supplied the music. Indeed, Homer provided the melody that went with Oswald's ballad-lyrics of 'Then Jesus Came'.

As a gospel communicator and songwriter, Homer Rodeheaver (along with his preaching partner, Billy Sunday) was a huge influence in the USA in the decades before World War II. He often brought a smile to faces when he would say, *"My motto is every cloud will wear a rainbow if your heart keeps right!"*

Born in 1880 in Union Furnace in Ohio, Homer said that he realised early-on the importance of gospel singing as a vital part of revival meetings. The composer-performer's new emphasis was to change the face of evangelistic meetings. Homer served in the Spanish-American War as a trombonist with the 4th Tennessee Regimental Band. Later during World War I, he served with the

'Young Men's Christian Association' in battle-scared France from August to December of 1918. He became the renowned evangelist, Billy Sunday's song-leader in 1909 (which is incidentally, the year of George Beverly Shea's birth). This association between Billy and Homer lasted until 1931.

Homer's evangelistic music spread widely in homes through the use of the new phonograph invention. Across the USA and Canada in the 1920s and 1930s, thousands thrilled to hearing Homer for the first time on record singing songs such as 'Sunrise'. The inspiring sound of Homer came from new wind-up Victrola phonographs. These highly prized mahogany instruments at the time were given pride of place in the nation's sitting rooms. Meanwhile, Homer himself was touring the world with evangelist W. R. Biederwolf from 1923 to 1924. A 'man with a missionary heart', Homer visited the Belgian Congo in 1936. All the while, his moving gospel songs were gaining popularity in the 'civilised world'. This came via the newly sprouting radio stations and new singers like the Blackwood Brothers, Gypsy Smith, George Beverly Shea and, of course, Homer himself.

Those attending his meetings found Homer to be a short, stocky, smiling individual whose sincerity was infectious. In his years of service, Homer developed the full art of audience participation in gospel singing. His innovative style and his God-given ability to draw even the most reluctant individual into taking part in the services was a totally different style to that of other song-leaders before his day. He would often prelude the meetings with a musical quiz or parts-singing, drawing on the audience to participate. An accomplished trombonist, Homer's trombone with piano accompaniment, provided dramatic background to the gospel singing. Such a sound was unheard of before in revival meetings.

Musically, George Beverly Shea and Cliff Barrows of the Billy Graham evangelistic team followed closely the team experiences of Sunday and Rodeheaver. The latter duo were exponents of a more relaxed version of revival meetings. This contrasted greatly with the rather staid dignity of previous days. Years later, George Beverly Shea openly gave credit to the gospel music pioneer for his distinctive way of singing. *"I loved to listen to Homer Rodeheaver singing. He was an early inspiration. Long ago, Homer would sing every week on the radio when the radio was America's only source of entertainment. Homer died in 1950 but in his day, America wanted to hear oldies like 'Amazing Grace" and 'Blessed Assurance' plus his new favourites like 'Then Jesus Came' and 'Precious Memories'. The dust bowl and the Great Depression left folks simple in their joys and pleasures. They did not want the taint of Hollywood's values or news of approaching world war."*

Mister Shea also credited Oswald Smith songs as being a comfort, inspiration and blessing to many at the Billy Graham crusades in the latter part of the 20th century. Few wee used as frequently as 'Then Jesus Came'.

Copyrighted in 1940 by the Rodeheaver Publishing Company, the opening verse of 'Then Jesus Came' musically retold the story of the last of the great healing miracles in Mark's gospel. The miracle took place near Jericho. The ancient city was located five miles west of the River Jordan and about fifteen miles northeast of Jerusalem. There was an 'old Jericho' and a 'new Jericho', built by King Herod. It is said by the experts that possibly the miracle was performed by Christ Jesus somewhere between the old Israelite city and the new city. Luke records this miracle as Christ went *into* the city and Mark, as He was *leaving*. Mark gives the name of the blind man as Bartimaeus, the son of Timai. In the Middle East, a blind man sitting along the road begging was a common sight.

This poor beggar, Bartimaeus must have heard of Christ's nationwide reputation as a healer. When he discovered that Jesus was coming by, he boldly seized the opportunity of approaching Him. The title of 'Son of David' that he used to address Jesus was messianic in origin. The pious pilgrims going up to Jerusalem for the Feast of Passover did not applaud Bartimaeus's loud shouting. On the contrary, they tried to silence him, but he shouted all the more, *"Son of David, have mercy on me!"*

Unlike the uncaring crowd, Christ Jesus did not try to silence the pleas of Bartimaeus. Incidentally, this implies too that He did not reject the title of 'Son of David' as He was now getting closer to the fulfillment of His messianic mission's First Advent. It was no longer necessary to keep the secret. The shouts continued and the beggar's loud cry stopped the busy Christ Jesus in His tracks. In compassion,

He called blind Bartimaeus to Him. The surprised crowd then completely changed their attitude and encouraged the beggar to approach the Master. Bartimaeus's response was immediate. The dust-covered cloak, his outer garment (that he probably spread regularly on the ground to receive the alms) was enthusiastically cast aside.

Before Christ healed the poor blind beggar, He asked him a probing question to stimulate the man's faith. Having done that, without any overt action or healing word on His part, He sent Bartimaeus away with the words, *"Go! Your faith has healed you!"*

As the beautiful song, 'Then Jesus Came' so graphically illustrates, the cure of Bartimaeus from blindness was immediate, and the elated man joined the busy crowd going up to the feast to worship. This wonderful miracle set the stage for the climax of Christ's earthly story. The eventful journey to Jerusalem was completed and Christ Jesus, Israel's promised Messiah entered the Holy City where the last tragic acts of the drama of redemption took place amid Jewish and Roman cruelty. The Messiah's miraculous opening of the eyes of the blind man stands in sharp contrast to the self-imposed-blindness of the religious leaders that He encountered there in Jerusalem during Holy Week.

One sat alone beside the highway begging,
His eyes were blind the light he could not see;
He clutched his rags and shivered in the shadows,
Then Jesus came and bade his darkness flee.

When Jesus comes the tempter's power is broken;
When Jesus comes the tears are wiped away.
He takes the gloom and fills the life with glory,
For all is changed when Jesus comes to stay.

From home and friends the evil spirits drove him,
Among the tombs he dwelt in misery;
He cut himself as demon powers possessed him,
Then Jesus came and set the captive free.

Unclean! Unclean! The leper cried in torment,
The deaf, the dumb, in helplessness stood near;
The fever raged, disease had gripped its victim,
Then Jesus came and cast out every fear.

So men today have found the Saviour able,
They could not conquer passion, lust and sin,
Their broken hearts had left them sad and lonely,
Then Jesus came and dwelt Himself within.

There Is Power In The Name Of Jesus
Noel Richards

And at the end of the days,
 I Nebuchadnezzar lifted up mine eyes unto heaven,
and mine understanding returned unto me, and I blessed
the most High,
 and I praised and honoured Him that liveth for ever,
whose dominion is an everlasting dominion,
 and His kingdom is from generation to generation:
And all the inhabitants of the earth are reputed as nothing:
and He doeth according to His will in the army of heaven,
and among the inhabitants of the earth:
and none can stay His hand, or say unto Him, 'What doest
thou?'
Daniel 4:34-35
Let every soul be subject unto the higher powers.
For there is no power but of God:
the powers that be are ordained of God.
Romans 13:1

With tongue-in-cheek, Noel Richards (the composer of 'There Is Power In The Name Of Jesus') laughingly remembered, *"When I was young, it seemed that most of the songs used in church worship were written by oldies like Charles Wesley and such. I genuinely believed that you had to be dead to be a hymnwriter!"*

Noel said that he never dreamed that he could write worship-songs and praise-hymns that churches worldwide could sing. Therefore, the numerous songs that Noel wrote in the early days tended to be evangelistic, mainly majoring on the Gospel message.

Many years ago as a young fledging singer-songwriter, Noel stated that providentially he received some good advice from a mature worship-leader friend. This good friend said, *"Noel, always remember that if a good song works for guitar and solo voice then it'll work for a band!"*

Because of that advice, Noel became convinced that the greatest resource that he had to offer was the song itself. *"It's the specialness of the song's lyrics and melody that's important not the arrangement or the instrumental toys that may augment the song. Therefore, I enjoy writing personal worship songs that can also be used in churches and even in big stadium meetings. I like hearing other worship leaders say, 'Yes, that's a song that'll work well for us'."*

Although one could say that Noel has written many gospel 'hits', he definitely does not want to get into a 'hit-factory-syndrome'. He always keeps in mind the local churches and their modest expressions of praise. Sensitive to good theology, he stated, *"My song, 'There Is Power In The Name Of Jesus' speaks of Christ's great authority. His legal and moral right to exercise power is rightly His possession. In the Bible, God is presented as the ultimate, personal authority and the source of all authority. This authority and power are related but different!"*

In his Bible studies, Noel came to understand that Christ Jesus as a man was 'under authority' and 'with authority'. Clearly, Christ did what only God could do when He forgave sins, controlled nature and even exercised power-over-death. As the Resurrected Lord, He now has all authority and power in earth and heaven. After Jesus' glorification, the apostles advanced the topic of the authority of Christ Jesus. Indeed, they displayed Him as the co-regent of the Father, possessing supremacy over the whole cosmos. They also taught that the transitory custody of authority and power by Satan was abused and will be punished.

The Early Church proclaimed that the purpose of Christ's exaltation is that all beings might bow in acknowledgment of the

Name that belongs to Christ Jesus and confess that "Jesus Christ is Lord!" Because of what the name Jesus (the Saviour) represents, the time is coming when every knee will bow before Him in recognition of His sovereignty. This universal acknowledgment will include angels and departed saints in heaven, people still living on earth, the satanic hosts and the lost humanity in hell. Such submission will also be expressed by verbal confession. This confession will not imply a universal salvation, but means that every personal being will ultimately confess Christ's Lordship, either with joyful faith or with resentment and despair.

This decisive assertion that *"Jesus Christ is Lord"* is the Apostle's Paul's indication of the special 'Name' granted Christ at His exaltation following the Cross. Every creature will eventually acknowledge that Name with all the dignity and divine prerogatives implied. Of course, the Son in His divine nature was always deity, but the exaltation (subsequent to the Cross) bestowed on Him the dignity of a station commensurate with His original nature. This is far superior to His humble state while on earth.

'There Is Power In The Name Of Jesus' composed by Noel Richards speaks of Christ's great power and authority. It represents the best of this worship troubadour's songwriting and performing ability. It speaks of affirming that Jesus is fully God and that His Name, status and privileges are deserved. Consequently, God's design is that all people everywhere should worship and serve Jesus as Lord. Ultimately all will acknowledge Him as Lord, whether willingly or not.

Noel's regular albums formed the foundation of his aspiring career in Christian music during the 1990s. His success was well-deserved. Since 1986, he recorded numerous albums and was featured on scores of 'live recordings' from various major events. Co-writing sometimes with his wife Tricia, their worship songs became used in thousands of churches around the world at the start of the third millennium AD. Indeed, his compositions traveled to more than 25 countries and to every continent. Yet, surprisingly he is not the author of all his album songs! When he writes songs such as 'There Is Power In The Name of Jesus', 'To Be In Your Presence', 'All Heaven Declares', 'You Laid Aside Your Majesty' and 'By Your Side', it is often said that it is a wonder why he has to dip into other people's repertoire!

Noel's childhood was spent in the Land of Song (Llantrisant near Cardiff, Wales) where he attended the local, lively Pentecostal church. Around the age of eight or nine years old, he became a Christian but made a more definite re-commitment at the age of fifteen. This decision coincided with the advent of a new church minister, John Glass, fresh out of Bible college. John really took an active role in discipling Noel. John was in his early twenties and became Noel's role model. Also, being a guitarist himself, he began to teach Noel to play, sing and present himself publicly. John acquainted Noel with the swelling contemporary Christian music scene in the UK. This was in 1971, the early days of new visionary organisations that gave birth to music ministries.

The first big Christian concert that Noel ever attended was at the Colston Hall in Bristol where Musical Gospel Outreach's Pete Meadows hosted an 'It's Buzz!' event. One of the artistes paraded was a young aspiring Graham Kendrick. As Noel watched him perform, he thought to himself, *"This is what I want to do!"*

Clearly, God planted a seed-of-vision in Noel's life at that juncture. His earliest singing opportunities came through his home church and his travel with preachers including John Glass and other young men. Tirelessly, they ministered in other churches. On one occasion, John introduced him to an associate who was organising the 'Youth for Christ' set-up in Bristol. Soon Noel became involved with schools evangelism and eventually entered into full-time Christian work.

Initially on leaving school, Noel worked in a drawing office for three years but found it incredibly boring! He then progressed to something marginally more interesting, selling toiletry products to supermarkets! However, all his excess time was consumed doing concerts. His day job was simply a way of making ends meet. When he was summoned to work full time with 'Youth for Christ', he went for it with great enthusiasm!

He recalled, *"I spent a year on-the-road going from mission to mission, event to event, on a very steep learning curve! But overall it was a good time! I had to learn a lot and did a lot of growing up.*

*I'm grateful to the people who had input into my life at that stage.
YFC leader, Clive Calver in particular was a great encourager!"*

Romantically, Noel met his pretty darling wife-to-be, Tricia on
his very first schools' mission in Plymouth in 1975 while working
with Phil Vogel (National Director of Youth for Christ). Tricia was
one of the senior girls at the first school he visited and was sent out
to meet him. She stood outside the school with a friend who was not
a Christian. As Noel walked across the car park, she said something
very strange to her friend, *"You see that guy there! I'm going to
marry him!"*

"She had never met me", says Noel, *"but obviously her prophetic
gifting was in operation! Three years later in September 1978, we
were married, going on to parent two children, Sam and Amy!"*
Noel and Tricia resided in Plymouth until 1980. Amid demanding
pressures, their local church grew quickly but they felt themselves
in need. Leadership was young and inexperienced. Their Church
had only one senior leader and eventually the workload proved too
great. Another church leader, Gerald Coates (from Cobham, Surrey)
came to their church several times to speak and it was to him that
they turned for advice. He suggested that the senior leader should
take a sabbatical. *"Why don't you let him come to Cobham for a
couple of years?"* Gerald said. *"Let the others continue to lead the
church in Plymouth and we can support and help them!"*

Everyone liked the idea of the senior leader's move but they also
wanted to remain a community too and be committed to staying
together. *"If one goes, we all go!"* was their response. Suddenly,
Gerald had the senior leader, the leadership team and congregation
all expressing a desire to move to Cobham, a small town just outside
the London area. The result was that they closed the Plymouth church
and fifty people moved to Cobham, 200 miles away! Hence, Noel,
Tricia and the others became part of Cobham Christian Fellowship
(now Pioneer People), led by Gerald.

"Imagine the shock", says Noel, *"of telling the Cobham
Fellowship that they were about to be invaded by about fifty people
from the other end of the country! They were around 200 people
then, so it was quite a large extra number to absorb! Cobham remains
our home base, after all those years. I led the worship team there*

from 1991 until 1996 and still regularly lead the church in worship. I've worked on a full-time basis with Gerald Coates from 1983 until the present time!"

In 1997, Noel and Gerald organised and hosted 'Champion of the World' at London's Wembley Stadium. Almost 45,000 people attended, the biggest contemporary worship event ever staged in the UK. Their vision is to *"summon the youth-of-the world and the young-at-heart"* to worship! As the new millennium dawned, it hailed Noel Richards as one of Britain's leading contemporary Christian songwriters with a diary full of major bookings to places throughout the world plus untold local churches throughout the UK.

There is power in the name of Jesus; we believe in His name.
We have called on the name of Jesus; we are saved! We are saved!
At His name the demons flee. At His name captives are freed.
For there is no other name that is higher than Jesus!

There is power in the name of Jesus, like a sword in our hands.
We declare in the name of Jesus, We shall stand! We shall stand!
At His name God's enemies shall be crushed beneath our feet.
For there is no other name that is higher Than Jesus!

Thief In The Night
Paul Field

"But, beloved, be not ignorant of this one thing,
that one day is with the Lord as a thousand years, and a
thousand years as one day.
The Lord is not slack concerning His promise, as some men
count slackness;
but is longsuffering to us-ward, not willing that any should
perish,
 but that all should come to repentance.
 But the day of the Lord will come as a thief in the night;
 in the which the heavens shall pass away with a great
noise,
and the elements shall melt with fervent heat,
 the earth also and the works that are therein shall be
burned up.
Seeing then that all these things shall be dissolved,
what manner of persons ought ye to be in all holy conversation and godliness,
Looking for and hasting unto the coming of the day of
God,
wherein the heavens being on fire shall be dissolved, and
the elements shall melt with fervent heat? Nevertheless we,
according to His promise,
look for new heavens and a new earth, wherein dwelleth
righteousness.

> *Wherefore, beloved, seeing that ye look for such things,*
> *be diligent that ye may be found of Him in peace, without*
> *spot, and blameless.*
> *II Peter 3:8-14*

Martin Luther is said to have had only two days on his calendar: 'today' and 'that day', 'that day' being 'the Day Of The Lord. In scripture, the 'Day Of The Lord' was an eschatological term referring to the consummation of God's kingdom and triumph over His foes and deliverance of His people. The Biblical teaching that 'the Day Of The Lord will come as a 'thief in the night' was the inspiration behind Paul Field's song 'Thief In The Night' popularised by Sir Cliff Richard and Sheila Walsh in the 1990s.

Paul Field in Bible study discovered that the 'Day Of The Lord' begins at the Second Coming. It will be accompanied by social calamities and physical cataclysms. It includes the millennial judgment and culminates in the 'new heaven and the new earth'. The 'Day Of The Lord' also speaks of God's judgment on all the nations including Israel.

Experts tell us that the Apostle Peter's reference to a future inferno to destroy the present cosmos is highly unusual. The Old Testament also speaks of fire in the 'Day Of The Lord'. Matthew's Gospel speaks of the future baptism-of-fire by the Messiah in which He will destroy the 'chaff'. Peter reasons that, just as in the old times God purged the then-existing world of Noah's day by His word and by water (the Flood), so in the future He will purge the world by His word and by fire.

Peter denounced the false-teachers' scoffing at the 'delay' of the Lord's coming. He reminds believers that in Psalm 90:4 we discern that 'a thousand years in God's sight are like a day that has just gone by, or like a watch-in-night'. God's on-going postponement of intervention is benevolent and compassionate; it is not caused by impotence or unconcern.

The Apostle Peter's letter reaffirms the Early Church's teaching that the 'Day Of The Lord' will come unexpectedly. Christ Jesus taught too that His Coming would be as unexpected as the coming of a thief, an analogy often repeated in the New Testament. In that catastrophic day 'the heavens will disappear' with a loud noise made by something passing swiftly through the air. Then in Revelation 6:14 and 20:11, the Apostle John teaches that the sky will recede 'like a scroll, rolling up', and the earth-and-sky will flee from the presence of God.

Paul Field's song, 'Thief In The Night' lyrically and musically points to the ominous disintegration of the universe that brings ethical implications to all mankind. This 'Day Of The Lord' focuses down to an individual challenge to every believing Christian. With respect to what is reserved for the world, the Apostle Peter demands of his readers, *"What kind of people ought you to be?"*

Inasmuch as the 'Day Of The Lord' will soon come to discipline the wicked and recompense the righteous, believers should live 'holy and godly lives'. Such holiness makes necessary separation from evil and dedication to God. A great motivating component of godly living is the contemplation of the prospective 'Day Of The Lord'.

Born in South London, England in1954 and raised in a caring Christian home, Paul Field attended the local Baptist Church where his Father played the organ and his Mother led the Sunday school. At the age of thirteen came his nervous introduction to performing before an adult audience. It initially came when he played music at his church in a trio formed with the minister's daughter and another girl-friend. Although he was composing his own songs by this time, they were not rooted in his own personal experience. Paul admits, *"I didn't have a very real understanding of what I was doing or what a Christian was!...The songs I was writing probably had the right lyrics but that was purely because of my upbringing. Most of my social life was in the church. It was easy to pick up the right phraseology and words."*

It was not until Paul attended an exciting church house-party at the age of seventeen that he says that he committed his life fully to Christ. His first music group (with Pam May and Heather Barlow) was called *Jesus Revolution*, a musical image of the Jesus Movement of that period of time. Their first album was released in 1973 although the group still retained their day-jobs as teachers. It was not until 1976 that they decided to go into their musical career full time with a name-change.

The group that became known as Nutshell began to tour extensively all over England and Europe followed by appearances on ITV's *Pop Gospel* programme. Nutshell featured Paul Field with two replacement singers, Mo McCafferty and Annie McCraig. Eventually, the group toured extensively with superstar, Sir Cliff Richard during 1979-80 and changed their name to *Network 3*. Despite success, it was not long after that the strains of being on-the-road started to impinge on plans. Then came the dawning realisation in the trio that things needed to change. Paul recalled, *"Purely and simply, the trio came to an end because it was meant to! There was a sense of disappointment, but it also felt like a sense of release for me. I think it's very hard for Christians involved in the arts to maintain a steady walk-with-God. A steady walk-with-God should be the core of a Christian's very existence!"*

Paul has since concentrated on being known more for his songwriting and producing abilities rather than as a performer in his own right. *"Writing is far more important to me"*, says Paul, *"and performing before smaller more intimate audiences causes one to be honest because you are not hiding behind the performance. The reason I still play concerts is that I want to share the gift-of-song that God has given to me. If there are things that people in the audience can find useful or beneficial in the songs then they can take them and use them in their own walk with God!"*

Paul Field, a deep thinker, agreed with the Apostle Peter's teaching that the contemplation of the coming 'Day Of The Lord' is a great motivating incentive to godly living and that is connected to the idea of speeding the coming Day. *"But, some ask, how can Christians hasten what God will do? The Apostle Peter would doubtless make reply by saying that prayer and preaching are the two prominent means to introduce people to repentance and thus to hasten the 'Day Of The Lord'."*

Study of the scripture (Acts 3:19-20) revealed that to the masses that thronged after the healing of the lame beggar at the Beautiful Gate in Jerusalem, Peter announced, *"Repent . . . so that your sins may be wiped out, that times of refreshing may come from the Lord, and that He may send the Christ"*. Paul Field noted that over and over again, Peter described this future 'Thief In The Night' will set off a series of events in 'Day Of The Lord' including a fiery disintegration of the very heavens of celestial bodies. *"Then after the ultimate resurrection, the concluding judgment and the regeneration of the heavens and the earth, this fated fleeting kingdom of Mankind will finally merge into God's Eternal Kingdom. Then the Lord will reign forever on the new earth."*

I could take for hours but you wouldn't hear a word your own opinions make you blind.
There will come a morning when the sand has all run out
There will be no time to change your mind.
Like a thief in the night He will come, there will be nowhere left you can run
You can fall with the night or you can rise with the Son
He will come in glory a rider in the sky The Lion and the Lamb rest side by side.
Children of the Kingdom He will gather to Himself
Children of the darkness He will leave behind.

Thou Didst Leave Thy Throne
Emily Elizabeth Steele Elliott & Ira Sankey

Let this mind be in you, which was also in Christ Jesus:
Who, being in the form of God, thought it not robbery to be
equal with God:
  But made Himself of no reputation, and took upon Him the
form of a servant,
  and was made in the likeness of men:
  And being found in fashion as a man,
  He humbled himself, and became obedient unto death,
  even the death of the cross.
Philippians 2:5-8

A dedicated, Victorian Anglican poetess, Emily Elizabeth Steele
Elliott was born in Brighton, Sussex, England on July 22nd 1836.
The daughter of the Reverend Edward Bishop Elliott (Rector of St.
Mark's Church, Brighton), Emily was the niece of the famed
hymnwriter, Charlotte Elliott who authored 'Just As I Am'.

Emily loved to compose sacred poetry but also, on the practical
side, had a highly developed social conscience. She nurtured an
interest in the charity work of the Mildmay Park Mission. For six
years she edited 'The Church Missionary Junior Instructor'. While
also serving at her father's St. Mark's Church in Brighton, she
dedicated herself to writing hymns for the local church services and
school. Her hymns included 'A Needy Sinner At Thy Feet', 'O For

A Heart To Praise My God' and 'Thou Didst Leave Thy Throne'. These were later published in books with grandiose titles, typical of Victorian days, such as 'Chimes of Consecration and their Echoes' (1873), 'Chimes For Daily Service' (1880) and 'Under The Pillows'. The latter book and others were published for hospitals and infirmaries for those that Emily described as 'the sick and sorrowing'. In Victorian and Edwardian societies and throughout the 20th century, Emily's poetic gem, 'Thou Didst Leave Thy Throne' gained wide popularity particularly at Christmas time. Emily died in Islington, London on August 3rd 1897, just over two years before the 20th century dawned.

Gospel singer, Ira David Sankey penned one of the tunes for 'Thou Didst Leave Thy Throne'. He was born on 28th August 1840 in Edinburgh, Western Pennsylvania. Ira Sankey lived into the 20th Century, dying on August 13th 1908 in Brooklyn, New York City.

Ira Sankey's 68 years, packed full of dedicated work, popularised a new style of gospel song designed to awaken the apathetic, melt the cold heart, and guide the honest seeker in repentance and faith to the Saviour of the World. As a *performer* of powerful revival songs, he became as effective a gospel communicator as his preaching associate, Dwight L. Moody. In his heyday untold multitudes heard Ira's richly inspired voice sing 'The Ninety And Nine', 'Under His Wings', 'Hiding In Thee', 'A Shelter In The Time Of Storm', 'God be With You 'Til We Meet Again' and 'Thou Didst Leave Thy Throne'. Since his time, such songs became well-beloved, evergreen classics of hymnology, recorded by countless performers. Indeed, Ira gave birth to many vocalising-successors. Subsequent decades saw many performers successfully fulfil their gospel-singing or song-leading ministries usually in the evangelistic arena.

Serving in the American Civil War that tore communities apart, Ira's regiment was deployed to Maryland. Christian services, held among the tents of the camp, called upon him to lead the singing. Soon he found several young soldiers with fine voices and a sense of harmony. A 'boys-in-blue' choir - led by Ira - was formed that gained neighbourhood renown. Ira said he owed his life to *divine protection* and to his *popular singing voice*. His closest call was while on sentry duty. He came into the rifle sights of a Confederate sniper. He almost fired but heard and was moved by Ira's beautiful, baritone singing. Instead the gunman lowered his rifle and the vulnerable Union soldier's life was spared for *a lifetime of gospel song*.

Leaving the army, Ira chose to return to Pennsylvania as a tax collector for the *Internal Revenue Service*. In the local Methodist Episcopal church, he was elected as superintendent of the Sunday school and leader of the choir. Soon his rich baritone voice began to attract attention and people would come from miles around just to hear his singing. Unbeknown to him during these years, he was unconsciously making preparation for his lifetime's work. Jovial and elegant, he was well known for his emaculate dress-sense. At the age of twenty-one, he met the challenge-of-a-lifetime at the '1870 International YMCA Convention' in Indianapolis. Up-and-coming preacher, Dwight L. Moody recognised Ira Sankey's God-given musical gift. Thus the powerful partnership was forged that was took Ira and Dwight all over the World.

Ira sang to hundreds of thousands before the stocky, no-nonsense D. L. Moody mounted the pulpit and preached. Initially, their audiences drew from the very poor of Victorian society. However, soon the audiences included members of Queen Victoria's Royal Family and America's President U.S. Grant himself. This relatively new phenomenon of 'white-gospel-music' professionals prospered essentially through the pious efforts of highly motivated, evangelistic singers after Sankey. Ira's *gospel music train* included Charles Alexander, Homer Rodeheaver, Gypsy Smith, the Blackwood Brothers, Cliff Barrows, George Beverly Shea and many more.

Ira is recognised as the greatest Victorian pioneer of inspirational sacred music, perhaps the greatest of all time. Much of the sacred music of the 20th century era was inherited from his dedicated labour. Sankey's story illustrated how useful gospel music could be. Ira believed ardently that in periods of 'sunshine-or-tempest', gospel music acted as a 'salt-and-light' both for individuals and society.

Not only a hymnal poet and performer, Ira Sankey also wrote impressive melodies such as the impressive tune to Emily Elizabeth Steele Elliott's 'Thou Didst Leave Thy Throne'. The song speaks clearly of the First Advent of Christ but also of His Second Advent.

Emily was fully aware that in scripture, Christ's various 'I Am' sayings asserted His 'pre-First Advent-existence' in terms of fellowship with the Father God. Indeed, she knew that the scripture stated that all created things came into being through Him and in Him continue to have their cohesive principle.

Emily was always excited to read that the Bible experts believed that manifestations of God in the Old Testament were of the preincarnate Christ. For instance, she said, when Isaiah glimpsed the glory of God, he was seeing Christ Jesus. Moses and the prophets spoke too of Him with special reference to His sufferings and the glories that would follow. Fully persuaded, Emily could clearly see that the prophetic predictions about Christ Jesus abounded. Emily declared, *"Then He came in the Incarnation to reveal God and to redeem people from their sins. Today the God-man is in heaven, representing the saints before the throne of God."*

Emily loved to hear her father strongly preach in church on the tried-and-tested subject of the Messiah. Speaking in authoritative, sonorous terms, his deep voice echoed around the historic Anglican Church rafters. *"My dear friends, one purpose of Christ's Incarnation was withheld for His second coming. There's coming a great day when His kingly rule will be introduced following His work as judge. Get ready to meet Him! His future coming is one of the major truths set forth in the epistles and is the leading theme of Revelation. Then after the 1000 year-millennial kingdom, Christ will enter with His people into the sanctity of our blessed eternal state! What a blessed day that will be! Heaven will be unmarred by the inroads of sin or death! Hallelujah!"*

Emily's 'Thou Didst Leave Thy Throne' described poetically how the long-heralded Christ came in the fullness of time. The humble birth of the Saviour was humanly-speaking a natural birth, but His conception was supernatural, by the power of the Holy Spirit. Emily clearly stated in her lyrics how Christ was not merely a messenger of God, like the ancient prophets, but more accurately the eternal Son of God now clothing Himself with human nature, yet free from any stain of sin. He manifested a divine and a human nature united in one person. His messianic message was that 'the kingdom of God' (the rule of God in human life and history) had come! This kingdom of God was both future and present. Emily's 'Thou Didst Leave Thy Throne' stressed how the free entrance into the present aspect of the kingdom comes solely through faith in Christ Jesus, the Son of God.

> *Thou didst leave Thy throne and Thy kingly crown,*
> *When Thou camest to earth for me;*
> *But in Bethlehem's home there was found no room for Thy holy nativity:*
> *O come to my heart, Lord Jesus! There is room in my heart for Thee.*
>
> *Heaven's arches rang when the angels sang,*
> *Proclaiming Thy royal degree;*
> *But of lowly birth cam'st Thou, Lord, on earth, and in great humility,*
> *O come to my heart, Lord Jesus! There is room in my heart for Thee.*
>
> *The foxes found rest, and the birds had their nest,*
> *In the shade of the cedar tree;*
> *But Thy couch was the sod, O Thou Son of God, in the deserts of Galilee.*
> *O come to my heart, Lord Jesus! There is room in my heart for Thee.*
> *Thou camest, O Lord, with the living word*
> *That should set Thy people free;*
> *But with mocking scorn, and with crown of thorn, they bore Thee to Calvary.*
> *O come to my heart, Lord Jesus! Thy cross is my only plea.*
>
> *When heaven's arches ring, and her choirs shall sing,*
> *At Thy coming to victory,*
> *Let Thy voice call me home, saying, 'Yet there is room, there is room at My side for thee.'*
> *And my heart shall rejoice, Lord Jesus, When Thou comest and callest for me.*

Emily Elizabeth Steele Elliott/Ira Sankey

Through It All
Andrae Crouch

*"And when they had preached the gospel to that city,
and had taught many, they returned again to Lystra, and
to Iconium, and Antioch,
Confirming the souls of the disciples,
and exhorting them to continue in the faith,
and that we must through much tribulation enter into the
kingdom of God.
And when they had ordained them elders in every church,
 and had prayed with fasting,
they commended them to the Lord, on whom they believed."*
Acts 14:22-23

Los Angeles-born in 1945, Andrae Crouch was not born-by any stretch of imagination-with a proverbial 'silver spoon in his mouth'. World War II was still raging on the Pacific front and the civilian USA was hard at work building battleships, tanks and warplanes for the military cause. Indeed, life's early experience was tough enough to give Andrae a considerable degree of 'street-sense'. His powerful song, 'Through It All' speaks of endurance amid all the adverse circumstances of life including persecution and tribulation.

In later years, an avid Bible student, Andrae discovered that the Hebrew and Greek words for 'tribulation' have a large variety of meanings in the scripture, but usually they refer to trouble of a general sort. As Andrae stated, *"Once in a while this suffering is just the natural quota of one's life while at other times it is looked on in the Bible as a definite discipline or chastening from the Lord for wrongdoing."*

Andrae agreed that Christ and the scriptures foretold that adverse circumstances-of-life including persecution and tribulation would occur to all believers. Christ taught that they should be calmly endure *through it all'*. Andrae stated, *"Persecution of Christians takes many forms and ranges from lying accusations to cruel unwarranted acts of violence. Praise God that Christ offers us all consolation and gives strength to persevere and endure through it all!"*

Persecution of Christians is not new to the 20th and 21st centuries, it was common in every century. To the Early Church of the first century, systematic persecution began with the oppressive Roman imperial government. Although prominently broad-minded and tolerant toward alien religious beliefs in general, the Romans clashed fiercely with the Christian believers over the formalities of Caesar worship. The reason was that Romans saw Emperor Nero as a divine god. Hence, he is now regarded in history as the Church's first persecutor. In 64 AD he utilized the small Christian community as a scapegoat for a cataclysmic fire in Rome, placing on all Christians the indictment of arson that was in truth popularly leveled against him. History records how the Early Church came *'through it all'* victoriously.

Piano-playing Andrae Crouch told me that he first received the divine call into the gospel music ministry at the tender age of eleven. About that time, his dear father - Rev. Benjamin Crouch - was managing a family cleaning business in east Los Angeles. He also preached on the streets of the city at weekends. From the converts, a church was forming and subsequently, Benjamin was called to take on the full time pastorship of the small church community. Initially, he was somewhat reluctant to take the position partly because the church did not have an available and competent pianist. Andraé remembered the time with a broad smile, *"My Dad called me up in front of the surprised congregation and asked me publicly that if God would give me the gift of music, would I use it for the rest of my life to His glory? When I said 'Yes!', he prayed for me and I knew right then that God was going to do something special in my life!"*

Within a week a tremendous miracle had taken place. Young Andraé was playing age-old hymns on his newly acquired piano. The instrument came as a gift from a local lady who felt led to donate it to the local church. Instantly, Andrae became the church's new pianist under his father's new pastorship. The fledgling church was zealous but poor. Therefore, the small congregation had no hymnals to sing from on Sundays. Seizing the opportunity, the resourceful Andraé used his God-given, personal ability to 'play-by-ear'. Using the piano, he pitched his new easy-to-sing songs to the surprised congregation and soloists. Very soon the gospel song material penned by Andrae increased in popularity not only in the local church but also beyond. His undoubted skills began to be noticed further afield.

Under the enthusiastic, evangelistic preaching of his father, Andrae was convicted of his sin and the need to gain peace with God through Christ. By faith, he become a 'born-again-Christian' one eventful Sunday night and says he has never looked back since. *"I remember,"* Andrae reminisced, *"I sat there in the church congregation listening under conviction. When my father finally gave the invitation in an altar call, I willingly went forward. I just felt so close to the Lord...I cried and cried...Then when everybody started singing, I was so happy! I started jumping around the church and split my new shoes!"*

Andrae continued with his basic education. Finally, with great expectations, he left college in 1965. Madly keen on music, he soon formed his own vocal group-The Disciples. Together, they enjoyed considerable local success in California and helped popularise Andrae's repertoire with the help of Hal Spencer of Manna Music Publishing Company. At about this time, the Los Angeles 'Teen Challenge Center' offered Andrae a position in their growing organisation. The work was a spin-off from the endeavours of the preacher, David Wilkerson. His successful work among the youth gangs of New York City was made famous by his book entitled 'The Cross And The Switchblade' later made into a movie starring Pat Boone in the David Wilkerson role.

Andrae's 'Teen Challenge Center' knew that work among drugs addicts would be tough and demanding. Consequently, he hesitated as he knew that his commitment to the Christian vision was not absolute. He remembered his fight to subdue his conscience and the call of the Holy Spirit. *"It took several months of soul searching before I finally ceased my struggle and committed his life wholly the Lord and His service. Joining Teen Challenge, I formed a choir (from among the drug addicts) that performed regularly in the Southern Californian area. While at Teen Challenge, the Lord really put a burden on my heart for needy people everywhere. I saw the good effect my music had on people that didn't know the Lord personally. So I began to write more songs that would be a blessing to others."*

At first national doors then international doors started to open. Soon Andrae's unique song-writing ability became appreciated from shore-to-shore in many areas of the globe's vast gospel music spectrum. Much of this success was due to the help gained from his song-publishing friends, Hal and Judy Spencer. It seemed as though Christian people everywhere fell in love with Andrae and his songs like "Bless The Lord" and 'Through It All'. Amazingly, the repertoire was as much at home in 'Southern Gospel' conventions as it was in his 'Black Gospel' music circles. Folk everywhere, whether in progressive or traditional churches, seemed to recognise Andraé's God-given ability to marry a heart-warming melody with powerfully subtle theological lyrics.

Thus his 'Andrae Crouch' songbook published by 'Manna Music' produced many of the 20th century's most familiar black gospel hit songs. The fine repertoire was recorded widely by countless artistes ranging from Elvis Presley to the Blackwood Brothers to Pat Boone to George Beverly Shea.

One of Andrae's earliest and most popular songs, however, remained 'Through It All'. The plaintive words of this modern hymn tells of how faith triumphs. God's love and compassion toward His persecuted peoples corporately and individually always succeeds.

The lyrics rally believers with a call-to-endurance *'through it all'*! Additionally, the song testifies-to and celebrates-in God's ongoing mercy and compassion displayed in the blessing of unending perseverance on His part.

*I've had many tears and sorrows, I've had questions for
tomorrow,*
There've been times I didn't know right from wrong;
But in every situation God gave blessed consolation
That my trials come to only make me strong.

Through it all, Through it all,
I've learned to trust in Jesus, I've learned to trust in God;
Through it all, Through it all,
I've learned to depend upon His Word.

I've been to lots of places, and I've seen a lot of faces,
There've been times I felt so all alone; But in my lonely hours,
Yes, those precious lonely hours,
Jesus let me know that I was His own.

I thank God for the mountains, and I thank Him for the valleys,
I thank Him for the storms He brought me through;
*For if I'd never had a problem I wouldn't know that He could
solve them,*
I'd never know what faith in God could do.

Till The Storm Passes By
Mosie Lister

*Now it came to pass on a certain day, that He went into a
ship with His disciples
and He said unto them, "Let us go over unto the other side
of the lake."
And they launched forth. But as they sailed He fell asleep:
and there came down a storm of wind on the lake;
and they were filled with water, and were in jeopardy.
And they came to Him, and awoke Him, saying, "Master,
Master, we perish!"
Then He arose, and rebuked the wind and the raging of
the water:
and they ceased, and there was a calm.
And He said unto them, "Where is your faith?"
And they being afraid wondered, saying one to another,
"What manner of man is this!
for He commandeth even the winds and water, and they obey
Him."
Luke 8:22-25*

Southern-gospel hymn-writer, Mosie Lister must have read many
times that God promised His chosen people protection in all the
storms-of-life. For instance, via the prophet Isaiah (4:5-6), He said,
"And the LORD will create upon every dwelling-place of mount Zion,

and upon her assemblies, a cloud and smoke by day, and the shining of a flaming fire by night: for upon all the glory shall be a defence. And there shall be a tabernacle for a shadow in the daytime from the heat, and for a place of refuge, and for a covert from storm and from rain."

After hearing a moving sermon in his local church on how Christ stilled the storm on the Lake of Galilee, the outstanding poet and composer, Mosie Lister took up the theme of the storms in believers lives and wrote 'Till The Storm Passes By'. It was a consoling anthem that was subsequently recorded by many artistes ranging from the Don Gibson to the Statesmen Quartet featuring Jake Hess.

A child of the 1920s, Mosie is undoubtedly one of the finest and most abiding of the Southern gospel tunesmiths of the 20th Century. Still very active in the Third Millennium, more than 500 wonderful sacred songs have streamed from his aesthetic pen. For many years, Mosie promoted the gospel-in-music as the tireless choir director of the Riverside Baptist Church in sunny Tampa, Florida, the town of his residence.

A few years later in the midst of the Civil Rights controversy of 1960s, Mosie received an unexpected phone call from an old acquaintance living in the 'Big Apple' otherwise known formally as New York City. The familiar voice was excited. *"Hey, Mosie have you thought about writing a song for Mahalia Jackson? She is such a quality singer, man! She's recording some great gospel albums on Columbia records and is always on the lookout for new repertoire!"*

Mosie's inventiveness was provoked. It was true that Mahalia was becoming a familiar face on television singing her sacred songs and spirituals. He had heard and seen her also on the news bulletins. There was little doubt that Mahalia's renown was expanding especially in the context of the times. Anxiety was swelling nationally over the Civil Rights issues.

For the American government, 1964 was a fearful year of social unrest and occasional violence as the issue of human rights continually took centre-stage across almost every high street in almost every state of the USA. Much overdue, tolerant legislation and determined municipal application was needed to redress the regressive human rights and social conditions of the South.

By this time, the adolescent musical taste of 'rock 'n roll' (coined by the legendary DJ, Alan Freed) was certainly in vogue popularising the black 'rhythm and blues' music of the South. Before the 'rock 'n roll' term was introduced, 'rhythm and blues' music was actually called 'race music'. Such demeaning racist terminology perplexed many including Mosie and was indicative of unchristian attitudes.

Mosie brought the troubles before the Lord in prayer. Consequently, he felt that God desired him to say something comforting and prophetic in a song. The outcome was the birthing of the song-'Til The Storm Passes By'. Ironically, Mosie at no time succeeded in getting Mahalia to record the song as she died soon after. Nevertheless, hundreds of diverse vocalists did record it. Their versions became blessings to millions of people predominantly in the USA during the difficult days of social division and civic unrest. Later Mosie said the great song was exported and became a blessing overseas even in countries as far away as New Guinea.

Mosie Lister ensured that his comforting theme of 'Till The Storm Passes By' harmonized with the words of the prophet Isaiah who described fellowship with God as a divine covert from the fiercest storm and from the driving rain. The prophet envisioned Mount Zion in Jerusalem as being elevated above the surrounding hills protected by the divine emblems reminiscent of the pilgrim journey of God's People out of Egypt to the Promised Land. These protective emblems represented God's glory and would not move, no matter what the provocation.

For God's people in every age, God's protective faithfulness was continually absolute just as it was during the Exodus. In the context of the present-day believers, in the future, Mount Zion is our 'journey's end'. The prophet Isaiah saw God's glory as providing a covering over all Jerusalem. This protective a canopy was reminiscent of that used for Jewish weddings and royal occasions. This divinely appointed canopy would continually provide protection, to the city's inhabitants, from the natural elements including rain and storm.

Born in 1921 in Cochran, Georgia where his beloved father was a singing instructor and choir director, Mosie Lister's elementary and secondary education qualifications were gained in Middle Georgia College where he majored in harmony and counterpoint, and arrangements for piano and organ. His first aspiring song was published at the age of eighteen years. Following national service, Mosie was additionally motivated by his darling wife to score music more seriously.

Consequently, from 1939 onwards, he accrued a relish for the discipline and fulfilment of songwriting, pitching his creative writing to the Atlanta gospel soloists, choirs and quartets of the late Forties. Before long he gained substantial radio experience.

By 1948, he was enthusiastic to discharge his gospel music 'on-the-road' in churches, theatres and schools. Initially, he was a vocal part of the early Statesmen Quartet line up with Hovie Lister (who was surprisingly no relation). Then after just a short time, he determined, following much prayer and consideration, to discontinue his gospel music on-the-road. Instead he decided to focus on songwriting forming the Mosie Lister Publications in1953. *"Looking back,"* he declared, *"I have written so many songs that even I have lost count!"*

He wrote 'Where No One Stands Alone', another one of his classics, in 1955. As Mosie was driving lazily down a north Georgia highway alone, he started to gently hum to himself in tempo with the rhythm of the car as he often did. Then without warning, inspired words-and-music percolated into the world of his gray matter as the chorus of 'Where No One Stands Alone' took shape. A year later, he wrote the verses inspired by the Psalmist David's words recorded in Psalm 27:9-10. Imagining himself in David's shoes, Mosie recalled the product of his meditation. *"Placing myself in David's frame of mind, the words to the verses of 'Where No One Stands Alone' came easily!"*

Ever since he was a child in Sunday school, Mosie was familiar with the story of how Christ quelled the storm on the Sea of Galilee. In his account of the calming of the tempest in his Gospel, Doctor Luke illustrated the powerful, authoritative word of Christ Jesus. Vividly Luke portrayed the Lord Jesus in complete control of His environment. However, the climax of the event comes not with the miracle itself but with the questioning of the disciples concerning the identity of the Master. It was a natural-setting miracle affirming Christ's sovereignty over wind-and-waves.

Christ Jesus' proposal to His followers, *"Let us go over to the other side of the lake"* should have guaranteed to the disciples that they would indeed conclude their voyage safely across the billows. The dread and incredulity of the disciples are in sharp contrast not only to the calm repose of their Master but also to the coolness-under-fire that they themselves should have had in the hour-of-trial. Their dread of being lost-at-sea is a prevalent mortal anxiety, representative of the powerlessness felt by an individual in the enormity of life's everyday circumstances.

Outstanding quality songs of Lister vintage include 'How Long Has It Been', 'Then I Met The Master' and, of course, 'Til The Storm Passes By'. It is perhaps Mosie Lister's most popular song, featured time and time again on the very successful Gaither Homecoming videos! In due time, this deserving songwriter was nobly initiated into the Gospel Music Hall of Fame. At the presentation, the playing of the recorded version by the Blackwood Brothers of Mosie's 'His Hand In Mine' forged part of the induction protocol. 'His Hand In Mine' was the classic title-song of Elvis Presley's first gospel album for RCA Victor recorded at the height of his high-flying career. Artistes who have recorded Lister materials through the years are legion but include BJ Thomas, Jim Reeves, Elvis Presley, Faron Young, Jan Howard, Jimmie Davis, Jimmy Dean, Webb Pierce, and Bev Shea. At the start of the new millennium, Mosie resided in Tampa, Florida. Even in old age, he still produced quality material and was a frequent guest-celebrity on the Gaither 'Homecoming' videos.

In the dark of the midnight have I oft hid my face,
While the storm howls above me and there's no hiding place.
'Mid the crash of the thunder Precious Lord, hear my cry,
Keep me safe 'til the storm passes by.

'Til the storm passes over, 'til the thunder sounds no more,
'Til the clouds roll forever from the sky, hold me fast, let me stand
In the hollow of Thy hand;
Keep me safe 'til the storm passes by.

Many times Satan whispered, 'There is no need to try,
For there's no end of sorrow; there's no hope by and by."
But I know Thou art with me, and tomorrow I'll rise
Where the storm never darkens the skies.

When the long night has ended, and the storms come no more,
Let me stand in Thy Presence on that bright, peaceful shore.
In that land where the tempest never comes, Lord, may I
Dwell with Thee when the Storm passes by.

To God Be The Glory
Fanny Crosby & William H. Doane

"Now unto Him that is able to keep you from falling,
and to present you faultless before the presence of His glory
with exceeding joy,
To the only wise God our Saviour,
be glory and majesty, dominion and power, both now and
ever. Amen."
(Jude 24-25)

History records that distinguished sacred music celebrities first appeared in abundance in Victorian times. Two of the greatest bridged the end of the 19th century and the start of the 20th century. Fanny Crosby epitomised the best of the newly evolving gospel songwriters, and Ira Sankey - the best of the gospel music performers. Both were still alive when George Beverly Shea, the soloist for Billy Graham was born in 1909.

Beyond any other sacred songwriter, Fanny Crosby captivated millions with her uncomplicated yet eloquent gospel songs. Miss Francis Jane Crosby was born on 24th March 1820. She died on 12th February 1915, just forty days before her 95th birthday, a year after the start of World War I in Europe. She followed two main personal pursuits. Firstly, she served the dropouts and drunks of New York's inner city missions. Secondly, she devoted herself to the ministry of transposing the great spiritual Bible truths into singable rhyme and melody. Fully persuaded of these truths, her life radiated humility and the quotation from her famous song –'To God Be The Glory Great Things He Has Done'! This was despite her songs outselling secular hits of her day such as 'In The Good Old Summertime', 'When You And I Were Young Maggie' and 'Silver Threads Among The Gold'. If there had been a pop chart in the music industry of those days, she would be a regular at the top!

A hero-of-the-faith, the Fanny Crosby story is often retold in church and Sunday school circles. Notwithstanding her blind affliction, never self-pitying, she lived out a remarkably normal life demonstrating confidence in Christ. A highly competent poet of worldwide influence with a stunning memory, her poems were composed and edited in her mind then dictated. She rose to be a personal friend and social guest of six USA presidents yet she humbly accepted merely about two dollars for each of her compositions, deliberately choosing to live simply and soberly.

Her many distinguished associates included such people as mass evangelist, Dwight L. Moody and his song leader-Ira Sankey. Her emotion-tugging songs translated into many languages attracted world attention via their meetings. Countless celebrated recording artistes of the 20th century articulated her song material, some of whom devoted entire concept albums to her compositions including Pat Boone, Eddy Arnold and George Hamilton IV. Her legacy was approximately 9,000 hymns and poems, over sixty of which are still in common church-usage throughout the globe in the third millennium. In spite of being physically blind, almost all of her songs refer to *seeing, watching and looking*. Her eyes-of-faith were always keenly vigilant and attentive.

Fanny Crosby turned tragedy to triumph as her visual disability drew her more closely to the Saviour she loved. Casting aside any thought of handicap, Fanny simply got on with her life! Using her talents for the Lord in the way she knew best, her first song appeared in print in 1828 when she was only eight years old! Even in youth, she evidently enjoyed closeness to her Saviour. This divine fellowship became the anchor of her life and her songwriting inspiration. She penned the song 'Rescue The Perishing' that speaks of the under-privileged and disadvantaged of society. She became a champion of second-class citizens knowing that a personal life-changing encounter with the Lord Jesus Christ could bring a new quality to any life. The Bible story of blind man Bartimaeus whom Jesus healed, was the basis of her beautiful song 'Pass Me Not O Gentle Saviour'.

She had every reason it seems to be bitter with her fortune. Born of humble stock in Putnam County (mid-way between Boston and New York City in New York State), baby Frances initially gazed around her, absorbing the colour and texture that surrounded her. Then tragedy struck...

Sadly, at six weeks old she developed an eye infection and the local unqualified doctor was urgently called. In error, he foolishly prescribed a hot mustard poultice to be placed on her inflamed eyes. This incorrect treatment blinded her for life. Despite the handicap, she was converted to Christ at an early age. Hungering and thirsting after spiritual truth, she wholeheartedly surrendered herself (including her so-called handicap of blindness) to her Saviour. In return, she was given two wonderful gifts. The first was 'spiritual sight'. With clear spiritual vision she gazed on truths that Christless eyes never see. Secondly, she was gifted with the ability to simply express the truths she perceived in rhyme and melody. Her life-long aspiration would be to serve the Saviour she saw clearly by faith.

Gathering every cent they could muster, her dear family plagued by guilt and remorse for what the medical blunder had done to her sight, sent the little blind lass to New York to see the noted eye surgeon, Dr. Valentine Mott. Perhaps, he could offer a cure for her blindness. After careful examination of her eyes, the surgeon turned to her parents and said, *"I'm sorry there's nothing I can do for this poor little blind girl!"*

She entered the New York School For The Blind at the age of twelve, becoming a very successful scholar. One of her teachers, Grover Cleveland later become a USA President. At the age of 27, she was invited back to become a teacher. It was there that she met the man who in 1858 was to become her husband, blind teacher and fellow musician, Alexander Van Alstyne.

Beset it seemed by so much false teaching and sin, Fanny Crosby often pondered, *"How could Christians ever reach heaven?"* The answer she said was only in 'the power of God'. Therefore she declared, *"To God Be The Glory Great Things He has done! Our salvation is entirely by His grace alone!"* Turning truth into poem, her musical doxology has surely become one of the greatest in hymnology reminding the listener of God's willingness and ability to bring every one of His own people safely to Himself. Quoting scripture, the old blind lady would say, *"My God is able to keep us all from falling and He is able to present us all before His glorious presence without fault with great joy...To God be the glory!"*

Born in 1832 in Preston, Connecticut, William Howard Doane scored the anthem-like tune. The song was first published in the 'Brightest And Best' songbook of 1875. Educated at the Woodstock Academy, he conducted the school choir at the age of fourteen. In his last year of school, he testified to 'coming to faith in Christ as his Saviour' at the Baptist Church of Norwich, Connecticut. As a young man, he did three jobs in his father's cotton manufacturing business. Later in 1860, he moved to Connecticut and joined the J. A. Fay Company who manufactured woodworking machinery. He rose to become president of the company. Later still, a beloved civic leader and benefactor, William served as superintendent of the Mount Auburn Baptist Sunday School in Auburn, Ohio and wrote about 2200 gospel song melodies, co-writing with many gospel poets. He died in South Orange, New Jersey on Christmas Eve 1915, the same year as Fanny Crosby.

Re-popularised by songleader, Cliff Barrows in the Billy Graham London Crusade meetings of 1954, the song was proposed to him by British clergyman, the Reverend Frank Colquhoun. He said that the Crosby/Doane song was objectively addressed to God, pointing out that the Father is 'the Saviour' as well as 'the Son'. He added that Fanny Crosby clearly understood that whatever the false teachers said, there is only 'one God and Saviour'. To God the Saviour, through Jesus Christ, belongs 'the glory'.

'Glory' is a word with so many associations and connotations, it is difficult to capture its fullness of glory. It speaks of radiance, splendor, majesty, greatness, transcendence, power and authority. Of course, God suffers no change and therefore His divine plan will surely be carried out. To Fanny Crosby, salvation was completely secure because God's own purpose stands firm and He is able to do all that He wills.

To God be the glory! great things He hath done!
So loved He the world that He gave us His Son,
Who yielded His life an atonement for sin,
And opened the life-gate that all may go in.

Praise the Lord! Praise the Lord!
Let the earth hear His voice!
Praise the Lord! Praise the Lord!
Let the people rejoice!
O come to the Father through Jesus the Son;
And give Him the glory, great things He hath done!

O perfect redemption, the purchase of blood!
To every believer the promise of God;
The vilest offender who truly believes,
That moment from Jesus a pardon receives.

Great things He hath taught us,
Great things He hath done,
And great our rejoicing through Jesus the Son:
But purer and higher and greater will be
Our wonder, our transport, when Jesus we see!

Fanny J. Crosby/William. H. Doane

Today I Followed Jesus
Erv Lewis

*'For I know that in my flesh dwelleth no good thing:
for to will is present with me, but how to perform that which
is good I find not.
For the good that I would, I do not:
but the evil which I would not, that I do.
Now if I do that I would not, it is no more I that do it,
but sin that dwelleth in me'. Romans 7:18-20*

Written by South Carolina hymnwriter, Erv Lewis' 'Today I Followed Jesus' has been recorded by many Christian artists in the USA as well as in far-flung places such as Sweden (Eric Anders), Wales (Bryn Yemm) and Northern Ireland (Eric Black). 'Today I Followed Jesus' speaks of being a disciple or a learner-of-Christ. In the scriptures, a disciple was a pupil of a teacher. For example there were the disciples of John the Baptist and disciples of the Pharisees, and even of Moses. 'Today I Followed Jesus', however, refers to the adherents of Christ Jesus. The song applied to the twelve apostles and to believers in general. Interestingly, the first century followers of Jesus were not called 'Christians' until the founding of the church at Antioch.

These Christians were known widely as disciples because they followed Christ Jesus in evangelism and in turn by making disciples of others. Being a disciple required personal spiritual growth. This was and is characterized by putting Jesus first in all things, by following His teaching and supremely, by displaying love for other disciples.

Erv Lewis was born in his old grandmother's old home 'way-out-in-the-country' at Hemingway, South Carolina on August 19th 1936. *"There was no hospital nearby and the only local doctor made house calls back then. Later my family kept re-locating to several towns in South Carolina as my father sought work. I attended first grade school in Charleston, South Carolina, second and third grades in Lake City, South Carolina and fourth grade through high school graduation in Hemingway, South Carolina."*

Erv's father owned a country store for a short while where Erv worked after school. For another period, he owned a farm where Erv worked summers and after-school gathering crops. Circumstances changed again as his father later worked for the US Postal Service and his mother worked in a retail store. Erv recalled, *"I worked in a retail clothing store after school and during summers until my last two years of high school. During those last two years I worked with a local photographer in his studio, becoming a commercial photographer."*

More education followed as Erv attended college at The Citadel, a military college in South Carolina. He married after completing two years of college then dropped out to go to work as an insurance salesman. *"I saw how difficult it would be to attain position in work without a college degree so I began taking educational courses, eventually leading to 'Associates in Industrial Engineering' and in 'Textile Engineering'. In 1954 I started work with a wool processing company called Wellman Inc and held positions in Industrial Engineering, Manufacturing Management, and Purchasing Management. I later earned a Master's Degree in Business Administration as a working adult from the University of South Carolina."*

Erv received no formal musical training, but started playing 'piano-by-ear' in his early teens. He became interested in guitar during college and began to tinker' around with it. Then, after college, he developed an interest in folk music, teaching himself how to play guitar by watching others and getting tips from anyone who would help. He was thrilled when he received an invitation to play and sing for a local civic club. Then quickly following came an invitation to appear on local television. That appearance led to a regular weekly booking on the local 'Showtime' TV program for three years. The exposure led to other invitations and, gradually, he began playing regularly at clubs and colleges around the Southeast USA gaining in demand as a folk entertainer.

Over the course of his musical career he appeared in just about all of the major folk music festivals in the USA (the Smoky Mountain Festival, the National Folk Festival, the Canadian-American festival, etc.). Erv remembered, *"I was the subject of three television specials featuring just me and my music and appeared on shows with Doc Watson, Merle Watson, Earl Scruggs, Randy Scruggs, Coleen Peterson, Guy Carawan and many others. Later I directed and produced the nationally recognized Canadian-American Folk Festival for eight years and received the 'National Communication's Award' for excellence in communication through music."*

After becoming a Christian in 1968, Erv began writing and playing Christian music and the musical career gradually changed from secular to Christian. Erv recalled, *"I was active as a secular folk-singing entertainer for several years before I accepted Jesus Christ as my Saviour and, like so many others in that music, wrote and sang songs about the world's ills and man's inhumanity to man. I was successful in music and in business, but could not find the satisfaction I needed. There was no peace in my life. Though I tried very hard to do so, I could not fill the void in my life through worldly pursuits. God and His Spirit worked with me through many channels including a local minister, Sam Anderson, who was also a friend; my wife who had already accepted Christ as Saviour and was a visibly and emotionally different person; and other Christian friends. Though I attended church regularly and was a model citizen in the community, I was spiritually lost. As I listened more and more to God's Word, I was convicted to seek a relationship with Him."*

Asked why he chose gospel music, Erv replied, *"After becoming a Christian I felt compelled to share my testimony and the gospel story with others. Since I was recognized as a musical artist, it seemed expedient to use music as one of the vehicles for that message. Simply stated, it was more important to me that I share the gospel story than to just entertain, as I would be doing through secular music. I was based in Johnsonville, South Carolina and was represented as a Christian musical artist by New World Productions. An active concert schedule ensued that included Christian clubs, churches and festivals. This was followed by television in many parts of the world including regular appearances on the 'Christian Broadcasting Network, with Pat Robertson on the '700 Club', and regular appearances on the PTL TV network as a musical guest on the 'PTL Club'.*

Six record albums and two songbooks (Singspiration Music and Benson Publishing) of Erv's work followed. He formed The Herald Association, a Christian music outreach that included publishing companies and a roster of fifteen Christian musical artists including Jerry Arhelger, Judy Herring, The Ruppes, Rick Eldridge and many others. Over the decades, Erv's songs have been recorded by many artists including George Hamilton IV, Judy Herring, Jerry Arhelger, Amy Roberts, Sandy Bond, Eric Black, Anders Erickson, The Providence Quartet, Woody Turner, the Harmonettes, Delores Taylor, Rick Eldridge, Johnny Sales, Sydna Taylor and many more.

Erv stated that like so many other young Christians, after his acceptance of Christ as his Saviour, he had the notion that he must work hard at living a Christian life. *"I felt that I should somehow deserve salvation. What a mistake that was! First of all, the temptations I believed would leave me did not go away. In fact, I became more acutely aware of them and I came to feel something of what the Apostle Paul must have felt when he wrote to the Romans in 7:15 '.....for what I would, that do I not; but what I hate, that do I.'"*

Lovingly, God continued to minister to Erv through the scriptures and he slowly came to realize that he would never be able to please God through his deeds. Erv clearly felt that the Apostle Paul summed it up very well in Romans 7:18-20 when he wrote, *"For I know that in my flesh dwelleth no good thing: for to will is present with me, but how to perform that which is good I find not. For the good that I would, I do not: but the evil which I would not, that I do. Now if I do that I would not, it is no more I that do it, but sin that dwelleth in me".*

Erv later declared that he was continuously amazed over the years at how God "sends the right message at the right time"! He realised that God let him come to grips with the fact that his salvation had nothing to do with his abilities. Instead, it had a lot to do with his availability. *"I came to realize that by grace are we saved through faith: and that not of ourselves: it is the gift of God. Looking back over the years, the search for these truths was intense, and sometimes confusing. But, the scriptures also teach that God is not the author of confusion, but of peace. Evidently, the confusion came from Satan, who knows more about our weaknesses and how to exploit them than we know ourselves!"*

Erv stated that Christians cannot arm themselves to deal with Satan's onslaught through some periodic infusion. It requires a daily, personal walk with Jesus Christ and the guidance of the Holy Spirit. *"That's the message of 'Today I Followed Jesus'. The walk is personal. A successful Christian life demands that the walk take place continually. As I sat down to finish the song I had the thought that, at the end of each day, I want to look inward and know that 'Today I followed Jesus'."*

My path through life was a lonely one,
With my trials I'd walked along with no way to rid my soul of guilt and shame,
And then my life crossed His and I heard Him gently say,
'Come to me, I'll make you whole again!'

And today I followed Jesus on a path made just for me,
And He led me gently up a hill to the base of a nail-scarred tree;
And there in that quiet place I met the Master face to face.
Today I followed Jesus and He led me to Calvary

My broken life has been born again,
Since Jesus took my sin and He nailed it with His body to a tree.
Praise God, He shed His blood to plunge me beneath the flood,
Of redemption on the cross of Calvary.

Erv Lewis/Silhouette Music

Until Then
Stuart Hamblen

"And I saw a new heaven and a new earth:
for the first heaven and the first earth were passed away;
and there was no more sea.
And I John saw the holy city, new Jerusalem,
coming down from God out of heaven, prepared as a bride
adorned for her husband.
And I heard a great voice out of heaven saying,
Behold, the tabernacle of God is with men,
and He will dwell with them, and they shall be His people,
and God Himself shall be with them, and be their God."
(Revelation 21:1-3)

By the latter 1940s, the fledgling evangelistic trio (Billy Graham, Cliff Barrows and George Beverly Shea) worked together in increasingly larger missions. In September 1949 came the famous Los Angeles tent meetings that catapulted Dr. Graham and his associates to national media attention. Secular Los Angeles was massive step-up from ministering in smaller 'Bible Belt' towns. Fashion, style and slick-efficiency seemed everywhere. The massive meeting tent, pitched at the junction of Washington Boulevard and Hill Street, became known as the Canvas Cathedral.

It was Billy Graham's first really major city crusade and overnight the Team trio was making national headlines. It caught the attention of James Blackwood of the Blackwood Brothers in far off Memphis, Tennessee. He told me, *"The meetings kicked up a storm of media attention and were headline news even in the South of the USA. Apparently, the famed newspaper publisher-William Randolph Hearst in Los Angeles- was so impressed by the Billy Graham phenomenon that he gave the instruction to all his newspapers to 'puff Graham' nation-wide! That meant provide positive nation-wide media publicity!"*

Because of the fruitful success, the three weeks of LA meetings were extended to eight weeks. News of Billy's powerful evangelistic preaching spread to every corner of the USA and even abroad. Attracted to the hyped newspaper publicity of the LA event was the locally well-known cowboy singer, Stuart Hamblen.

Born on 20th October 1908 in Kellyville, Texas, as Stuart grew, he loved the freedom of the open Texas range and the songs of the cowboys. Show business beckoned to the young man and soon he was making a name for himself as a very popular singer on the USA's West Coast. He came to great radio fame in the 1930-1940s during the golden age of Hollywood's singing cowboys. Movie stars such as Gene Autry, Roy Rogers, John Wayne, Tex Ritter, Rex Allen, Randolph Scott and the like were his close buddies. He rode alongside with them in their movies usually playing one of the bad guys! Songs such as 'Remember Me, I'm The One Who Loves You', 'Texas Plains' and 'My Mary' penned by Big Stu became established standards. Indeed, Hamblen material was regular repertoire for all the silver screen cowboys, the country stars of Nashville and the great crooners of the time.

Stuart's dear long-suffering wife, Suzy knew that drink-and-horses were tempting passions that led Big Stu into various moral pitfalls. She prayed that somehow he would be convicted in his conscience of his sin and waywardness of life. Intrigued by publicity, he finally attended a Graham meeting and heard the gospel challenge. Angrily stomping out of the tent, Cliff Barrows told me that Stuart initially responded to Billy's 'call to repentance' by literally shaking his fist in the face of the young blond evangelist.

Troubled, unable to sleep that night and deeply challenged in his conscience, Big Stu eventually decided to yield to the 'claims of

Christ'. In the middle-of-the-night, he phoned the hotel and asked Billy to pray and counsel with him. More publicity followed as the Graham Crusade and the Hamblen conversion hit the national headlines. As far as Stuart was concerned, his friends and foes were bitterly cynical! *"How long would it last?"* was their cynical question.

"But last it did!", said his western friend, Redd Harper, *"My cowboy buddy rode into sunset's old-age testifying to his new Christian lifestyle. Amazingly, it was clear to see that Big Stu was radically converted, changed dramatically for the better."*

In latter years, Stuart penned many quality sacred songs such as 'It Is No Secret', 'Known Only To Him', 'My Religion's Not Old Fashioned' and 'He Bought My Soul At Calvary' (recorded by hosts of top personalities including Elvis Presley, Sir Cliff Richard, Kate Smith, Stu Phillips, Pat Boone, Slim Whitman, Jo Stafford and many others). His best known composition was 'This Old House' that hit the charts big-time, decades apart via Rosemary Clooney (of Hollywood) and Shakin' Stevens (of Wales). Movie star, John Wayne gave his friend Stuart the idea for the song 'It Is No Secret'.

Stuart lived the rest of his years as a singing and testifying Christian pilgrim. From 1949 to his death decades later, Stuart said his greatest love was to sing gospel songs and tell what Christ had done for him.

Stuart's song, 'Until Then' beautifully anticipates the New Jerusalem. He said that the city's name was found only twice in the Bible, but that it is also called the Holy City. Scripture described it as coming down out of heaven from God. Indeed, the Apostle John received the vision of the new heavens, the new earth, and the New Jerusalem. 'Until Then' like innumerable productions of art and music have through the ages been inspired by this vision. John's imagery reflected the multiple Old Testament promises fulfilled in the New Jerusalem. At that future day, creation will be restored to its pristine character as God dwells with His people as in Eden. Significantly, there's an absence of death and suffering and the 'curse of sin' is removed.

Stuart Hamblen died in 1989 but he understood the connection of this heavenly vision with the promises to the Christian 'overcomers'. But the reality is now present only in a promissory way, not in actual fulfillment. Therefore, believers, like Abraham, are looking forward to the Holy City with foundations, whose Builder and Maker is God. This City and the new heavens and earth were also foreseen by the prophet Isaiah but Saint John's picture of the final age to come focuses not on a platonic ideal heaven or distant paradise but on the reality of a new earth and heaven, the believer's permanent home.

Stuart declared, *"God's abode will be among His people. This Holy City is not only humanity's eternal home but also the City where God will place His own name forever! The Bible reveals God will wipe away every tear from our eyes and finally liberate His people. Until that day, my heart will go on singing!"*

The cowboy songwriter recognised encouraging reassurance in the promise of heaven.

But ye are come unto mount Zion, and unto the city of the living God,
*   the heavenly Jerusalem, and to an innumerable company of angels,*
*   To the general assembly and church of the firstborn, which are written in heaven,*
*   and to God the Judge of all, and to the spirits of just men made perfect,*
*   Hebrews 12:22-23*

We'll Understand It Better By And By
(Trials Dark On Every Hand)
Charles A. Tindley

Blessed be God, even the Father of our Lord Jesus Christ,
the Father of mercies, and the God of all comfort;
Who comforteth us in all our tribulation,
that we may be able to comfort them which are in any
trouble,
by the comfort wherewith we ourselves are comforted of God.
For as the sufferings of Christ abound in us,
so our consolation also aboundeth by Christ.
And whether we be afflicted, it is for your consolation and
salvation,
which is effectual in the enduring of the same sufferings
which we also suffer:
or whether we be comforted, it is for your consolation and
salvation.
And our hope of you is stedfast, knowing,
that as ye are partakers of the sufferings,
so shall ye be also of the consolation.
II Corinthians 1: 3-7

A distinguished black Methodist pastor from Philadelphia, Pennsylvania, Charles A. Tindley wrote 'We'll Understand It Better By And By' as a means of helping Christians come to terms with trials, disasters and afflictions. These types of events are common to all mankind and assault the rich and poor, old and young, and the known and the unknown. After a fire had destroyed two million dollars worth of his equipment, the famous US inventor of the phonograph, electric light bulb and the electrical storage battery, Thomas Edison (1847-1931) stated, *"There is great value in disaster. All our mistakes are burned up. Thank God we can start again!"*

Experience and Bible reading taught Charles A. Tindley that, when trials are dark on every hand with disasters and afflictions, God is the Author and Giver of consolation. In 2 Corinthians 1: 3-4, the Apostle Paul generally followed his greeting to the church in Corinth with thanksgiving for the divine grace evident in the lives of his converts. In the letter, he offered praise to God for consolation and encouragement. He highlighted the aspects of God's personality that he had come to prize in deeper measure as a result of personal need and divine response, namely, God's limitless compassion and never-failing comfort. Indeed, Paul saw his suffering not merely as personally advantageous, driving him to trust God but also as directly benefiting all believers too.

The Apostle Paul felt that God's support, consolation, and fortitude in the midst of affliction equipped him to communicate the divine comfort to others in their trials, disasters and afflictions. He knew that the greater the suffering, the greater the comfort would be. Indeed, the greater the comfort is, the greater is the ability to share with others the divine sympathy under the Holy Spirit. As a minister of the gospel, Charles A. Tindley told his listeners that he actively prayed for the presence and support of God, and that the Holy Spirit may not be withdrawn in times of trials, disasters and afflictions. He would say, *"Brothers, even if we don't understand what we're going through, we can always turn to God for protection and preservation, and deliverance from troubles! Consequent to the Fall- trials, disasters and afflictions are visited upon us all. Man is born to trouble as the sparks fly upward! Are these things but temporary? They will one day end in joy and blessings in the glory of God!"*

Charles A. Tindley wrote both the words and the tune entitled 'We'll Understand It Better By And By'. He was born on 7th July

1851 (some books says 1856!) in Berlin, Maryland, USA. The poor son of slave parents, Charles and Esther Tindley, his early life was full of trials and tragedy. His mother died when he was just four years old leaving him in the care of his father. Moreover, a year later he was separated from his father too. He grew up not having any formal education and like many others of his generation could neither read nor write. Undeterred, Charles determined in his heart that he would just have to teach himself these skills. Therefore, he would collect written material of any kind he could find, even collecting scraps of newspaper from the roadside to take home and try and decipher the words for himself. His patience and dedication to the task paid off and he became known in his locality as 'the boy with the bare feet who could read the Bible'. He met and married Daisy Henry and together they moved to Philadelphia. He secured a job as a hod-carrier and later took up the position of a janitor of a small church. However, with education still on his mind, Charles attended night school to further his education. Sights were set even higher when he decided to also take a correspondence course from the Boston School of Theology.

Studies successfully completed, he was later ordained as a minister in the Methodist Church and joined the Delaware Annual Conference in 1885 serving in many towns as an itinerant pastor in the States of Delaware, New Jersey, and Maryland. Seventeen years later in 1902 he was appointed pastor of the Calvary Methodist Episcopal Church of Philadelphia in Bainbridge Street. By this time black Americans were slowly starting to impact on mainstream society in many spheres ranging from show business to politics. Indeed, 1902 saw the black fun-song 'Bill Bailey Won't You Please Come Home' hit the best-sellers list, and President Teddy Roosevelt state that skin colour was no bar to public office.

Coincidentally, Calvary Methodist Episcopal Church was the very same little church where Charles Tindley had once been the janitor! Under his leadership the church began to outgrow its premises and so a new building was built to accommodate the burgeoning congregation. The new building was finished in 1924 at Broad and Fitzwater Streets where he preached the gospel to thousands of people. The church was named later renamed the Tindley Temple

Methodist Church, in his honour.   The congregation was multi-cultural in its congregation, with both black-and-white folk serving in positions of authority in the church. Reflecting the neighbourhood it served, there were also lots of Italians, Jews, Germans, Norwegians, Mexicans and Danes among the congregation. Charles noted that 1924 was a key year in the evolution of black roots music particularly jazz. Composer, George Gershwin, best known previously for his song, 'Swanee', was the sensation of New York City in February when with jazz band and piano, he introduced 'Rhapsody In Blue'. He said that the piece was a *"kaleidoscope of America, our pep, our blues, and our metropolitan madness"*.

There was more than a hint of jazz in the music of Charles Tindley too. Although he was well known for his eloquent sermons, he would intersperse them with new self-penned gospel songs and choruses. During the singing of these songs, Charles would encourage and lead the congregation to join in with him. This type of service became known as a 'gospel songfest' by the 1950's. In the 1920s, however, black gospel music was successfully being commercially sold via groups such as the Jubilee Singers. Their recordings for the 'Paramount' record label included Charles Tindley's 'Stand By Me'. His original version of 'We'll Understand It Better By And By' was slightly amended in 1940 by B. B. McKinney for inclusion in the 'Broadman Hymnal'.

As well as 'gospel songfests', Charles has also been credited as being the first person to combine black-folk imagery and blues-formats-and-styles with spirituals and classic hymn themes. He thus created an entirely new genre in Christian song. It was not yet fully recognised as gospel music, but when sung by artistes such as Marie Knight, Roberta Martin, Washington Phillips and even Louie Armstrong, his songs become like the contemporary gospel songs of today.

To communicate the gospel in the best possible way to his congregation, Charles would use tuneful melodies and harmonies, provoking his people to worship fully. He would often take a passage from the Bible and translate it into everyday language that people could relate to and sing along to. He would also tell a story or bring out a strong moral point using his songs.

Charles was also acutely aware of the low standing and of the lack of respect that his fellow black Christians had to endure at that time. Consequently, he would encourage them by incorporating their everyday struggles as themes of spiritual conflict in his new songs. Thus his repertoire could be sung by anyone and be given individual interpretation in delivery.

His first published collection of hymns and songs came out in Philadelphia in 1916 entitled 'New Songs of Paradise'. His jazz-influenced gospel songs were also included in a hymnal specially written for black congregations called 'Gospel Pearls'. He wrote such favourites as 'Stand By Me', 'Nothing Between', 'I Have Found at Last A Saviour' and 'Leave it There'. In 1902, Tindley wrote the song 'I'll Overcome Some Day'. The obvious meaning and spirit of the song was to be the inspiration behind the 1960's anthem of the Civil Rights Movement entitled 'We Shall Overcome'. The first verse reads, *"I'll overcome, I'll overcome, I'll overcome some day. In my life I do not yield, I'll overcome some day."*

Charles Tindley was also to influence another great black gospel writer of the 20th century, Thomas Dorsey. It has been said that more than any other, Tindley inspired Dorsey to become a gospel songwriter. Charles Tindley was a great champion for the civil rights of black Americans right up to the day that he died. He passed away on July 26th 1933 in Philadelphia, Pennsylvania at the height of the Great Depression that impoverished millions of black citizens due to loss of jobs. A few days later, President Franklin D. Roosevelt ordered $75 million to be spent on clothing and the feeding of the unemployed as his 'New Deal' began.

For we know in part, and we prophesy in part.
But when that which is perfect is come, then that which is in part shall be done away.
When I was a child, I spake as a child, I understood as a child, I thought as a child: but when I became a man, I put away childish things.
For now we see through a glass, darkly; but then face to face: now I know in part; but then shall I know even as also I am known. II Corinthians 13:9-13

We've Come To Worship You, Lord
David Moody

> '*I will give thanks to You, O Lord,*
> *call upon Your name and make known to others what You*
> *have done.*
> *I will sing to You, sing praises of You,*
> *and tell of all Your wonderful acts!*"
> *1 Chronicles 16:8-9*

Songwriter, David Moody was one of the three Moody Brothers from Charlotte, North Carolina who gained international acclaim in the latter quarter of the 20th Century with what they called their 'Americana Music'. They performed in many distinguished venues such as Wembley Arena (London), the White House (Washington DC) and Disneyland (Paris). The trio's undoubted talents earned them two Grammy Award nominations and three 'International Country Music Association' awards.

Dave and his brothers started in the early 1970s performing on their parents' local TV show in their hometown of Charlotte. Dave himself made his first stage appearance at the tender age of four! His Methodist minister father, Dwight L. Moody Jr, himself a old-time fiddle player, taught all his sons to play musical instruments. Dave recalls, *"Music was everywhere in my family. It was our life and livelihood!"*

At sixteen years of age, Dave headed up a folk band in Carolina. Whilst studying American History at the University of North Carolina, he developed an educational programme aimed at primary school age children. Geared to teaching American History using the medium of folk music, it was widely used throughout the State. After college, he went on to teach American History at Independence High School in Charlotte for several years. During this time, the Moody Brothers gained a recording contract and went on to Grammy Award nominations and a Gold Disc. They were closely involved in the 'Take Pride In America' campaign from 1987-1992, serving as national spokesmen and performing twice at the White House for two Presidents, Ronald Reagan and George Bush.

Dave left the Moody Brothers to concentrate on a solo gospel music career. His first gospel album 'I Will Follow You', recorded in Nashville and Charlotte, showcased his many musical talents-vocals, acoustic guitar, electric guitar, dobro, lap slide guitar, mandolin, dulcimer, percussion, bass and keyboard! Such instrumental prowess made Dave a popular session musician on recording sessions being featured B. J. Thomas, Paul Overstreet, Radney Foster, George Beverly Shea, Charlie Daniels, Johnny Cash, Doc Watson, Thrasher-Shriver, and the Dixie Chicks, among others. Dave testifies, *"God has truly blessed my life! At every step of my career, when one door seemed to be closing, we'd trust God to show us the way...and another opportunity would present itself. It is great to be singing and playing for the Lord. I feel God has truly led me to this point in my life - opening and closing doors at every turn."*

The music director of 'Praise Street Music' (a company dedicated to provide new 'praise and worship' music to churches worldwide), Dave Moody declared, *"'We've Come To Worship You Lord' was written as I was preparing to record my first solo CD entitled 'I Will Follow You'. It was in the morning, as our family returned from our Methodist church just outside Charlotte, North Carolina. I begin to play my guitar in our sunroom. I had heard several powerful messages in the weeks prior to this Sunday by various ministers including Glenn Wagnor, Lynn Upchurch and Wayne Detzler where they had all talked about how we should seek to become complete worshippers of God in all that we do, praising and worshipping*

Him not only on Sunday, but in everything we do - everyday! The song was finished in minutes, as it seemed to be my personal extension of the service and response to God that day. Worship is a loving act of a willing heart. Sincerely, we honour, reverence, and pay homage paid to Christ. Worship is an old English word meaning 'worthship' and denotes the worthiness of the Lord Jesus, the One deserving of receiving the special honour. We give God the praise for all!"

Dave met his pretty wife, Susan (nee Davis) in 1981 while he was a musician and she was working in the costume department at 'Carowinds' (a theme-park similar to Disney on the border of North and South Carolina). They were married in 1984. Their son, Joshua was born in 1988 followed by a daughter, Rebecca in 1992. The Dave Moody family (Dad and the kids) often performed and ministered together in churches throughout the USA. Joshua became more and more efficient on bass, drums and guitar, while Rebecca honed her singing skills piano-playing. Meanwhile, Susan worked behind the scenes, running 'PowerPoint' picture presentations of the ministry, as well as coordinating events.

With his wife Susan, Dave launched 'Word On The Street Ministries' in 2001 with the help of their friends, the Bryan family - Dana and Pam. Dave stated, *"Our purpose behind 'Word On The Street Ministries' was to reach non-Christians in their own environment through music and God's word. We want to reach them just as they are and just where they are! We basically create music festivals in cooperation with local churches and other outreach organizations on the streets of the USA, Canada and Europe. We want to celebrate the love of Christ. In 'Word On The Street Ministries', Christians can learn to 'share Christ' with neighbours and friends, We desire to teach local churches to reach out beyond their four walls. In this way, we hope to share the Good News of Christ with people who are searching for answers in a world that has left them empty and longing for more."*

Susan recalled, *"When we started, we focused on several Bible verses as guideposts for our daily lives and our young ministry. As we looked at them, many of them focused on giving thanks, praising and worshipping our Lord for all that He has done for us. One of our favourites was from King David's 'Psalm of Thanks' in 1*

Chronicles 16:8-9. The verses say, 'I will give thanks to You, O Lord, call upon Your name and make known to others what You have done. I will sing to You, sing praises of You, and tell of all Your wonderful acts!"

In 2002, Dave Moody was nominated in the Gospel Music Association's 33rd Annual Dove Awards for his tribute to the legendary guitarist Chet Atkins. The project entitled 'Will The Circle Be Unbroken' was nominated in the 'Country Recorded Song of the Year' category. The Dove Award nominations were voted on by the 5,000 members of the GMA, an association dedicated to educating the public and the music industry concerning the mission and role-of-gospel-music in the world. The GMA's Dove Awards, annually recognises achievements in various genres of Gospel music via its premiere television show. Dave expressed his joy in being nominated. *"It was an honour just to be nominated! It's wonderful to be recognised this way by ones peers in the industry. It is truly a great feeling. 'Will The Circle Be Unbroken' was recorded as a tribute to Chet Atkins after his death in 2001. It was my way of saying 'thanks' for all the years of inspiration he brought to me and so many other musicians around the world."*

Earlier in the summer of 1999, Dave Moody led a group of enthusiastic Christian musicians on a mission trip with the Reverend Dana Bryan to sunny Northern Spain. According to Dave, numerous Spaniards made commitments to accept Christ during the activities! As well their listeners, the trip proved a major influence on the missionary team too. Many on the team chose to go on more mission-outreaches at home and aboard. Dave is clear about the value of Christian music in evangelism. *"Message Music can influence someone's life forever. My missionary trips truly altered my perception helping me realise how I can best utilise my talents to bring people into the acceptance of Christ in their lives!"*

Back home, Dave continues to lead worship at various churches, and teach praise-and-worship teams to reachout through various styles of music. Supremely, he says that he encourages who he calls 'pre-Christians' to seek God the truth of God in their lives. Lastly, he still finds time to produce Southern gospel albums with his friend Wesley Pritchard of the Gaither Vocal Band.

We've come to worship You Lord and praise Your Name
We've come to lift our voices high and proclaim
That we will follow You today, Oh Jesus guide our way
We've come to worship You Lord and Praise your Name
We've come to worship You Lord and praise Your Name.

We've come to worship You Lord here on our knees
We've come to bow before You now humbly
Now we offer You our praise, for it is us you came to save
We've come to worship You Lord and praise Your Name,
We've come to worship You Lord and praise Your Name.

We praise Your Name,
There's so much we're thankful for
We praise Your Name as well call to You our Lord.

We've come to worship You Lord and praise Your Name
We've come to lift our voices high and proclaim
That You are truly God with us, our Emmanuel Jesus
We've come to worship You Lord and praise Your Name
We've come to worship You Lord and praise Your Name.

David Moody ©1999 Mallie B Music (BMI),
P. O. Box 1636, Indian Trail, NC 28079 USA
Used with permission

We Shall Behold Him
Dottie Rambo

And it shall come to pass in that day,
that I will seek to destroy all the nations that come against
Jerusalem.
And I will pour upon the house of David,
and upon the inhabitants of Jerusalem,
the spirit of grace and of supplications:
and they shall look upon Me whom they have pierced,
and they shall mourn for Him, as one mourneth for his
only son, and shall be in bitterness for him,
as one that is in bitterness for his firstborn.
Zechariah 12:9-10
Behold, He cometh with clouds;
and every eye shall see Him, and they also which pierced
Him:
and all kindreds of the earth shall wail because of Him.
Even so, Amen.
I am Alpha and Omega, the beginning and the ending, saith
the Lord, which is, and which was, and which is to come, the
Almighty.
Revelation 1 :7-8

'We Shall Behold Him', written by Kentucky-born-and-bred Dottie
Rambo, is an engaging truth that she heard first in Sunday school in

her home church as a child. Her minister declared, *"One day in the future will be heard the dramatic cry: 'Look, Christ is coming!'...And we shall behold Him!"*

The expressive preacher went on to emotionally declare that even in the Old Testament, there is the oft-repeated pronouncement of Christ's coming rule over the all the earth's kingdoms. *"More so"*, he said, *"the New Testament teaches that we Christians will share in His messianic kingdom!"*

A Grammy winner and multiple Dove award-winner, Dottie was considered by her peers as one of the most inspired Christian songwriters of her time. Scores of beautiful songs are credited to her including 'He Looked Beyond My Faults' (set to the tune of Northern Ireland's beloved 'Londonderry Air') and 'If That Isn't Love'. She was elected as a member of the 'Gospel Music Hall Of Fame' and the 'Southern Gospel Music Hall Of Fame' (which is located at Dolly Parton's theme park Dollywood in Pigeon Forge, Tennessee. As a songwriter, she has written over 2,500 songs recorded by Elvis Presley, Whitney Houston, Jerry Lee Lewis, Dottie West, Barbara Mandrell, The Oak Ridge Boys, Johnny Cash and many more. The ASCAP Foundation awarded Dottie with their prestigious 'Lifetime Achievement' award in 2001. As a recording artist, she recorded over 80 albums over a career spanning almost fifty years at the turn of the new millennium.

In the 1970s and 1980s whoever had the opportunity to attend a Singing Rambos' concert in a church, hall, arena received a triple treat. On stage, the Rambo family represented a wide spectrum of sound that uniquely showcased three shades of gospel music - country, soul, and contemporary. In addition they cleverly interwove the traditional and modern sounds into a unique, blended sound. The Rambos special sound of gospel was a soul-penetrating, soft-ballad style, tailored to a classic, close-country-harmony pattern.

The 'Daddy-of-the-family', Buck roamed the world of country-gospel; the 'Mother-of-the-family', Dottie searched the deep-running reaches of gospel-soul; and their daughter Reba, added the third dimension with Bible-anchored, contemporary gospel material.

Although Dottie Rambo is now recognised as one of America's top Christian songwriters, surprisingly she readily admits her humble start. Additionally, she says that she cannot read or write a note of music, and she doesn't make any big secret of it either! *"I was really shocked the first time that I was asked to teach at the Stamps School of Music. I couldn't believe that they would want to hear me because I don't know anything about the technical part of music. When I explained this to the directors, they still insisted I talk about the beautiful inspiration of God in my songwriting. I suppose one reason that God has so abundantly blessed me with my songs is because I have always been so eager to share what He gives me with others. When I have written a new song, I can't wait to sing it for someone and tell the circumstances surrounding the song. Most of my songs come from actual experiences. It makes the pain, the trouble, the disappointments of life somehow seem worthwhile. After they are over, God sweeps my soul like a clean refreshing rain sweetens the earth, and inspires me to write lyrics that I could never think of on my own. Sometimes when I have finished a song that has a very special meaning to me, I sit and look at it and think, 'I didn't write this, I couldn't have!' So often I just say that I take dictation from the Lord. He writes my songs."*

Dottie states that most of the time when that 'cool freezing' feeling of inspiration comes to her, she remembers the first time she felt it. At the time, she was sitting with her feet dangling in the small brook behind her parents' Kentucky home. She was then nine years old. At other times, she says that she can still almost hear the deep, yet faltering voice of her dying eighty-seven years old Grandfather, who was a blind minister, saying, *"Little Dottie, make Jesus a good soldier when you are older and come to know Him!"*

In addition to its undoubted singing talents, the Singing Rambos' group members were also quality musicians. Buck played rhythm guitar, Dottie lead guitar and Reba classical guitar and percussion. Originally, the initial group first consisted of just Buck and Dottie. Then in due time, they were joined by daughter, Reba. Dottie recalls their start with a smile. *"When we first started singing, we worked with guitars. The regular quartet groups laughed at us and said that we'd never make it with guitars. We're still working with guitars today, and so is almost every other major group in Christian Music!"*

Dottie states that the spiritual emphasis of their song-material was always the most important aspect of their work. Indeed, they formed the Rambo Evangelistic Association to make the point accordingly in the mid-1970s. As Buck once said, *"We feel the Rambos are a ministry in gospel song, and all that we want is the opportunity to reach out for the lost, the weary, the broken-hearted and the wayward souls and say the thing that we think will inspire them to grasp the only permanent solution to their problems is Jesus Christ."*

In 1967 at the height of the Vietnam War the three Rambos decided to cross the Pacific to visit the Allied troops on the front lines. Seemingly, they became the first gospel music messengers to entertain the troops in that war-torn land. The tour literally took them to within seven miles of the DMZ (demilitarized zone) line, landing in aircraft for the scheduled concerts. The homesick troops reacted enthusiastically and gave the visitors standing ovations at the climax (and often at various other portions) of every concert.

As well as overseeing the Rambo Evangelistic Association for many years, Buck managed the Rambo Music Publishing company too that enriched the Christian music field with many fine songs recorded by diverse artists from the religious and secular fields. Artistes included Elvis Presley, Dolly Parton, Pat Boone, Connie Smith, Andrae Crouch and Jerry Lee Lewis.

The group, right from the start, made it a priority not to try and emulate any other gospel groups in style and kept their uniqueness by only singing material written by Dottie or Reba. Dottie stated, *"Our goal was always to be creative. That is why the Rambos didn't use songs that other artists recorded. Usually every album of ours was new material. We believe people liked to hear new material as well as old."*

Always trendsetters, the Rambos were the first to dress the girls in long dresses to protect their modesty due to high stages they were called to perform on! They were also among the first to work primarily by themselves. *"To be the first in any business means to be original. But originality without the Spirit of God and a definite calling from Him in anyone's life and heart would be putting the cart before the horse."*

Born in Madisonville, Kentucky in 1934, Dottie was one of eleven children. By the age of eight years, her poems were being performed to her mother as she busied herself cooking in the kitchen. As Dottie grew and read the scriptures for herself, she understood that Christ's coming 'with the clouds' would be supernatural and openly known to all. With guitar-in-hand, she wrote 'We Shall Behold Him' in 1981 in Ohio while traveling to a meeting in a car. Her friend was driving as Dottie put the song together. Clearly, historically-speaking, she understood that 'openly known to all' included those who pierced Him and were directly responsible for His death such as Pilate, Annas, and Caiaphas and the other Roman and Jewish leaders of the Sanhedrin who proclaimed Him guilty. The Bible attests that when He comes, there will be mourning among 'all the peoples of the earth'. As Dottie said, *"Every eye, even to those who put Him to death will behold Him... 'We Shall Behold Him' speaks of the divine promise of Christ's return, given by the Father."*

In every succeeding generation since the great promise was given, often amidst the oppression and suffering of believers, the promise brought hope to believers. Little wonder that prophets, preachers and congregations, empowered in their royal and priestly status, cry out the words, *"So shall it be! Amen!"*

Dottie said that she loves to read the word of God. She said that in the closing verses of the Bible, God Himself has spoken and, with His own signature, vouches for the truthfulness of the Coming of Christ. God's spectacular promise of Christ's Return comes with more than the prophet John's own signature or even Christ's "Amen!", it comes with God's guarantee. Jesus Christ is The Lord Of History! All the many names of God reveal His multi-sided character and commemorate His great deeds. Christ declared Himself to be 'Alpha and Omega' (the first and last letters of the Greek alphabet) or in other words, the 'First and the Last'. Further more, He declared Himself to be the 'Beginning and the End'. He is the absolute source of all creation and history, and nothing lies outside Him. Thus He is the 'Lord God of all', the One who is, and who was, and who is to come! Indeed, one day in the future will be heard the dramatic cry: *"Look, Christ is coming!"* ...And we shall behold Him!

Sadly, the Rambo family split-up before the close of the 20th century but Dottie continued to write successfully. In 2002, she teamed up with country music legend, Dolly Parton in the recording studio dueting on an up-tempo gospel tune written by Dottie. The pair originally met in the 1960s. Dolly stated, *"Dottie Rambo is a special and precious person. I have always loved her and her writing. I think she is one of the most incredible writers of our time or anybody's time!"*

Immediately after the tribulation of those days shall the sun be darkened,
*   and the moon shall not give her light, and the stars shall fall from heaven,*
*   and the powers of the heavens shall be shaken:*
*   And then shall appear the sign of the Son of man in heaven:*
*   and then shall all the tribes of the earth mourn,*
*   and they shall see the Son of man coming in the clouds of heaven with power and great glory.*
*   Matthew 24:29-30*

We Will Glorify The King Of Kings
Twila Paris

*"Whoso offereth praise glorifieth Me:
and to him that ordereth his conversation aright
will I show the salvation of God."*
Psalm 50:23

Hymnwriter, Twila Paris always believed that Psalm 50 was a psalm that speaks of a believer's grateful heart and true loyalty to God. Such loyalty was incompatible to formalism and hypocrisy in worship. As Twila stated so clearly, *"When we glorify the King Of Kings, the Lord requires hearts of gratitude. God's relationship with us, His people is very special to Him."*

Twila healthy Christian family heritage, she stated, was the clue to her strong motivation. *"My dear Father was an evangelist and pastor, one of a family of ministers!"* Twila's preaching-father was often heard by her, expounding the scriptures to his congregation. He declared that God's covenant people were consecrated by covenant and sealed by 'the blood of the covenant'. Unlike the pagan religions, God needed naught from His subjects. Indeed, He did not even need offerings, not even specifically dedicated ones. God's desire was that all worship signified true thankfulness and exultation from the worshipers. The message of the psalmist was that the whole complex world belongs to Him! Therefore, the question should be asked, *'What are the tens of thousands of animals from Israel's folds and pens compared with the millions of living things in the forests and fields, on the hills and mountains, that already belong to him?'*

As she grew, Twila came to understand that God always desired sweet communion with His people inviting them to enjoy His presence. Offerings to Him were to reflect true love and thankfulness not a spirit of self-sufficiency. Despite their shortcomings, God's grace was apparent to His people in His patience. Though they continued to have problems, he was still patient with them. Constantly, He invited them to repent and to devote themselves to lives of godliness. Those that heeded the word of prophecy and honoured God witnessed the fullness of His salvation and glorified God accordingly.

The psalmist David was one who heeded the word, honoured God and glorified Him. Not only did King David write lyrics that still soar after thousands of years, he was also a gifted musician who played his instrument as worship-to-the-Lord. His music lifted the spirits and calmed the hearts of those around him. Twila, the writer of 'We Will Glorify The King Of Kings', declared, *"Using David as our example, I hope and pray that my music will inspire worship in the listener's spirit, lighten his heart and minister peace."*

Early in years, Twila Paris committed her voice and life to worship-and-praise. In the process she gained several Dove Awards including 'Female Vocalist of the Year'. Her songwriting sensibilities and fervent faith made her an inspiration to millions. Yet even though Twila made her mark singing and writing about the 'presence-of-God' in lives, there were times when the songstress said that she found Him distant as she searched for God's answers to her own questions about life.

After fifteen years of marriage, Twila and her husband, Jack Wright had come to terms with the disappointment of the possibility of never experiencing parenthood. She confided, *"My mentality was that there was only a couple of minutes left on my biological clock. So parenthood wasn't completely out of the question. I was grappling with childlessness. I remember there were times when I thought that my calendar was out of whack. It was getting way behind. All my friends had two and three children and I don't have any! But God had a calendar too and His was much bigger than ours. He never gets behind.''*

Twila and Jack Wright prayed that God would do what He knew was best. Hard as it was, they trusted God, seeking to embrace His plan. Meanwhile, Twila never let go of her desire to create an album of recordings of lullabies for little ones. For years she tucked away kiddies' melodies-and-lyrics, and waited. Although she was not quite sure just what she was waiting for, Twila was excited to learn that the timing of the record company for that 'lullabies album' was right in her schedule. However, it seemed like she was making it for other people's children. At peace with God's will, it was just an offering for others.

No sooner were the songs written, chosen   and production began, Twila discovered she was pregnant! Not long after, she hit the road with the Christmas musical, 'Child of the Promise', playing the role of Elizabeth - a part she accepted prior to learning her own good news. She laughed, *"I think it just demonstrated God's faithfulness and His sense of humour!"*

Twila's laughter quickly turned to awe. The dreams of her heart for her life and career came true. The Wrights saw tangible reminders of God's goodness and remarkable purposes in their new son and the lullaby album. This experience caused Twila to glorify God in worship more and more. To her, worship always remained central. She received numerous songwriter awards and her music found a home in many hymnbooks around the world. Twila's heart, artistry and love-for-God created the perfect backdrops for worship. She displayed an obvious love and desire to glorify her Saviour. She explained, *"I always wanted to grasp celestial concepts of worship in very basic ways....I always felt like the Lord was directing me to songs that are worshipfully filled foundational truths."*

After Twila was born on 28th December 1958, it soon became apparent that this fair little lass was endowed with an admirable singing voice. Even from a very early age the capability was gradually perfected. In her cute 'Shirley Temple' dresses, she loved to perform for audiences no matter how small. At the age of four years, bolstered by her father's encouragement, she charmingly recorded an album for children entitled 'Little Twila Paris'!

When she was seven, the family moved to Springdale, Arkansas where her father pastored a church. It was a trying time for the youngster as she sought to make new friends in a new community. She found consolation in music, being taught to play the piano by her father. An accomplished pianist and composer, himself, he wrote what were (in his day) contemporary Christian songs.

Twila remembers that her father was a great inspirational and discipling influence in her life and music. *"My father always encouraged me! When I questioned him about the future, the questions I had about my life involved God's will, and whether I should be singing. Questions never involved whether or not I could do it! My Dad had always told me I could and I believed him!"*

Entering high school, teenager Twila studied computer programming. But during one semester, she swapped from a maths class to a chorus class. The notion of a musical career began to develop in her adolescent mind. By this time, her Father was now director of the Springdale base of the very active 'Youth With A Mission' organisation. As its name implies, YWAM evangelisticly concentrated on discipling and the sending out of mainly young people into the mission field. So subsequent to her graduation, Twila resolved to join a YWAM training school touring with a music-and-drama team. Her solo performing endeavours proved to be very acceptable to audiences wherever she went. People kept questioning her. They asked whether she had recorded any of her songs and where could they purchase them. With such a demand building, a friend and confidant suggested that she record a custom album (one paid for and distributed by the artist). Adventurously, this she did! When finished, the Christian recording product was dispatched to a record company. Its executives quickly recognised Twila's qualitative potential so she was duly signed up. Soon she was one of the record company's top-selling contemporary Christian artists.

Twila continued to minister with Youth With A Mission and not surprisingly perhaps, her songs mirrored her deep commitment to her Lord. Her Christian priorities majored on worship, praise and the importance of missions. Twila said, *"Maintaining Christ Jesus at the heart of my musical message was always my top priority. The Church too should be serious in its commitment to keep Christ and*

His objectives in their sight! His purposes should always be our ultimate goal! The bottom line is not WHAT we do, but WHY we do it! It's very important to retain the right motivation!"

Coming to terms with that belief was, she says, the turning point in the musical career of this attractive singer and composer of contemporary Christian music. With her winsome looks and musical quality she could easily have been engulfed in showbiz pursuits. But, as she explained, she remained jealous of her 'heavenly calling'. *"I really felt there was a call on my life from God, to be used in music. I think, in one sense, that's why I wanted a music career so badly! But somehow, in between, I let my own personal ambitions creep in. Then I had to determine what was from God and what was from me! I had to come to the place where I was able to say, 'God, if You don't want me to have a career in music, that's okay! I want to do with my life whatever will serve You and Your kingdom'."*

We will glorify the King of kings; we will glorify the Lamb.
We will glorify the Lord of lords, Who is the great I AM.

Lord Jehovah reigns in majesty; We will bow before His throne.
We will worship Him in righteousness, We will worship Him alone.

He is Lord of heaven, Lord of earth; He is Lord of all who live.
He is Lord above the universe; All praise to Him we give.

Hallelujah to the King of kings; Hallelujah to the Lamb.
Hallelujah to the Lord of lords, Who is the great I Am.

When The Roll Is Called Up Yonder
(When The Trumpet Of The Lord Shall Sound)
James Milton Black

He that overcometh, the same shall be clothed in white raiment;
and I will not blot out his name out of the book of life,
but I will confess his name before my Father, and before his angels.
Revelation 3:5
And I saw the dead, small and great, stand before God;
and the books were opened:
and another book was opened, which is the book of life:
and the dead were judged out of those things
which were written in the books, according to their works.
And the sea gave up the dead which were in it;
and death and hell delivered up the dead which were in them:
and they were judged every man according to their works.
And death and hell were cast into the lake of fire. This is the second death.
And whosoever was not found written in the book of life was cast into the lake of fire.
Revelation 20:12-15
And the city had no need of the sun, neither of the moon, to shine in it:

*for the glory of God did lighten it, and the Lamb is the
light thereof.*
*And the nations of them which are saved shall walk in the
light of it:*
*and the kings of the earth do bring their glory and honour
into it.*
*And the gates of it shall not be shut at all by day: for there
shall be no night there.*
*And they shall bring the glory and honour of the nations
into it.*
*And there shall in no wise enter into it any thing that
defileth,*
neither whatsoever worketh abomination, or maketh a lie:
but they which are written in the Lamb's book of life.
Revelation 21:23-27
*And if any man shall take away from the words of the book
of this prophecy,*
*God shall take away his part out of the book of life, and out
of the holy city,*
and from the things which are written in this book.
*He which testifieth these things saith, Surely I come
quickly. Amen.*
*Even so, come, Lord Jesus. The grace of our Lord Jesus
Christ be with you all. Amen.*
Revelation 22:19-21

James M. Black, poet and composer of 'When The Roll is Called
Up Yonder' was fully persuaded that the believer's sacred unalloyed
kinship to Christ Jesus is forevermore guaranteed. He declared, *"To
us as citizens of the heavenly kingdom, Christ gave us the great
promise that He will never erase our names from the Book of Life!"*

Born in South Hill, Sullivan County, New York State on August
19th 1856, James gained an early education in the skills of singing
and playing the organ. Actively involved in his Methodist
denomination, he progressed to become an itinerant teacher of
successful singing-schools. Soon he was editing many gospel
songbooks that were published in the latter half of the 19th Century

by the 'Methodist Book Concern' (of New York and Cincinnati), the Hall-Mack Company (of Philadelphia) and the McCabe Publishing Company (of Chicago). In 1894, his collection entitled 'Songs Of The Soul' sold no less than 400,000 copies. Appointed by the bishops of the Methodist Episcopal Church to the 'Joint Commission for the Methodist Hymnal' of 1905, amazingly James was apparently the only gospel songwriter on the board.

James recounted the heart-warming story behind his song, 'When The Roll is Called Up Yonder' to his great friend, gospel soloist Ira Sankey...One day, while a teacher in a Sunday school and president of a young people's society; James encountered a poorly-clad teenage girl of fourteen years of age. Soon he discovered that her ill fortune was due considerably to the waywardness of her father who was a drunkard. In compassion, he invited her to attend his Sunday school and young people's club. She responded positively and attended regularly. Later at what James called a 'consecration meeting'; the teen members of the group answered the roll call by quoting scripture texts aloud. The shy teenage girl, however, did not participate due to her sense of unworthiness.

James saw the opportunity to apply a lesson to his class. Smiling kindly he spoke softly and clearly to his assembled group. *"In ancient metropolises of the past, the names of citizens were duly chronicled in a city-register until their death; then their names were ceremonially signed out of that book. Young people, there's a corresponding concept that appears in the Old Testament. It speaks of God's people being recorded in God's 'book of the righteous'. This brings to you and me the wonderful sense of personally belonging to God's eternal kingdom and personally possessing eternal life!"*

James explained how Christ pledges to believers that He will never blot out any Christian's name from the Book of Life. *"This is an pronouncement from the Almighty Himself! It means that even death can never separate us from Christ and the life He offers us. It's wonderful to know that any person, rich or poor, enrolled in the Book of Life by faith remains in it by faithfulness. We can only be erased by unfaithfulness."*

The teenagers drank in every word as James enthusiastically continued his discourse. *"Young people, historians tell us that in the ancient cities of the past, citizens' names were ceremonially expunged from the city register before death if anyone was convicted of a crime or fell foul of the authorities. That's likely the reason that we don't read about Moses in Egyptian literature as the authorities attempted to blot his name from Egyptian history!"*

The eyes of his listeners watered as he explained how sadly, in the first century, Christians who were devoted to Christ were under continual jeopardy of being branded as political and social rebels. *"To be a Christian meant torture and death. Authorities also would then ceremonially confiscate them of their citizenship. The good news of the Gospel is that Christ Jesus offers Christians an eternally safe citizenship in His everlasting kingdom if they remain faithful to Him."*

Bathed in Holy Spirit conviction, James recounted to the young group of teenagers how on Judgement Day in his vision, the Apostle John saw moments of trepidation among some believers. *"We know,"* James continued, *"that when The Books are opened it will be serious business. God in His sphere of perfect and comprehensive vision misses nothing in history. Every human being will have to give an explanation to God of individual actions. God's divine judgment will be based on the sum and substance of all our human deeds and motives, recorded in The Books containing both good and evil works. But young people, don't be fretful; true believers on that day will be more thrilled about another book, the Lamb's Book of Life."*

Although it was difficult for his young teenage class to grasp, James continued to unpack further truth. *"God as our Judge will have is no difficulty in harmonizing the judgment between 'works' and 'grace'. Our good works as Christians are the clear confirmation of the faithfulness of our hearts. Our lives today express our belief or our unbelief, our faithfulness or our unfaithfulness. Take special note, this judgment by God is not going to be a tallying-up of 'good works' over 'bad works'. No, indeed, as Christians, our names are already in the Lamb's Book of Life and it also contains records of righteous deeds!"*

Under on-going Holy Spirit conviction, the teenage class was transfixed and spellbound by James impromptu address. He then furrowed his brow as he eyed his class with a misty stare. He declared how sad it would be if even one of their number was absent when the roll is called from the Lamb's Book of Life. Looking heavenward he cried, *"O God, I pray that when our names are called up yonder, we'll all be there ready to respond!"*

Looking back on that day with his teenage class, James remembered how he dearly wished for something suitable to sing to round off the anointed session. Scouring the songbooks, he found nothing apt and so closed the meeting without a hymn. On his way home, he pondered the lack of a suitable sacred song for such an occasion. Inspired, the thought came to him. *Why shouldn't he write such a song?* He dismissed the idea as being merely fanciful. *How could he write such a song?*

Arriving home, his wife recognised her husband's preoccupied anxious air and questioned James accordingly. But he held his counsel. Inspired, the first verse of a song was crystallizing in his heart as he moved to the parlour's piano seat. Within fifteen minutes at the keyboard, two more verses and the melody arrived as nowadays recorded note for note. He felt that he dare not change a single note. In a letter to the publisher, Robert H. Coleman dated January 7th 1913 that James wrote from Williamsport, Pennsylvania, he granted permission for 'When The Roll is Called Up Yonder' to be printed in 'World Evangel' for the unprincely sum of merely $20. Later he upped the price to $25 as the song started to appear in many, many songbook collections! James was a deeply committed member of the Pine Street Methodist Church in Williamsport, Pennsylvania from 1904 until his death on December 21st 1938.

Among his friends in the Methodist Church, James loved to speak publicly about 'When The Roll is Called Up Yonder'. He would tell how the Apostle John in his resplendent vision, foresaw the accomplishment of Christian hopes in the undiminished presence of God with His purified people. *"When the roll is called up yonder in the Holy City"*, declared James, *"there'll no longer be any impurity. Nothing impure will ever enter the city's gates. Only those can enter whose names are in the Lamb's Book of Life! These are they that belong to Him through redemption."*

Even as an old man, James loved to repeat to his friends and associates that the only way they could participate in the future Holy City would be to turn their total loyalty to the Lamb of God now.

With a twinkle in his eye, He would say, *"Friends, up there when the roll is called up yonder there'll be no further need for any natural or artificial lighting! The glory of God will dull the strongest earthly light into dimness. The redeemed peoples of the earth will bring their offerings to the throne of God in worship. That's not all, our activity in that heavenly age to come will doubtlessly encompass ongoing spiritual activities and associations that promote the glory of the Holy City throughout eternity. I can't wait, can you!"*

When the trumpet of the Lord shall sound, and time shall be no more,
And the morning breaks, eternal, bright and fair; When the saved of earth shall gather
Over on the other shore, and the roll is called up yonder; I'll be there.

When the roll is called up yonder, when the roll is called up yonder,
When the roll is called up yonder, when the roll is called up yonder,
I'll be there.

On that bright and cloudless morning when the dead in Christ shall rise,
And the glory of His resurrection share; when His chosen ones shall gather
To their home beyond the skies, and the roll is called up yonder,
I'll be there.

Let us labour for the Master From the dawn till setting sun;
Let us talk of all his wondrous love and care. Then when all of life is over,
And our work on earth is done, and the roll is called up yonder,
I'll be there.

James M. Black (Copyright © Hope Publishing Co.)
Administered By Copycare, PO Box 77, Hailsham, BN273EF, UK
music@copycare.com / Used With Permission

Without Him
Mylon Lefevre

Jesus said: 'Abide Me, and I in you.
As the branch cannot bear fruit of itself, except it abide in
the vine;
no more can ye, except ye abide in Me.
I am the vine, ye are the branches:
He that abideth in Me, and I in him, the same bringeth
forth much fruit:
for without me ye can do nothing.'
John 15:4-5

The French humanist simply known as Lefevre (1455-1536) shared more a merely a name with modern gospel songwriter, Mylon Lefevre when he said, *"Unutterable exchange! The Sinless One is condemned, the guilty go free. The Blessed bears the curse, the cursed bears the blessing. The Life dies and the dead live. The Glory is covered with shame, and the shame is covered by Glory!"*

Baby Mylon Lefevre was born four hundred years later than Lefevre. In 1944, Mylon was birthed at born, at the height of World War II hostilities between the Western Allies and the Axis forces, into a gospel-singing family in the USA's famed 'Bible Belt'. The pilgrimage-of-life before him provided the adult songwriter, Mylon with (in the words of the Beatles' song) a 'long, winding road' that was hard and at times strange to travel. He had to prove by personal, private and painful experience that without Christ he could do nothing, as the Saviour declared to His disciples in John 15!

Christ's words came at the point in His life when He planned leaving the Upper Room in Jerusalem after the Last Supper for the Garden of Gethsemane. His momentous words to the eleven disciples were spoken en route to the Garden place of suffering and arrest. Known as 'the Farewell Discourse' to His disciples, Christ Jesus dealt with three relationships that involved the disciples. The first was their *'relationship with Him'*. The second was their *'relationship with one another'*. Lastly, the third was their *'relationship with the world around them'*. Christ Jesus knew that His disciples would soon establish a manifest community with a definite function. Therefore, He desired to make them ready for the change that His departure would make in their manner of living.

Christ made it clear that their *'relationship with Him'* was a relationship that was chief. The very presence of the group depended on the union of each individual with Christ. To explain by example, Jesus used the analogy (or parable) of the Vine and Vineyard, a prevalent feature of Palestinian life, familiar to the disciples. Thus using the Vine metaphor, Jesus augmented its scope to include all *'born-again'* believers. Individualizing its teaching application, Christ emphasized specific features in the cultivation of healthy vines. The first was that there must be an authenticated stock. A gardener must plant the right kind of vine or tree in order to guarantee the proper quality of fruit, for no fruit can be better than the vine that produces it. Jesus then said, *"I am the true vine... without me ye can do nothing!"*

Mylon took up this declaration as the inspiration for his gospel song, 'Without Him'. He personally discovered that in the 'crucible of his unique experience' that unless individual believers are indispensably linked with Him, the quality of an individual believer's fruitfulness will be unsatisfactory. He knew that there may be many branches including Mylon, but if branches are to bear the right kind of fruit, they must be a part of Christ - the real Vine.

In John 15, Christ's next teaching lesson was that God the Father is the Divine Gardener. Achievement in raising any harvest depends largely on the competence of the farmer or gardener. The relation of the 'believer to God' is that of the 'vine to the Owner of the vineyard'. God lovingly tends it; waters it; guards it, and cultivate it. His purpose is to secure a maximum harvest. Inevitably, this involves pruning: the withdrawal of dead wood and the trimming of live wood so that its potentiality for fruit-bearing will be improved. Christ was saying that pruning was necessary for all vines. Indeed, dead wood is worse than fruitlessness, for dead wood can conceal disease and decay. An untrimmed vine will develop long rambling branches that bring forth little fruit because most of the strength of the vine is given to growing wood. The Divine Gardener too is concerned that His vines are healthy and productive. This tender and affectionate process is a picture of God's dealings with humankind. He removes the dead wood from His church and disciplines the lives of believers so that they are directed into fruitful activity.

Mylon was raised in a 'hothouse' of Christian heritage in the large gospel-singing family known as the Singing Lefevres. Their gospel music traditions went back to the early 1920s and many family members including his parents participated down through the decades of the century. In due time, Mylon showed as a youth in the 1950s and 1960s that he was not only a gifted performer but a songwriter too. Indeed, back then and more so in later life, his songs were recorded by the likes of Mahalia Jackson, the Blackwood Brothers, Pat Boone, the Oak Ridge Boys, The Imperials and many others. One of his compositions, 'Without Him', was even picked out for recording by non other than Elvis Presley at the height of his career. Subsequently, more than a hundred more other artists in the studio covered 'Without Him'. The resultant sales almost immediately made Mylon a rich man. Despite the fame and fortune, in the late 1960s and 1970s traditional gospel music held little appeal for the handsome young man with the stylish sideburns. After more than three dozen albums with the Lefevres, Mylon left to find his own way-in-life and his own sound. Music was programmed it seemed in his DNA so he kept on writing, kept traveling and doing concerts and finally he released 'Mylon' in 1970, a solo effort. However, the further away Mylon got from his God-fearing roots, the harder he found it was to hold on to his personal faith. Sadly, he slipped into a deep miry pit of drugs and other excesses. His musical ability still shone brightly and he came to the attention of the secular record labels that clamoured for his talents. With them he produced sometimes brilliant and sometimes confused rock albums with the likes of Eric Clapton, Alvin Lee, George Harrison, Duane Allman, The Who and many more. By this time, Mylon found that he had slipped so far away from his faith that he felt his life was dangerously slipping away, getting more and more out of his control.

Looking back over those painful years, he said, *"I stayed stoned twenty four hours a day for ten or twelve years!"* Sadly he recalled, *"My heart finally stopped one day because of an overdose. At that point I realised that I didn't really know whether or not I would get to Hell. That scared me."*

The road-to-repentance was long and painful. His pruning and renewal process began in 1974. It was slow and sure but not without many setbacks along the way. He said that the breakthrough came when he was asked to perform on a Phil Keaggy Christian album produced by Buck Herring. Mylon said that he discovered that Buck was willing to take a chance on him as a musician who by then was 'long on talent' and 'longer on problems'. Mylon commented, *"Buck was leading me to the Lordship of Christ. He did it unselfishly. He worked me harder than I had ever allowed. But I knew that he was a 'Man of God', so I could take discipline from him that I couldn't take from anyone else!"*

Finally on New Years' Eve in 1978, Mylon surrendered and decided to perform what he said would be his last secular rock concert. He decided to make a permanent commitment to follow God's calling. He explained simply, *"I needed to stop my career and follow Jesus!...For the next few years I threw myself into church work, working with young people, playing for free, and mending bridges long-broken with my family!"*

In time, Mylon became an ordained minister and joined the Mount Parin Family Life Centre in Atlanta as a counselor. Music was still an ever-present constant and he recorded again in 1982. This time it was an outstanding gospel album entitled 'Brand New Start', an apt title that said it all. The album was picked as one of the year's best seven albums in 'Contemporary Christian Music' magazine. Predictably it was followed by an album called 'More'.

Mylon had discovered that fruit-bearing for a Christian is not only possible but also certain if 'the branch remains in union with the vine'. Christians are not individually promised a uniformity of quantity and quality of fruitfulness but they are promised a harvest. Mylon stated, *"If the life of Christ permeates a disciple, fruit will be inevitable. I've discovered that a Christian's connection to Christ the Vine is maintained by obedience and prayer. To remain in Christ and to allow His words to remain in one means a conscious acceptance of the authority of His word and a constant contact with Him by prayer. Without Him we can do nothing!"*

The explorer and evangelist associated with Moody and Sankey, Henry Drummond (1851-1897) stated, *"Will-power does not change men.... Time does not change men.... Christ does!"*

I can do all things through Christ who strengthens me.
Philippians 4:13

Ackley, Alfred Henry - He Lives! (I Serve A Risen Saviour)

Alphabetical Songwriter Index

Baker, Marilyn - Jesus Is Lord Of All
Bilbrough, Dave - I Am A New Creation
Black, James - When The Roll Is Called Up Yonder
Bowater, Chris - Here I Am Wholly Available
Brock, Blanche & Virgil Brock - Beyond The Sunset
Brock, Virgil & Blanche Brock - Beyond The Sunset
Brumley, Albert - I'll Fly Away
Carter, Russell Kelso - Standing On the Promises-
Chapman, Wilbur & Charles H. Marsh - Living He Loved Me (One Day When Heaven …)
Crosby, Fanny & William Doane - To God Be The Glory
Crouch, Andrae - Through It All
Doane, William & Fanny Crosby - To God Be The Glory
Dorsey, Thomas - Take My Hand Precious Lord
Fellingham, Dave - God Of Glory -We Exalt Your Name
Field, Paul - Thief In The Night
Gabriel, Charles - The Glory Song (When All My Labours And Trials…) Gaither, Bill - He Touched Me
Garrett, David & Dale Garrett - Hallelujah For The Lord Our God The Almighty Reigns
Garrett, Dale & David Garrett - Hallelujah For The Lord Our God The Almighty Reigns
Green, Keith - O Lord You're Beautiful
Hamblen, Stuart - Until Then
Hansen, Paul & Susan Hansen - The Lord Is Good
Hansen, Susan & Paul Hansen - The Lord Is Good
Hayford, Jack - Father God
Hawkins, Edwin - Oh Happy Day
Hoffman, Elisha Albright - Are You Washed In The Blood?
Jones, Ruth - In Times Like These
Kendrick, Graham - Jesus Stand Among Us
LeFevre, Mylon - Without Him
Lewis, Erv - Today I Followed Jesus
Lister, Mosie - Till The Storm Passes By
McGuire, Barry - Take This Bread I Give To Thee (Communion Song)
Marsh, & Charles H. & Wilbur Chapman - Living He Loved Me (One Day When Heaven …)

Moen Don & Paul Overstreet - God Is Good All The Time
Moody, David - We've Come To Worship You Lord
Norman, Larry - I Wish We'd All Been Ready
Orr, Edwin - Search Oh God
Overstreet, Paul & Don Moen - God Is Good All The Time
Owens-Collins, Jamie - In Heavenly Armour
Pantry, John - King Of Kings and Lord Of Lords
Paris, Twila -We Will Glorify The King Of Kings
Peterson, John - It Took A Miracle
Pollard, Adelaide Addison & George Stebbins - Have Thine Own Way, Lord
Rambo, Dottie - We Shall Behold Him
Redman, Matt - The Heart Of Worship
Richards, Noel - There Is Power In The Name Of Jesus
Rodeheaver, Homer & Oswald J. Smith - Then Jesus Came
Sankey, Ira & Emily Elizabeth Steele - Thou Didst Leave Thy Throne
Smith, Oswald J. & Homer Rodeheaver - Then Jesus Came
Stanphill, Ira - Room At The Cross
Stebbins, George & Adelaide Addison Pollard - Have Thine Own Way, Lord
Steele, Emily Elizabeth & Ira Sankey - Thou Didst Leave Thy Throne-
Tindley, Charles Albert - We'll Understand It Better By And By (Trials Dark On
Every hand)
Townend, Stuart - How Deep The Father's Love
Wilkin, Marijohn - I Have Returned
Zschech, Darlene - Shout To The Lord

Scripture Index

Genesis 1:1-5, 14-19 / IT TOOK A MIRACLE
1 Samuel 16:7 / THE HEART OF WORSHIP
1 Chronicles 16:8-9 / WE'VE COME TO WORSHIP YOU, LORD
Psalm 9:1 / THE HEART OF WORSHIP
Psalm 27:4-6O / LORD YOU'RE BEAUTIFUL
Psalm 34:1-8 /GOD IS GOOD ALL THE TIME
Psalm 50:23 / WE WILL GLORIFY THE KING OF KINGS
Psalm 96 : 1-13 / SHOUT TO THE LORD
Psalms 106:1 / THE LORD IS GOOD
Psalm 139:7-10 / TAKE MY HAND PRECIOUS LORD
Psalm 139:23-24 / SEARCH ME O GOD
Psalm 146:5-8 / O HAPPY DAY
Isaiah 6:1-8 / HERE I AM WHOLLY AVAILABLE
Isaiah 55:7/I HAVE RETURNED
Jeremiah 18:1-6 / HAVE THINE OWN WAY
Daniel 4:34-35 / THERE IS POWER IN THE NAME
Zechariah 12:9-10 / WE SHALL BEHOLD HIM
Matthew 8:1-2 /HE TOUCHED ME
Matthew 24:29-30 / WE SHALL BEHOLD HIM
Matthew 24:38-44 / I WISH WE'D ALL BEEN READY
Mark 9:27 / TAKE MY HAND, PRECIOUS LORD
Mark 10:46-52 /THEN JESUS CAME
Luke 8:22-25 / TILL THE STORM PASSES BY
Luke 15:11-24 /HOW DEEP THE FATHER'S LOVE
John 15:4-5 / WITHOUT HIM
John 19:25-26 / ROOM AT THE CROSS
John 20:19-23 / JESUS STAND AMONG US
Acts 3:19 / IT'S THE PRESENCE OF YOUR SPIRIT
Acts 10:34-36 / JESUS IS LORD OF ALL
Acts 14:22-23 / THROUGH IT ALL
Romans 7:18-20 / TODAY I FOLLOWED JESUS
Romans 8:14-17 / FATHER GOD
Romans 13:1/ THERE IS POWER IN THE NAME OF JESUS
I Corinthians 15:54-58 / BEYOND THE SUNSET
I Corinthians 11:23-26 / TAKE THIS BREAD I GIVE TO THEE (Communion Song)
I Corinthians 13:9-13 / WE'LL UNDERSTAND IT BETTER BY AND BY

I Corinthians 15:52-55 / I'LL FLY AWAY
II Corinthians 5:16-17 / I AM A NEW CREATION
II Corinthians 1: 3-7 / WE'LL UNDERSTAND IT BETTER BY AND BY (Trials Dark)
Ephesians 2:13-18 / ROOM AT THE CROSS
Ephesians 5:19-20 THE LORD IS GOOD
Ephesians 6:10-17 /IN HEAVENLY ARMOUR (The Battle Belongs To The Lord)
Philippians 2:5-8 / THOU DIDST LEAVE THY THRONE
Philippians 2:5-11GOD OF GLORY, WE EXALT YOUR NAME
Philippians 4:13 / WITHOUT HIM
Colossians 3:1 / THE GLORY SONG (When All My Labours And Trials Are O'er)
I Thessalonians 2: 16 / FATHER GOD
II Thessalonians 4:16-18 /I'LL FLY AWAY
I Timothy 1:14-17 / LIVING HE LOVED ME (One Day When Heaven)
II Timothy 3:1-13 / IN TIMES LIKE THESE
Hebrews 1:1-2 / IN TIMES LIKE THESE
Hebrews 12:22-23 / UNTIL THE DAY
James 4:8-10 / CLOSER TO JESUS
II Peter 1: 2-4 / STANDING ON THE PROMISES
II Peter 3:8-14 / THIEF IN THE NIGHT
1 John 1:4-7 /ARE YOU WASHED IN THE BLOOD? (Have You Been To Jesus?)
1 John 2: 28 I WISH WE'D ALL BEEN READY
Jude 24-25 / TO GOD BE THE GLORY
Revelation 1:5 / ARE YOU WASHED IN THE BLOOD? (Have You Been To Jesus?)
Revelation 1 :7-8 / WE SHALL BEHOLD HIM
Revelation 1:18 /HE LIVES! (I Serve A Risen Saviour)
Revelation 3:5 / WHEN THE ROLL IS CALLED UP YONDER
Revelation 19:5-8/HALLELUJAH, FOR THE LORD OUR GOD THE ALMIGHTY REIGNS
Revelation 19:11-16 / KING OF KINGS (He Came To Earth)
Revelation 20:12-15 / WHEN THE ROLL IS CALLED UP YONDER
Revelation 21:1-3 / UNTIL THEN
Revelation 21:23-27WHEN THE ROLL IS CALLED UP YONDER
Revelation 22:19-21WHEN THE ROLL IS CALLED UP YONDER

About The Author

Dr. Paul Davis is an author, journalist, broadcaster, record producer, tour organiser and music publisher of considerable experience. His books include the biographies of George Hamilton IV, Pat Boone, George Beverly Shea and the Blackwood Brothers plus projects for *Readers Digest* on several country music and gospel music themes. He has written for many of the top music and religious newspapers and magazines including *Music Week, Renewal, Country Music People, Christian Herald*, to name a few. He has broadcast over several decades on *BBC Radio, Trans World Radio*, and *United Christian Broadcasters* and others. He has produced hundreds of albums and organised concerts in hundreds of venues ranging from small town theatres and churches to prisons to the American Embassy in London, and to major Festivals. Happily married in 1965, he has three married children and two grandchildren. He and Hazel, his wife, have pastoral responsibilities in the Leighton Christian Fellowship, Leighton Buzzard, England.